Neurodiversity and Higher Education

Neurodiversity in higher education is gaining essential recognition, yet significant challenges remain. This book offers a comprehensive exploration of strategies and initiatives designed to foster inclusion for neurodivergent students. It is an invaluable resource for higher education academics and non-academics, illuminating pathways towards accessible learning environments and systemic institutional change.

This book delves into the multifaceted aspects of supporting neurodivergent students in higher education. It presents an array of topics, including the application of a bioecological theory for inclusive design, assistive technologies that enhance learning experiences and innovative work-integrated learning programmes. Key chapters explore accessible library design, tailored support for dyslexia and ADHD and successful mentorship initiatives. Through case studies and institutional profiles, it showcases practical strategies that promote neuro-inclusion, from flexible learning environments to institutional reforms. The book emphasises the importance of collaborative efforts, systemic approaches and leadership commitment to creating truly supportive educational programmes.

Highlighting both challenges and transformative strategies, this book underscores the necessity of systemic change for neuro-inclusion in higher education. It serves as a critical guide for institutions aiming to build equitable, inclusive environments, offering practical insights and evidence-based recommendations to empower neurodivergent students and staff to enhance their academic and professional success.

Andrew Eddy is the Co-founder of the Neurodiversity Hub community of practice, working with universities and employers to facilitate neurodivergent higher education students to become more work-ready and increase their employment opportunities. Andrew is retired but continues his interest in neurodiversity and advocating for more neuro-inclusive workplaces and learning spaces.

Timothy Frawley, DGov; MEd, BNS, RPN, RNT, is Associate Professor in Mental Health Nursing at UCD. A registered psychiatric nurse and educator, he has held leadership roles in curriculum development, governance and research. His work focuses on neurodiversity, nursing governance and service user involvement. He is committed to education, inclusion and issues concerning professional regulation.

Blánaid Gavin, PhD, is a child and adolescent psychiatrist who has worked clinically with children and teenagers for over 20 years. She is particularly interested in expanding understanding in relation to child and adolescent mental health. To this end, she has been involved in teaching and research focused on optimising outcomes for young people. She specialises in the area of ADHD.

Etain Quigley, PhD, is Lecturer in Law at Maynooth University, specialising in neurodiversity, mental health, youth justice and criminology. She has held Irish Research Council awards, worked on FP7 and H2020 projects and serves on Mental Health Tribunals. She is also a co-founding editor of *Neurodiversity* (Sage).

Charlotte Valeur is an investment banker and seasoned FTSE Chair, Non-Executive Director and governance expert. She is a professor, author and public speaker in corporate governance, leadership, equality and diversity. Charlotte is Autistic and ADHD, and the founder and CEO of the global Institute of Neurodiversity (ION).

Neurodiversity: International Perspectives on Theory Policy and Practice

Series Editors
Andrew Eddy, Timothy Frawley, Blánaid Gavin, Etain Quigley and Charlotte Valeur

About the Series

This five-book series explores neurodiversity across important and interconnected domains – mental health, higher education, the criminal justice system, gender, and relationships. The series grew from a series of annual international online conferences organised by University College Dublin, Maynooth University, ADHD Ireland, ION and the Neurodiversity Hub. The conference sparked significant interest and dialogue, leading to a series of follow-up masterclasses, and eventually, this book series.

At its core, this series seeks to push beyond traditional academic boundaries by creating a platform for neurodivergent and neuro-mixed voices to share research, lived experience, and critical reflections. Contributors were invited for their scholarly expertise, but also for their capacity to bring authentic, engaged, and at times challenging perspectives to the forefront. The resulting volumes reflect an inclusive and dialogic approach that takes on complexity, fosters respectful disagreement, and centres empowerment for those often marginalised by dominant systems and narratives.

The books are underpinned by a neurodiversity-affirmative framework, which seeks to move away from deficit-based thinking and clinical labelling, and instead recognises and values neurological variation as part of human diversity. While clinical terminology (such as "Autism Spectrum Disorder" or "ADHD") is used where chosen by authors, the editorial team encouraged contributors to adopt affirming, identity-respecting language and to situate their work within the broader goals of inclusivity and transformation.

Each book in this series focuses on a distinct yet overlapping domain in which neurodivergent individuals often experience systemic barriers, exclusion, and misunderstanding. These volumes seek to shift the paradigm:

- from assimilation to authentic inclusion;
- from pathologisation to validation;
- from silencing to co-production of knowledge.

The first book addresses the critical link between neurodiversity and mental health, where masking, marginalisation, and social exclusion can lead to significant distress. The second book turns its attention to higher education, interrogating how inclusive practices can be implemented and reimagined through neurodivergent-led scholarship. Future volumes will examine how neurodiversity intersects with the criminal justice system, with gendered experiences, and within the context of interpersonal relationships, bringing fresh perspectives to policy, practice, and daily life.

The editorial approach has been both rigorous and reflexive. Contributors were encouraged to draw on both empirical research and theoretical frameworks, while also writing in a style and structure that best reflected their message. In doing so, this series fosters an academic space that honours diversity not only in neurological profile but also in scholarly voice.

This series is grounded in the principle of 'nothing about us without us'. It champions a rights-based, community-led approach to knowledge and advocacy, promoting systemic change through informed dialogue and shared vision. It aims not only to advance academic and policy discourse, but to support a growing movement that reclaims space, agency, and dignity for neurodivergent individuals around the world.

This series is, unapologetically, part of a wider paradigm shift — one that affirms neurodivergent lives, challenges institutional norms, and creates space for critical and collaborative transformation.

Books in this Series

Neurodiversity and Mental Health
Andrew Eddy, Timothy Frawley, Blánaid Gavin, Etain Quigley and Charlotte Valeur

Neurodiversity and Higher Education
Andrew Eddy, Timothy Frawley, Blánaid Gavin, Etain Quigley and Charlotte Valeur

Neurodiversity and Higher Education

Edited by Andrew Eddy,
Timothy Frawley, Blánaid Gavin,
Etain Quigley and Charlotte Valeur

Routledge
Taylor & Francis Group

LONDON AND NEW YORK

Designed cover image: Getty © Caelestiss

First published 2026
by Routledge
4 Park Square, Milton Park, Abingdon, Oxon OX14 4RN

and by Routledge
605 Third Avenue, New York, NY 10158

Routledge is an imprint of the Taylor & Francis Group, an informa business

British Library Cataloguing-in-Publication Data
A catalogue record for this book is available from the British Library

ISBN: 9781032801971 (hbk)
ISBN: 9781032788241 (pbk)
ISBN: 9781003495925 (ebk)

DOI: 10.4324/9781003495925

Typeset in Galliard
by Newgen Publishing UK

Contents

Editor Biographies

Andrew Eddy, B Comm, FCA, FCPA, FAICD, is a senior finance professional passionate about neurodiversity and creating opportunities for neurodivergent individuals. He co-founded the Neurodiversity Hub initiative in Australia focused on working with employers and higher education institutions to develop a sustainable neurodiverse employment ecosystem to increase opportunities for Autistic individuals and those with other neurovariations, thereby realising their untapped potential. Before this, Andrew had a career in senior finance-related roles with global public companies and was also a Deputy Chancellor of La Trobe University in Australia. Andrew has now retired but continues his interest in neurodiversity and advocating for more inclusive workplaces and learning spaces.

Timothy Frawley is Associate Professor in Mental Health Nursing at University College Dublin, Ireland, with previous roles as Head of Subject and Associate Dean. He teaches on Ireland's only Neurodiversity Professional Certificate and Diploma programme and focuses on inclusive nursing practices in mental health care. His work is dedicated to advancing mental health nursing, neurodiversity awareness and education, aiming to improve support for people within healthcare settings. Dr Frawley's commitment to advancing neurodiversity is also shaped by personal experiences that have provided unique insights into the challenges and strengths of neurodivergent individuals.

Blánaid Gavin is Consultant Child and Adolescent Psychiatrist at University College Dublin, Ireland, who has worked as a clinician with children who experience mental health difficulties for over 20 years. Dr Gavin's clinical and research interests include service accessibility and outcome optimisation. Dr Gavin is also involved in teaching, training and research in the field of child and adolescent psychiatry. She works with a variety of voluntary organisations to support collaborative models of awareness and enable coproduction in system change. Together with Prof McNicholas, Dr Gavin has co-developed a project to heighten awareness of young people's mental health across a variety of sectors including health, education and justice. She led the development of the first interdisciplinary research in Ireland exploring the experiences of young people attending mental health services. As Chair of the University Equity, Diversity and Inclusion subgroup on Neurodiversity, she is co-lead of the research programme on Making UCD a Neurodiversity Friendly Campus.

Etain Quigley is Lecturer in Law at Maynooth University, Ireland. She teaches and conducts research in the areas of neurodiversity, mental health, youth justice and criminological theory and has been appointed and reappointed to sit on mental health tribunals for over a decade. Dr Quigley completed her PhD and postdoctoral work at University College Dublin, Ireland. She was successful in her application for the Irish Research Council Government of Ireland Postdoctoral Scholarship. She was also successful in receiving a Teaching and Learning Fellowship and two Irish Research Council New Foundations awards. Moreover, she has worked on an Fp7 and an H2020 research project. Finally, she is a co-founding editor of the Sage journal *Neurodiversity*.

Charlotte Valeur is a UK-based investment banker and seasoned FTSE Chair, Non-Executive Director and governance expert with a wealth of board experience across different sectors. She is a professor, author and public speaker in corporate governance, leadership, equality and diversity. A lifelong human rights advocate, Charlotte is driven to play her part in creating an inclusive society; she advocates for equality and inclusion for all, working at the intersection of Government, Industry, academia and the Third Sector. She founded Board Apprentice and the global Institute of Neurodiversity, ION.

Author Biographies

Megan Ames is Assistant Professor in the Department of Psychology at the University of Victoria, Canada. Dr Ames' research examines the support needs, accessibility and experiences of Autistic post-secondary students across Canada. Her research focuses on supporting Autistic post-secondary students with a focus on peer mentorship models. In her graduate work, Dr Ames was involved in developing and evaluating a peer mentorship model for Autistic postsecondary students. Dr Ames and the research team have also published an environmental scan of autism-specific postsecondary supports across Canada (see https://onlineacademiccommunity.uvic.ca/ames/autistic-student-resources/ for more information and resources).

Jenny Anderton is Head of Disability Services at York St John University, England.

Mercedes Bagshawe has a Master of Science degree in School and Applied Child Psychology from the University of Calgary, Canada, and is continuing her education there as a Doctoral Student, pursuing a PhD in School and Applied Child Psychology. Mercedes's graduate research focused on suicidality in youth with autism and youth with fetal alcohol spectrum disorder, and the barriers to mental health support during crisis. Mercedes continues to support neurodivergent students as the programme lead of the UCalgary Peer Mentorship Program for Autistic and Neurodivergent Students and as a group facilitator with the CanLearn Society.

Marlee Bickford Bushey is Career Advisor at Landmark College, USA. In her current role, Marlee uses her lived experience as an Autistic woman to support neurodivergent college students with fostering and developing self-advocacy and workplace transition skills. Marlee's unique career journey started with gaining her cosmetology license from CV-Tech, giving her a background in navigating technical colleges. Marlee then obtained a Bachelor of Science in Global Studies and Master of Science in Student Affairs in Higher Education from SUNY Plattsburgh where she developed cross-cultural knowledge while working with international students, first-gen students and students with disabilities.

Trevor Boland is an advocate for inclusion in education and over his 20 years in education he has worked with and for students on initiatives that include assistive technology, accessibility and universal design for learning. He is the AT Officer at Dublin City University, Ireland, and collaborates internally and externally on inclusion initiatives to enhance inclusion in education.

Sandra Connell qualified as a registered psychiatric nurse in 2003. She worked in rehabilitation and community settings before moving to the UK in 2010, where she worked as a lecturer/senior lecturer in nursing education for eight years. Sandra returned to Ireland in 2018. She held the position of assistant professor at University College Dublin, Ireland, from 2019 to 2020, where she continues to contribute to teaching and research. Sandra is currently pursuing a PhD in the UCD School of Medicine. Sandra holds a Diploma in Mental Health Nursing from DCU, a BSc (Hons) in Nursing from DKIT, and an MSc in Nursing (Education) from UCD.

Jan Coplan, MEd, has more than 27 years' experience in the field of education and has been a career counsellor for the past 11 years. She is currently the Senior Director of Career Connections and Employer Relations at Landmark College in Putney, Vermont, USA, an institution exclusively for students who learn differently, including dyslexia, ADHD or autism. Jan is passionately committed to creating greater awareness of the advantages individuals with learning differences bring to the workplace. During her eight years at Landmark College, she has worked fervently to increase the number of professional work experiences for neurodivergent individuals both locally and nationwide.

Adrienne Cornish Lucas is the Assistant Director for Spectrum Scholars at University of Delaware, USA. She coaches students one-on-one to help them develop self-advocacy and other skills that are vital to their success. She also develops and oversees other facets of Spectrum Scholars including group coaching and peer mentoring. Adrienne has delivered presentations on developing effective peer mentor programmes for neurodiverse students, ensuring accessibility in K-12 lesson planning, and fostering inclusive and accessible environments for neurodiverse students on college campuses. Adrienne holds an MEd in Exceptional Children and Youth from the University of Delaware and a BA in Sociology from the University of Maryland – Eastern Shore.

Claire Davill is a PhD student at Flinders University, Australia. Her research explores the experiences of higher education students with dyslexia in

Australian universities and technical and further education (TAFE) institutions. She has also analysed higher education support services for students with dyslexia, with a focus on how these supports are communicated and made available to students.

Cheryl Dissanayake, AM, FINSAR, FASSA, is Professor Emerita at La Trobe University, Australia, and was the inaugural Director and Olga Tennison Endowed Chair in Autism Research. She founded the Olga Tennison Autism Research Centre, Australia's first dedicated autism research facility. Her research focuses on early autism identification, development and supports, leading pioneering work on attachment in Autistic children. She has significantly influenced Australian autism policy and practice through interdisciplinary research and advocacy. An internationally recognised leader in autism research, she has been instrumental in shaping the field in Australia and continues to influence global perspectives on autism.

Winnie Dunn is Distinguished Professor of Occupational Therapy at the University of Missouri, USA, renowned for her research on sensory processing. She has authored over 100 publications, including the Sensory Profile, translated into numerous languages. Her research has been recognised with numerous awards, including the Award of Merit and the Eleanor Clark Slagle Lectureship. Dr Dunn is also a distinguished teacher, receiving the Chancellor's Excellence in Teaching Award and the Kemper Teaching Fellowship. Her book, *Living Sensationally*, has been widely acclaimed and featured in major media outlets.

Sonja Duric is a Director at the Australian architectural firm of Hames Sharley, with 20+ years of experience in design psychology. She excels at fostering consensus among diverse stakeholders and is passionate about research-driven design with a positive social impact. Sonja holds a Bachelor of Built Environment (Hons) from QUT and UNSW and is a member of the Golden Key Honour Society. Her work focuses on neurodiversity and mental health, exploring how sensory design can create inclusive and successful built environments. She has lectured at RMIT and the New York School of Interior Design.

Nicole Eddy is a first year MSc student in the Clinical Psychology programme at the University of Calgary, Canada, supervised by Dr McMorris. She completed her BA (Psychology) and MSc (Experimental Psychology) at Memorial University of Newfoundland. Nicole has gained extensive experience working with Autistic and neurodivergent youth and adults in supportive, community-based roles and in research and clinical contexts. With the UCAN Program, Nicole has assisted with organising and facilitating the group-based events to promote student connections with peers. She looks forward to expanding into the role of a Student Mentor, providing one-on-one support to neurodivergent students at the university.

Steve Edwards is Clinical Psychologist and Senior Lecturer in Psychology in the Institute of Health and Wellbeing at Federation University, Australia. He currently teaches and supervises in the honours and Master of Psychology courses as well as supervising higher degree research. Steve's clinical experience with disadvantaged groups in rural and metropolitan settings such as primary mental health, dual disability, chronically homeless men and neurodivergent adults informs his research interests. He is currently principal researcher on the Enhancing the Inclusion and Success of ND Students in Regional and Remote Higher Education project. Steve maintains national and international research collaborations as well as consulting on clinical and research matters.

Wes Garton is the Program Director for Spectrum Scholars college-to-career autism initiative at the University of Delaware, USA. Wes oversees the programmatic functions of Spectrum Scholars, including student support, marketing, recruitment, partnerships, training and more. Wes has worked with college students with disabilities for over ten years, starting as a note-taker for the Office of Services for Students with Disabilities at West Chester University in Pennsylvania. Wes has presented at multiple conferences about autism, inclusion, access and programme development. Wes holds an MS in Higher Education Counseling and Student Affairs from West Chester University.

Sonya Girdler is affiliated with the School of Allied Health at Curtin University, Australia, and is Director of the Curtin Autism Research Group (CARG). Sonya oversees all research activity and programmes within CARG. Sonya has extensive experience in the field of autism research and neurodevelopmental disorders more broadly. Sonya is particularly interested in understanding functioning in autism using the International Classification of Functioning, Disability and Health (WHO), the development, evaluation and translation into practice of evidence-based interventions (particularly social skills, strengths-based programmes and mental health), and research directed at improving the participation of Autistic individuals in major life areas such as employment and education. The work of CARG is underpinned by a philosophy of 'Nothing about you without you' with all projects either being co-lead or informed by Autistic individuals themselves (Photovoice study co-produced with Autistic adults). CARG is fundamentally committed to impact and translation, frequently holding community and virtual events, informing the community of the latest evidence-based practice.

Mary-Elizabeth Goodman MEd, started in the Disability Services field in 2014 as a student worker during her undergraduate years at the University of Tennessee at Chattanooga (UTC), USA. During this time, she was also involved with Mosaic as a peer mentor. She graduated with a master's degree in Clinical Mental Health Counseling and currently serves as the Assistant Director of the Mosaic Program at the UTC. She is passionate about advocating for neuro-inclusivity, educating about autism and celebrating neurodiversity.

Jessica Green is Associate Interior Designer at the Australian architectural firm of Hames Sharley with over ten years of experience in award-winning projects across various sectors. She holds a Bachelor of Interior Architecture (Hons) from Curtin University and is passionate about mentoring emerging designers. Jessica champions human-centred design, creating meaningful and engaging spaces for clients in education, workplace, hospitality and more. Her diverse portfolio spans projects across Australia, Singapore and India.

Jennifer Grelak is Academic Program Coordinator for Spectrum Scholars at the University of Delaware, USA. She supports students by providing one-on-one coaching focused on self-advocacy, executive functioning, academics, self-care, social engagement, career exploration and interdependent living skills. She has given presentations on topics related to academic integrity and classroom management strategies for addressing student conduct in an online environment. Jennifer received her BA in English Literature from the University of Baltimore, her MA in Leadership in Disability Services from the University of Delaware and is currently pursuing her EdD in Community College Leadership at Morgan State University.

Susan Hall is an occupational therapist (OT) working in Perth, Australia. Susan trained as an OT in Western Australia, completing a Master of Occupational Therapy at Curtin University, Australia. Susan currently works in Aged Care as an OT, and as a Research Assistant with the Curtin Autism Research Group. Susan also works as a Registered Nurse, and Undergraduate Nurse Clinical Facilitator, and has completed qualifications in Nurse Education and Perioperative Nursing. Susan has a special interest in rehabilitation, sensory processing, disability and working with older adults. Susan is passionate about working alongside individuals, their families and the wider community to develop inclusive environments that promote well-being and quality of life and enable individuals to participate in meaningful activities.

Jessika Hames is a highly experienced design leader at the Australian architectural firm of Hames Sharley with 20+ years of expertise in architecture and design. Her portfolio spans education, science and public buildings, with a focus on sustainability and community engagement. Jessika has led award-winning projects and fosters meaningful stakeholder dialogue. She serves on the Wesley College Council and has chaired the WA Australian Institute of Architects Awards jury. Her commitment to design excellence shapes meaningful and sustainable environments.

Lorna Hamilton is Professor of Developmental Psychology and Inclusive Education at York St John University, England, where she was formerly Head of the Psychology Department. Lorna's research focuses on understanding the educational experiences of neurodivergent children and young people, with a view to developing inclusive, neurodiversity-affirming educational environments and practices. She uses participatory designs and creative, accessible research methods to foreground first-person perspectives in her studies in schools and university settings. In her own teaching practice, Lorna draws on principles of compassionate pedagogy, universal design and strength-based assessment. She leads the Inclusive Neurodiverse Campuses project at York St John, working with neurodivergent members of the university community to improve accessible and inclusive practice across university systems. Lorna is a Principal Fellow of the Higher Education Academy and Associate Fellow of the British Psychological Society.

Anne Hill, BS, is an external programme specialist with the Mosaic Program at the University of Tennessee at Chattanooga, USA and served three terms on the Board of the Chattanooga Autism Center. She is the parent of three neurodivergent young people and has focused much of her adult life on improving the lives of Autistic individuals after her son's diagnosis in 2008.

Judith Hudson is an adjunct to the School of Education, University of Tasmania, Australia. She has worked in the field of dyslexia for more than 40 years in the UK and Australia, as a psychologist, specialist teacher and teacher educator, researcher and author. Over that time theories about dyslexia have informed universal consensus that dyslexia exists, even when theoretical debate continues to disagree on its causes. She is a dyslexia advocate and ambassador who strives to raise the social profile of dyslexia, particularly in Australia, where the understandings of dyslexic strengths are too often under-acknowledged, misunderstood or ignored.

Emil Jonescu is Head of Research & Development at Hames Sharley, a leading Australian architectural firm. He bridges academic research with industry practice, focusing on community needs, including isolation, placemaking and security. With a master's and PhD in specialised facility design, Emil possesses a unique blend of academic and industry experience. He is an Adjunct Senior Research Fellow at ECU, fostering collaborative research across sectors.

Milo Kat is a final-year undergraduate psychology student and founder of the Disabled Student Network and Neurodivergent Study Group at York St John University, England.

Adam R. Lalor, PhD, is an educational psychologist and Vice President for Neurodiversity Research and Innovation at Landmark College, USA. His research focuses on the college success and transition of neurodivergent and disabled college students. Dr Lalor is co-author of the book *From Disability to Diversity: College Success for Students with Learning Disabilities, ADHD, and Autism Spectrum Disorder* and co-editor of *The New Accessibility in Higher Education: Disrupting the System for an Inclusive Future*. He serves in leadership capacities within the Association on Higher Education and Disability, College Autism Network, Learning Disabilities Association of America and National Center for Learning Disabilities.

Elinda Ai Lim Lee is a research fellow and an executive member of the Curtin Autism Research Group (CARG), Curtin University, Australia. A trained teacher, she completed her PhD in Instructional Technology at Murdoch University in Western Australia. Since 2015, Elinda has been actively involved in autism research with a strong community focus, particularly in areas such as post-secondary school transition to employment, social skills development and strengths-based interventions for neurodivergent individuals, with an emphasis on a co-production approach. She has extensive experience collaborating with industry partners and international researchers. Additionally, Elinda developed online learning content for Curtin's learning management system, Global Challenge Platform, supporting research, learning and training initiatives for students, therapists and school teachers.

Rebecca W. Matte, MS, is Professor of Education at Landmark College, USA, who holds degrees from the University of New Hampshire and New England College. With 30 years dedicated to the fields of neurodiversity and learning disabilities, Rebecca is celebrated for her dynamic teaching and engaging speaking style. She advocates for strengths-based approaches and holds certifications in The Birkman Method and Gallup Clifton Strengths, in addition to being an ICF Certified Coach. Her educational philosophy promotes holistic, strengths-focused strategies specifically designed for non-traditional learners. Rebecca also contributes as co-principal investigator on the NSF's STEM education grant, creating supportive programming for neurodivergent, low-income students.

Jasmine McDonald has an extensive background in inclusive secondary, tertiary and home school education in her different roles as parent, educator, tertiary programme coordinator and researcher. Her Masters of Special Education thesis, an enlightened paradigm regarding effective inclusive education of children with disabilities from an autoethnographic, parental perspective, earned her the George Bradshaw Prize as the top student to complete the University of WA Graduate School of Education Masters course in 2001. Her 2010 PhD research resulted in a requested international publication, *How Parents Deal with the Education of Their Child on the Autism Spectrum: The Stories and Research They Don't and Won't Tell You.* From 2013 to 2022, Dr McDonald jointly developed and coordinated the innovative Specialist Mentoring Program (CSMP), Curtin University, Australia. Dr McDonald also co-devised a series of generic tertiary mentoring manuals based on CSMP for use by other Australian tertiary education sites currently available on the Autism CRC website.

Carly McMorris is Associate Professor in the School and Applied Child Psychology programme at the Werklund School of Education, University of Calgary, Canada. She is the director of the ENHANCE Lab and a registered child clinical psychologist. Dr McMorris' research and clinical practice focuses on improving mental health outcomes for neurodivergent youth and young adults, including autism. Her research identifies factors that might contribute to mental health challenges and develops evidence-based treatment and prevention strategies to promote positive outcomes. Over the last two decades, Dr McMorris' research has focused on improving the experiences of neurodivergent post-secondary students through peer mentorship, neuro-inclusive settings and pedagogical practices. Her collaborative network includes national and international researchers, community organisations and individuals with lived experience, highlighting her commitment to creating impactful, real-world solutions.

Aoife McNicholl is Assistant Professor of Psychology in Dublin City University, Ireland. Her research area of interest is disability and rehabilitation psychology, assistive technology and the psychosocial impact of living with an illness or disability. As a disabled person who is a wheelchair user, she has fronted national advocacy campaigns related to independent living and the United Nations Convention of the Rights of Persons with Disabilities.

Ben Milbourn is Associate Professor, (teaching and research) in Occupational Therapy, Curtin School of Allied Health, Curtin University, Australia. Ben trained as an occupational therapist (OT) in the United Kingdom (UK), working in New Zealand, Australia and the UK practicing occupational therapy in mental health and disability contexts. Ben undertook a PhD at Curtin University in occupational therapy, focusing on the occupational meaning of everyday activity of people who experience severe mental illness. Ben is Deputy Director of Curtin Autism Research Group (CARG) and is interested in research with a strong community focus, working alongside Autistic individuals to promote social inclusion, well-being and positive mental health. Ben is passionate about co-produced research and developing strengths-based programmes in the community.

Sylvanna Mirichlis was the joint Program Coordinator of CSMP (Curtin Specialist Mentoring Program, Curtin University, Australia), from 2021 to 2024, and previous to this, was a highly regarded mentor within the program to four mentees. Sylvanna is a proud neurodiversity advocate and a psychology academic at Curtin University. Sylvanna has a passion for neurodiversity and mental health, being a member of several professional working groups related to these matters. Sylvanna is currently working in a research capacity at the Curtin EnAble Institute, as project manager for a Medical Research Future Fund (MRFF) national project aimed at better understanding the transition to high school amongst children with language and reading difficulties.

Renu Pariyadath is Associate Professor of Communication and the Director of Neurodiversity at University of South Carolina Upstate, USA. She is an Affiliate Faculty member in the Women's and Gender Studies Program. Renu is a teacher-scholar active within the areas of environmental sustainability and justice; diversity, equity and inclusion (DEI) in higher education; communication ethics; non-profit organisational strategy; and transnational migration. Her research examines communication processes in non-essential identity formation, within the contexts of social and organisational change, development in the Global South, environmental health and justice, and sustainability. She is a qualitative researcher and heavily draws on a transnational feminist theoretical framework. Renu received her PhD in Communication Studies from the University of Iowa.

Beth Radulski is an Autistic researcher specialising in Neurodiversity inclusion. She holds a PhD in Sociology from La Trobe University, Australia, where she also served as the University's first Manager: Neurodiversity Inclusion, establishing and overseeing its Neurodiversity Project. Dr Radulski's work explores the intersectionality of neurotypical privilege, and its relationship to systemic inequality throughout society, with a focus on Autistic masking and camouflaging. Her research has been mobilised to address institutional barriers to inclusion in social, professional and educational settings. Dr Radulski's PhD developed Best Practice Principles for Neurodiversity Inclusion, and an award-winning Work Integrated Learning Program for university students.

Qona Rankin has spent 24 years of her life at Royal College of Art, England, first studying and then working as the SpLD co-ordinator. Her academic research is focused on the creative advantages unconventional cognitive processing enables, and she regularly contributes to academic journals and conferences. In 2021, she co-authored *Observational Drawing for Students with Dyslexia; Strategies, Tips and Inspiration.* In 2008, Qona founded Creative Mentors Foundation, a charity, which promotes the importance of the creative curriculum for school children with SpLDs. Qona continues her practice of designing and making jewellery and is a governor of a local primary school where she focuses on Special Educational Needs issues. She is a Fellow of the RCA and the Royal Society of the Arts.

Abbie Robinson is a PhD researcher in Dublin City University, Ireland. Her research focuses on adult ADHD and perceptual decision-making. After receiving an ADHD diagnosis in 2023, she has participated in ADHD Ireland events to share her experiences navigating higher education with ADHD.

Amy Rutherford, LPC-MHSP, MEd, is the Director of the Mosaic Program at the University of Tennessee at Chattanooga, USA. She co-authored *The BASICS College Curriculum* (a four-book series) which developed a curriculum for Autistic college students as they transition into and out of college. Amy is also a co-founder of Navigate U who has recently joined forces with College Autism Spectrum and a consultant with many universities and businesses, specialising in creating autism programming and neurodiversity hiring initiatives. She conducts a variety of programme evaluations, is proficient in project management and loves supporting study abroad possibilities for students. Her research focuses on autism and neurodiversity in higher education and mental health services, universal design and leadership studies. Amy is a licensed professional counsellor serving the greater Chattanooga area. At her core, she loves creating inclusive environments, equitable experiences and serving others as a neurodivergent advocate.

Jane Sedgwick-Müller is the Programme Lead for Mental Health Nursing, Government of Jersey. She also chaired Jersey's Neuroinclusive Strategy working group and the university students living with ADHD steering group, facilitated by Takeda. Jane serves as a Board Member of the UK Adult ADHD Network (UKAAN) and is a member of the National

Association of Disability Practitioners (NADP). She provides professional training and consultancy, delivers public talks, and speaks at national and international conferences. Additionally, she has published articles and book chapters and has been interviewed by media outlets including the Guardian, Times Radio, BBC, ITV news and Bailiwick Express Jersey.

Lucy Simons is an occupational therapist with a background in nursing. She completed her Master of Occupational Therapy at Curtin University, Australia, and is a research assistant with the Curtin Autism Research Group. Lucy is passionate about working alongside individuals and community groups to support their health and well-being and create environments supportive of their needs. She has a special interest in mental health, paediatrics and rehabilitation, and values utilising strengths-based, creative approaches to provide personalised supports.

Tele Tan is John Curtin Distinguished Professor and Deputy Head of School of Electrical Engineering, Computing and Mathematical Sciences, Curtin University, Australia. Professor Tan has over 20 years of research and development experience in the field of computer vision and pattern recognition. In 2009, Tele founded the Studio for Experiential Sensing and Virtual Environment (SESVE). The studio is now used as a platform to foster research in human factors studies associated with various forms of visual analytics. Tele co-founded in Autism Academy for Software Quality Assurance in 2015 to help support the transitioning of students with Autism to employment in the fast-growing IT industry.

Sandra Thom-Jones, MBA, MPH, PhD, is an Autistic author, artisan, academic and advocate. She is the author of *Growing in to Autism* (2022), *Autistics in Academia* (2025) and *Autistics at Work* (2025). Sandra worked for more than two decades in the university sector as a researcher and senior leader, most recently as Pro Vice-Chancellor, Research Impact at Australian Catholic University, Australia. She now works as a consultant providing a range of services for Autistic people – as well as professional development, research and consultancy services for education, employment and healthcare providers – through her website 'Autistic Professor'. Sandra is also an Honorary Professor at the University of Wollongong, Australia. She has undertaken numerous research projects in partnership with the Autistic community on the experiences of Autistic people, and the knowledge and attitudes towards autism in the broader community; including research that won the Autism Co-operative Research Centre's 2019 and 2021 awards for research translation and 2022 award for inclusive research.

Talia Uylaki is a Researcher at the Australian architectural firm of Hames Sharley. With a Bachelor of Arts (English) and Honours in Creative Writing from Flinders University, and a Graduate Diploma in Information Management from the University of South Australia, Talia brings strong writing and research skills to her role. She contributes to research papers and supports various projects within the architecture and design industry at Hames Sharley.

Shae Wissell is a thought leader, researcher and internationally recognised advocate for adults with dyslexia and neurodivergence. A certified practicing speech pathologist, she holds a Master of Public Health and Health Administration and a Doctor of Public Health. With extensive experience in health, not-for-profit and social enterprise sectors in Australia, Shae directs re:think dyslexia and is the founder and chair of the Dear Dyslexic Foundation, leveraging her lived experience and diverse expertise to provide coaching, advocacy and workforce solutions.

Her research focuses on the lived experiences of Australian adults with dyslexia, examining social inequalities in healthcare, education, employment, relationships and mental health. A published author and presenter, Shae's work has been recognised locally and internationally. Shae recently published her second book based on her research and lived experiences: *Dyslexia: Insights into the hidden disability in and out of the workplace.*

Katie Wright is an Associate Professor of Sociology at La Trobe University, Australia. Her research focuses on social change, social justice and the cultural impact of psychological knowledge. She is committed to interdisciplinary research that addresses complex social issues and is currently leading three major projects related to institutional child abuse. These include an Australian Research Council-funded study titled *Reclaiming Child Rights: Activism, Public Inquiries and Social Change* (2022–2025). Dr Wright has also published extensively on therapeutic culture and the history of psychology, with notable works including *The Rise of the Therapeutic Society: Psychological Knowledge & the Contradictions of Cultural Change.*

Mohd Syazwan Zainal is a renowned lecturer in Special Education and serves as the Coordinator of the Autism Research Centre at Universiti Kebangsaan Malaysia (UKM), Malaysia. He obtained his PhD from Universiti Sains Malaysia (USM) in 2024. In 2022, he was part of an esteemed attachment programme at the Olga Tennison Autism Research Centre (OTARC), La Trobe University, Melbourne, which further enriched his expertise in autism studies. His innovative research earned him the Best Research Idea Award at the 2023 Malaysia Young Scientist Network Award Program, organised by the Academy of Sciences Malaysia. Currently, Mohd Syazwan Zainal leads four impactful research projects focusing on autism and career transitions for individuals with disabilities, with a total funding of nearly RM150,000. His work significantly advances the understanding of autism and the challenges faced by individuals with disabilities, particularly in the transition to adulthood and employment, promoting inclusivity and empowerment in these critical areas.

Introduction

Background

This book is the second in a series of books in the area of neurodiversity that arose from a number of papers presented at an international online conference organised by University College Dublin, Maynooth University, Stanford University, ADHD Ireland, and the Neurodiversity Hub in December 2020. The conference was so successful that a series of masterclasses was organised whereby the speakers would enter into a dialogue about their areas and provide the audience with a more engaged format to discuss their topics. As a result of the success of the masterclasses and the conferences, it was decided to bring these diverse and important topics into an accessible book format to assist with the development of advancements, and indeed a social paradigm shift, in the area of neurodiversity. A number of the speakers and other practitioners were invited to contribute to the book series. The framework for the book series was one of inclusivity and respectfulness of others' opinions, even where there is disagreement, empowering individuals who are often disempowered by the system.

Terminology in line with the Neurodiversity Paradigm (Walker, 2014) was suggested by the editors and this has largely been adhered to. At points in the book more clinical terms, such as autism spectrum disorder or attention deficit hyperactivity disorder, have been used. The editorial team respected the authors' decision to utilise clinical terms but recognised that many within the neurodivergent community are advocating for a move away from deficit-based language.

It is also crucial to note the issue of neurodiversity and mental health, which is the topic and title of the first book in this series. Inclusion efforts have frequently focused on assimilating neurominorities into mainstream norms, often requiring them to mask their neurodivergence. This expectation to conform, however, can lead to significant mental health challenges such as anxiety, depression, and identity loss. Emerging research underscores the detrimental effects of masking and highlights the need for approaches that value

DOI: 10.4324/9781003495925-1

neurodiversity and support individuals in their authentic selves (Radulski and Jaworowski, 2022).

There is also now substantial evidence highlighting the role of social exclusion. This exclusion manifests across various domains, including social interactions, education, healthcare, employment, and even within families. Understanding how exclusion contributes to mental health difficulties is crucial for developing effective support systems and fostering inclusive environments. Social exclusion refers to the process by which individuals or groups are systematically marginalised from participating fully in societal activities. This marginalisation can occur through discrimination, stigmatisation, and the creation of barriers that prevent equal access to resources and opportunities. For the neurodivergent community, social exclusion often results in limited access to quality education, healthcare services, employment opportunities, and social networks. Exclusion serves as a mechanism to suppress neurological differences by enforcing conformity to societal norms. This suppression invalidates the unique experiences and contributions of neurominorities, pressuring individuals to mask or hide their differences. Such masking is mentally exhausting and can lead to increased stress and mental health issues.

The societal expectation to 'fit in' disregards the value of diversity and perpetuates a cycle of exclusion and mental distress. A study by Morgan et al. (2007), published in the *British Journal of Psychiatry*, highlights the complex relationship between social exclusion and mental health. If anything, the experience of social exclusion has become more acute since this paper was published almost 20 years ago. It outlines that social disadvantage, including mental illness, is both a cause and a consequence of social exclusion. This has led to growing efforts to promote social inclusion for those with mental health problems, who are often among the most excluded in society. The mental health difficulties experienced by the neurodivergent community are deeply intertwined with the pervasive social exclusion they encounter. By recognising and addressing the various forms of exclusion – as mechanisms that suppress neurological differences – society can take meaningful steps towards fostering inclusivity. Such efforts not only alleviate mental health challenges but also enrich communities by embracing the full spectrum of human diversity.

A central pillar of this book is that it is community-led wherever possible. In many cases, a neuro-mixed team authored or contributed to the chapters. Authors were provided with a wide scope to write about their experiences of neurodiversity and higher education in the areas of their interest/scholarship. Both identity-first (e.g. **Autistic**) and person-first language (e.g. with autism) have been used in the books as this is a global series, different authors have different preferences and there is no unified agreed approach. The editors were not prescriptive in relation to this as the approach taken was to provide a space where authentic scholarship could be developed in a manner that suited the author's drafting style. In this sense, the book is pushing the boundaries of typical academic work and providing a safe space where neurodivergent scholars and authors can write in a style that suits their message dissemination. The flexibility around this is to advance academic scholarship and be inclusive of diverse styles. While this flexible approach is being championed in this book series, there were clear guidelines around remaining faithful to empirical arguments and theoretical frameworks to guide work. The editors felt this was important as a step to highlight that more flexible and authentic scholarly work can still be evidence-based and theoretically framed.

The innovative approach to this book is driven by a wider paradigm shift where the voice and lived experience of researchers and scholars are coming to the fore in an activist and unapologetically authentic manner while remaining faithful to an empirical and theoretical framework. The conference, the masterclasses and now the book series allow for researchers and scholars to discuss the empirical and theoretical from the perspective of the lived world. Similar to the disability movement, this shift, and indeed this book series, aims to bring about change, challenge stigma, and break down presuppositions about neurodiversity. It brings together various voices and perspectives that are not always aligned and indeed can sometimes be at odds. This is intentional as it breaks down the echo chamber walls with a view to bringing about authentic critical dialogue and discussion with the objective of advancing this space. A case in point is the strength-based model, sometimes perceived as being based on a neurotypical perspective, risks perpetuating injustices. This has prompted a discourse within higher education about its reimagination to align with the Neurodiversity Paradigm and foster greater inclusivity. However, others contend that a strength-based approach is about challenging the idea that only neurotypical strengths are valuable and identifying the strengths that neurodiversity can bring if we value neurodivergence instead of attempting to eradicate or assimilate it.

The editors' call for student support programme profiles provided valuable insights, though it is important to note that most submissions came from programme managers who have not disclosed their neurotype. Therefore, the extent of neurodivergent input into the original development or the running of the programmes is not explicitly known. Many examples of impressive outcomes and evaluation designs were evident, and these are to be highly commended. In some cases, however, programme outcome evaluations were high-level and programme resourcing to undertake more comprehensive examinations may have been insufficient. Recognising the foundational importance of these programmes, especially those with longer histories, we strongly encourage the adoption of collaborative advisory structures, already in place in some, to ensure active incorporation of neurodivergent voices in future developments.

This book series is underpinned by the 'nothing about us without us' approach whereby no policy, practice, decision-making, or book writing should be undertaken without the central voice of those it is about and will impact. This is an important rights-based approach that upholds inclusivity, empowerment, and the right for people impacted by events and actions to have control over the decisions that affect their lives. Therefore, this book series aligns itself with an affirmative approach and is open to dialogue and inclusive advancement of societal change in this space.

Neuro-affirming language is a communication approach that emphasises respect and validation for individuals' neurological differences, particularly in contexts involving neurodiversity. It focuses on recognising and affirming each person's unique experiences and perspectives, avoiding language that is stigmatising or dismissive.

This type of language promotes understanding and acceptance, fostering an inclusive environment where people feel valued and understood.

Key principles include the following:

1 **Respect for individual experiences:** Acknowledging that everyone has their own way of processing and interacting with the world.
2 **Avoiding pathologising terms:** Using language that doesn't frame neurominority traits as deficits or disorders.
3 **Empowerment:** Encouraging self-advocacy and valuing diverse ways of thinking and being.

Overall, neuro-affirming language aims to create a supportive atmosphere that recognises and honours neurological diversity.

Finally, while the terms 'higher education' and 'university' are sometimes used interchangeably in this book, in some cases for brevity, it is important to note that 'higher education' encompasses a broader range of post-secondary institutions, whereas 'university' refers specifically to degree-granting academic institutions.

Neurodiversity and Higher Education

In a particularly insightful paper by Hamilton and Petty (2023) on the concept of compassionate pedagogy, the following scene is set for neurodivergent learners in higher education:

> Universities and other higher education institutions ought to be an ideal context for neurodivergent flourishing. Studying at post-secondary level allows for increased independence, autonomy and self-advocacy, ... On average, university settings likely exhibit greater tolerance of difference than other contexts, both preceding and following higher education. Universities can therefore play an important role in promoting lifelong wellbeing, holistic identity development and skill learning for neurodivergent students .... However, we know that not all neurodivergent students thrive at university, and the barriers to

thriving are complex. Many experience high anxiety about exposing their diffe-
rence, within systems and processes that highlight deficit and put the onus on
the student to obtain support. The hidden curriculum can disproportionately
exclude neurodivergent students.

(Hamilton and Petty, 2023, p. 6)

The landscape of higher education has the potential to undergo a profound transformation and recognise the diverse needs and strengths of neurodivergent students. Neurodivergence, as an umbrella term for autism, attention-deficit/hyperactivity disorder (ADHD), dyslexia, dyspraxia, dyscalculia, dysgraphia and other neuro-variations, acknowledges that neurological differences are not deficits but rather variations in human cognition. While neurodivergence brings a wealth of unique perspectives and talents, it also presents significant challenges for many individuals, particularly in academic settings that are mainly designed for the neurotypical population.

Systemic barriers within higher education contribute significantly to the underrepresentation of neurodivergent individuals. These barriers often manifest in ways that discourage neurodivergent people from even considering higher education as a viable pathway as they perceive higher education environments as inherently inaccessible. Moreover, even when neurodivergent students do pursue higher education, they frequently encounter challenges during their enrolment or face significant obstacles during the crucial early stages of their studies. These obstacles, which may include exclusionary pedagogical practices, inadequate support services, and unwelcoming campus cultures, frequently lead to academic failure and subsequent attrition and dropout. This highlights a critical need for institutions to address these systemic issues to improve access and support for neurodivergent students. Banerjee and Graham (2023) highlight how institutional barriers and procedures disproportionately affect disadvantaged students, which can include those with specific learning differences. The paper calls for a more nuanced understanding of these barriers to improve science, technology, engineering, and mathematics (STEM) participation for all students. In fact, in our Masterclass series, Professor Sara Rankin links the concept of the 'leaky pipeline' to specific learning differences in neurodivergence. In her session, Professor Rankin highlights the messaging and other barriers that can inhibit students from pursuing careers in STEM (UCD College of Health and Agricultural Science, 2022).

This book delves into neurodiversity within the higher education context, examining the unique experiences and challenges faced by neurodivergent students and staff. It explores how societal expectations, institutional practices, and individual support systems can either facilitate or hinder students' academic and personal growth.

The barriers confronting neurodivergent students and staff within higher education institutions are not merely incidental. They represent a systemic failure to cultivate truly supportive environments. These barriers manifest as an interplay of deficiencies across the physical, virtual, and cognitive realms – novelly conceptualised in this Introduction as the 'neuro-verse'.

Figure 1 depicts the physical, virtual, and cognitive environments of the 'neuro-verse', highlighting how the various components interrelate and either enhance or detract from its appeal, conviviality, and functionality.

Left unchecked, this neuro-verse can be an environment where neurodivergent individuals are consistently disadvantaged.

The 'physical environment', in its traditional configuration, often presents an overwhelming assault on the senses. The cacophony of sounds, harsh glare of lighting and strong colour palettes, pervasive presence of strong odours, varied textures encountered, and even the subtle nuances of taste within communal spaces can trigger sensory overload. This is further complicated by the fact that neurodivergent individuals may experience either hyper-sensitivity or hypo-sensitivity to these sensory inputs, resulting in a highly individualised and often unpredictable experience of discomfort and distress.

THE "NEURO-VERSE"

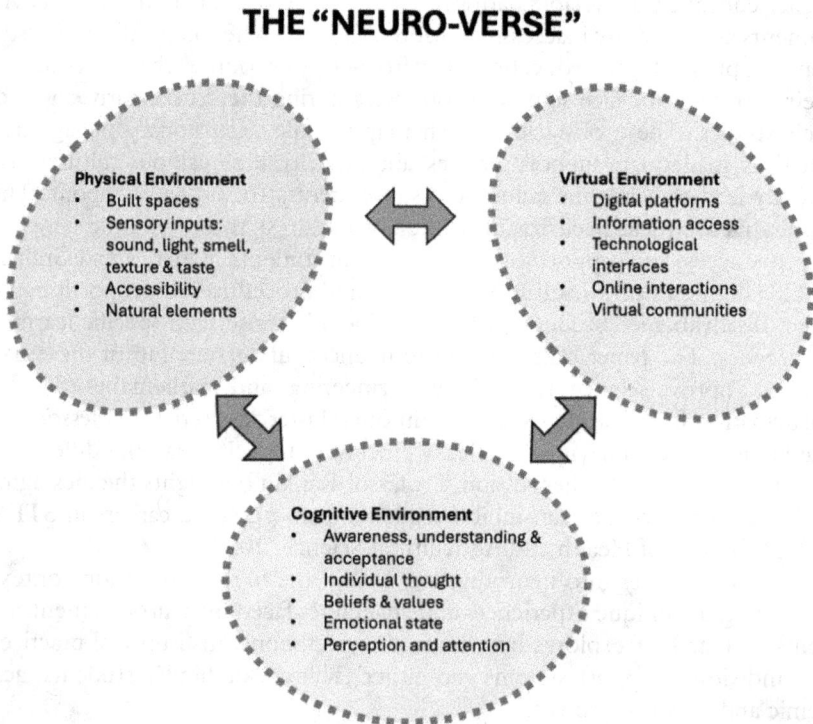

Physical Environment
* Built spaces
* Sensory inputs:
  sound, light, smell,
  texture & taste
* Accessibility
* Natural elements

Virtual Environment
* Digital platforms
* Information access
* Technological
  interfaces
* Online interactions
* Virtual communities

Cognitive Environment
* Awareness, understanding &
  acceptance
* Individual thought
* Beliefs & values
* Emotional state
* Perception and attention

Figure 1 The 'neuro-verse' – interrelated physical, virtual and cognitive environments.

While the integration of a thoughtfully designed virtual environment, complete with relevant and integrated assistive technology (AT) tools, holds the potential to mitigate some of the inherent accessibility challenges posed by the physical environment, this potential can be unrealised. This depends, at least in part, on the quality of training provided in the tools (McDowall et al., 2023) and how broadly available the tools are to students, the lack of understanding of AT by staff and the requirement for staff to create accessible and inclusive settings for all users (Zorec et al., 2024). The tools provided are often sub-optimally configured, poorly integrated with the physical setting, and an institution may fail to offer the necessary range of choices to accommodate the diverse needs and preferences of its neurodivergent population (Macheque, Kadyamatimba and Ochara, 2024). This lack of customisation and flexibility further exacerbates the challenges faced by these individuals.

A significant challenge also exists within the broader 'cognitive environment', defined here as the collective awareness, understanding, and acceptance of neurodivergent individuals within the higher education community. This community encompasses lecturers, tutors, student services personnel, and fellow students. The atmosphere they cultivate through their conduct and interactions, whether consciously or unconsciously, can greatly influence the sense of belonging and well-being of neurodivergent students and staff. When the understanding and acceptance of neurodivergence are limited, and efforts to develop and implement effective accommodations are insufficient, the environment may not fully support the diverse needs of all individuals.

This systemic failure is deeply rooted in structural biases that privilege neurotypical norms while marginalising neurodivergent individuals. In this context, Radulski (2022, 2024) argued that a Minority Group Model of Neurodiversity could help identify barriers to inclusion for neurominority cohorts. Radulski also introduced two new concepts, neurotypical hegemony, and neurotypical privilege: defined respectively as the cultural dominance of neurotypical norms throughout society, and the corresponding privilege this social group experiences because of their normativity. From another perspective, Nair et al. (2024) argue for a decolonial shift in neurodiversity scholarship, moving beyond Global North-centric perspectives to include Global Majority knowledge systems and address the intersection of race and neurodivergence, thereby expanding theoretical discourses and research implications.

The hegemonic position of neurotypical perspectives creates physical, virtual and cognitive environments that are both self-referential and self-reinforcing, thus perpetuating neurotypical norms and marginalising neurodivergent individuals.

Consequently, neurodivergent students and staff are often placed in an untenable position, forced to expend significant energy in an attempt to 'mask' and 'fit in' to an environment that was not designed with their needs in mind. Those who are unable to successfully navigate this inimical environment are often left to languish, their potential unrealised, their contributions lost and their well-being compromised. This is not merely a matter of inconvenience; it is a systemic failure to uphold the principles of inclusivity and equity that should underpin all institutions of higher learning.

> *Growing up neurodivergent, we are taught that our natural way of thinking, moving or communicating is 'wrong' or 'too much,' and we learn to hide part of ourselves to be tolerable to the neurotypical people who surround us. Like being expected to communicate in a second language that you were never explicitly taught but being expected to somehow automatically learn and punished when you make mistakes. Always exhausted – always frightened. Masking … every day I am accommodating the needs of the neurotypical people in my personal and professional life. But to ask to be accommodated in return has almost always been a fight. But is it asking for an accommodation, or am I asking in these little ways, to be able to safely stop accommodating the neurotypical people around me?*
>
> (Romy E. Cecil, Pre-Service Teacher, personal communication, 25 March 2025)

A deliberate change in the cognitive environment is necessary to prioritise neurodiversity. This will generate opportunities for more inclusive physical and virtual environments, which may further strengthen and solidify a neurodiverse cognitive environment, creating a more neuro-accepting neuro-verse.

Ultimately, this book aims to empower educators, administrators, and support staff, with knowledge and exemplars to inspire the creation of inclusive and supportive higher education experiences for neurodivergent students and an inclusive workplace for neurodivergent staff. By fostering a deeper understanding of the unique challenges and strengths of this population, we can work towards a future where neurodiversity is celebrated, and all students and staff have the opportunity to thrive.

Book Layout

This book is organised into two parts. Part I explores some fundamental topics relating to neurodiversity and higher education. Note that as there was a prominent focus on Autism in some of these chapters, separate chapters covering dyslexia and ADHD have also been included. Part II provides examples of what has been achieved in practical terms in a number of higher education neurodiversity programmes in various countries around the world.

References

Banerjee, P., and Graham, L. (2023) 'STEM education in England: Questioning the "leaky pipeline" metaphor', *Education + Training*, 65(8/9), 957–971. https://doi.org/10.1108/ET-03-2023-0079

Hamilton, L.G., and Petty, S. (2023) 'Compassionate pedagogy for neurodiversity in higher education: A conceptual analysis', *Frontiers in Psychology*, 14(1093290), 6. https://doi.org/10.3389/fpsyg.2023.1093290

Macheque, V., Kadyamatimba, A., and Ochara, N.M. (2024) 'Engineering modelling requirements for integration of assistive technology as a pathway for inclusive education in the disability unit', *International Journal of Research in Business and Social Science*, 13(6), 381–404. https://doi.org/10.20525/ijrbs.v13i6.3529

McDowall, A., Doyle, N., and Kiseleva, M. (2023) *Neurodiversity at work: Demand, supply and a gap analysis* (p. 56). London, UK: Birkbeck, University of London.

Morgan, C., Burns, T., Fitzpatrick, R., Pinfold, V., and Priebe, S. (2007) 'Social exclusion and mental health: Conceptual and methodological review', *British Journal of Psychiatry*, 191(6), 477–483. https://doi.org/10.1192/bjp.bp.106.034942

Nair, V.K., Farah, W., & Boveda, M. (2024) 'Is neurodiversity a Global Northern White paradigm?' *Autism*, 0(0). https://doi.org/10.1177/13623613241280835

Radulski, E.M. (2022) 'Conceptualising Autistic masking, camouflaging, and neurotypical privilege: Towards a minority group model of neurodiversity', *Human Development*. www.karger.com/Article/FullText/524122 (accessed: 26 April 2022).

Radulski, E.M. (2024) 'A sociology of Autistic masking and camouflaging: The intersectionality of neurotypical privilege and the neuroarchy', Thesis, La Trobe. https://opal.latrobe.edu.au/articles/thesis/A_Sociology_of_Autistic_Masking_and_Camouflaging_The_Intersectionality_of_Neurotypical_Privilege_and_the_Neuroarchy/27139314/1 (accessed: 16 October 2024).

Radulski, B., and Jaworowski, N. (2022) 'Neurodiversity as the next frontier: Part 1 – celebrating "all kinds of clever" in higher education'. www.latrobe.edu.au/mylatrobe/neurodiversity-as-the-next-frontier-part-1-celebrating-all-kinds-of-clever-in-higher-education/ (accessed: 11 March 2025).

UCD College of Health and Agricultural Science. (2022) 'Neurodiversity Masterclass 24th March 2022: Prof Sara Rankin'. www.youtube.com/watch?v=Op_udhJB0JE (accessed: 1 April 2025).

Walker, N. (2014) 'Neurodiversity: Some basic terms and definitions', https://neuroqueer.com/neurodiversity-terms-and-definitions/

Zorec, K., Desmond, D., Boland, T., McNicholl, A., O'Connor, A., Stafford, G., and Gallagher, P. (2024) 'A whole-campus approach to technology and inclusion of students with disabilities in higher education in Ireland', *Disability & Society*, 39(5), 1147–1172. https://doi.org/10.1080/09687599.2022.2114885

Part I

Fundamental Topics Relating to Neurodiversity and Higher Education

Chapter 1

Designing for Neurodiversity in Higher Education

A Bioecological Approach

Lorna Hamilton

With case studies contributed by Jenny Anderton and Milo Kat

Introduction

The number of neurodivergent students entering higher education has risen steadily in recent years. Accurate prevalence rates are difficult to ascertain; in one recent survey, 14% of university applicants in the United Kingdom identified as neurodivergent (using a limited operational definition encompassing autism and attention-deficit/hyperactivity disorder [ADHD] only) (Unite Students, 2023). This marks a significant shift in comparison with previous generations, when a diagnosis of autism, ADHD or 'specific' learning differences such as dyslexia or dyscalculia made access to university-level study a remote possibility for young people. This trend is likely attributable to a combination of factors, including changes to diagnostic criteria, increased awareness, as well as widening participation efforts across the higher education sector. Whatever the underlying reasons, neurodivergent students now constitute a sizeable minority within the university population. However, higher education institutions are often not well-equipped for the inclusion of neurodivergent learners, instead relying on established pedagogical practices, institutional processes, and structures that are inaccessible or even actively marginalising, for this group of students. Neurodiversity is rarely specifically considered as a dimension of difference within institutional equality, diversity, and inclusion policies; meanwhile, research suggests that neurodivergent students are at elevated risk of leaving before completing their course and tend to be less happy at university than neuro-majority peers (Anderson, Stephenson and Carter, 2018).

In this chapter, I draw on bioecological systems theory to frame the complex social ecology of universities, with consideration given to how they might be designed to better include neurodivergent learners. Drawing on case studies from student and staff perspectives in the context of a small, widening participation university in the north of England, I focus on three components of the higher education system through a bioecological lens: (1) learning and teaching, (2) professional support services, and (3) student advocacy underpinned

DOI: 10.4324/9781003495925-3

by changing societal discourses of neurodiversity. In adopting a bioecological lens, the chapter imagines a neurodiversity-affirming university education that actively welcomes neurocognitive difference, recognising strengths alongside support needs, and designing its programmes and systems to be equally accessible for students of all neurotypes.

Neurodiversity and Bioecological Systems

The neurodiversity paradigm shifts the focus of the study of neurodevelopmental difference from the individual to individual-in-context (Chapman, 2021; Pellicano and den Houting, 2022). Until recently, most psychological research relating to autism, ADHD, 'specific' learning difficulties and other forms of neurodivergence has sought to pinpoint cognitive causes of impairment, in order to inform evidence-based interventions. There have been important advances using this approach; for example, broad scientific consensus on the causal role of phonological processing in dyslexia has informed the development of effective reading interventions for dyslexic children (Snowling, Hulme and Nation, 2020). However, there is growing acknowledgement that many common neurodivergent characteristics and experiences – including sensory sensitivities, inconsistent executive functioning, and social communication challenges – are transdiagnostic (Astle et al., 2022). Furthermore, categorical diagnoses very often co-occur in the same individual and within-diagnosis profiles are highly heterogeneous (Thapar, Cooper and Rutter, 2017). Given this complexity, the search for simple explanatory models becomes less relevant.

Moreover, some interventions seeking to modify neurodivergent behaviours have been identified as causing long-term psychological harm in lived experience accounts (Anderson, 2023). Recent progress in scientific understanding, alongside a burgeoning research literature that foregrounds the experiences and priorities of neurodivergent communities, signals the need for a change in conceptualisation of what intervention should mean in relation to neurodivergence. A narrow focus on fixing within-person 'impairment' is insufficient and, in the worst cases, damaging. Researchers and practitioners seeking to improve outcomes must also consider how the contexts in which neurodivergent people live, study, and work can be modified to support individual strengths.

A useful framework in which to situate this necessary shift in focus is afforded by Bronfenbrenner's bioecological systems theory (Bronfenbrenner, 2005; Bronfenbrenner and Morris, 2006). This model conceptualises human development as the synergistic interaction of four components: *person-process-context-time* (PPCT). 'Proximal processes' are the mechanisms of interaction between the individual and the environment that drive development, thereby allowing genetic potential for psychological functioning to be actualised. The environment here comprises nested contexts that are more or less immediate to the individual; from microsystems (such as the family home or school class-room) to macrosystems (including socio-economic influences and cultural norms). Critically, environments both shape and are shaped by the individual through bidirectional, and progressively more complex, interactional processes that occur regularly and over extended periods of time. For these proximal processes to support positive psychological development, adequate resources and a degree of stability within the environment are necessary. Here, posi-tive developmental outcomes might mean acquiring new knowledge and skills (i.e. learning), establishing and maintaining reciprocally rewarding relation-ships, and the ability to cope under conditions of stress (Bronfenbrenner and Ceci, 1994). A key implication of this model is that it should be possible to increase the extent of actualised genetic potential for positive developmental outcomes by enhancing the quality of proximal processes and/or environ-mental contexts.

Most research relating to neurodevelopmental difference trains a spotlight on the centre of the bioecological model, that is, characteristics of the (neu-rodivergent) person. Adjustments within specific settings, such as schools or healthcare providers, in response to these individual characteristics are some-times considered, although intervention studies have more typically sought to effect change within the person. To achieve an inclusive, affirming educational culture in which neurodivergent people can flourish, a more holistic, system-wide approach is needed (Aitken and Fletcher-Watson, 2022).

A System-wide Approach to Inclusive Higher Education

Education is characterised by proximal processes: between learner and teacher, learner and technology, teacher and management, and so on. While bioecological systems theory has been influential in early childhood educa-tion research and practice, it has been applied to higher education settings relatively rarely, although it provides a theoretical account of development through the lifespan. Universities are made up of complex social ecologies, within which proximal interplay between students and their environments takes place. Educational outcomes are not simply the result of student compe-tence plus curriculum quality (Mulisa, 2019). Rather, students' learning and well-being at university is the product of personal characteristics (such as neu-rodivergent cognitive profiles) and interacting components of the university ecosystem (e.g. pedagogical practices, disability support, and cohesive working between these microsystems).

Hewett and colleagues used longitudinal interview data from visually impaired university students to formulate a bioecological model of inclu-sive higher education (Hewett et al., 2019, 2020). The learner sits at the centre of the model, with person characteristics (here specifically visual impair-ment) operating in bidirectional interaction with aspects of the environment. The authors identify salient aspects of university microsystems for inclusive higher education practice, including departmental academic staff, student peers, welfare and disability support services, and physical and digital university infrastructure. Mesosystems comprise the connections and communications between these components. Relevant features of the exosystem – directly influencing aspects of the microsystem, while more psychologically remote to the learner – include institutional disability policy and funding landscape. At the macrosystem level, national higher education policy, equality legislation and societal attitudes towards disability combine to influence proximal processes within universities. Finally, university study is situated within a developmental and educational timeline, such that learning interactions are influenced by students' prior educational experiences from early years through primary and secondary school.

Outcomes for neurodivergent students are likewise underpinned by proximal interactions within the complex social ecology of universities. Students must navigate multiple, interacting systems (e.g. learning spaces, disability services, accommodation, and pastoral support) that are often not designed with neurodivergent needs in mind (Clouder et al., 2020). For example, an Autistic first-year student midway through a lengthy assessment process, but not yet in receipt of a learning adjustment plan or disability support funding, who has slept badly in noisy accommodation and navigated busy hallways to reach the teaching room, may not be able to engage effectively in a discursive seminar. Likewise, a student with executive function challenges who is experiencing poor mental health may struggle to navigate pastoral support services that are not clearly signposted. Inclusion strategies that target specific neurodivergent diagnoses are unlikely to show consistent success, given very wide heterogeneity within diagnostic categories and frequent overlap between them (Sonuga-Barke and Thapar, 2021). Moreover, teaching staff report feeling overwhelmed by requirements to make multiple, sometimes seemingly conflicting, adjustments to their practice (Cook and Ogden, 2022). Instead, the ideal cross-institutional practice would involve both *universal* inclusion strategies and *personalised* support mechanisms tailored to individual profiles of strength and difficulty. Overarching principles for a neurodiversity-affirming university ecosystem might include the following:

- **Universal design** – campus spaces, pedagogical practices, technologies, policies, and processes that are intentionally constructed to be accessible to the widest possible range of people, including those with neurodivergent profiles (Burgstahler and Cory, 2010).
- **Anticipation of need** – expecting every group, setting, and network to be neurodiverse and planning accordingly. This would help to reduce sensory, social, and other common barriers to access and engagement, thus avoiding reactive problem-solving in response to exclusion, failure, burnout and distress.

- **Flexibility and choice** – supporting students' sense of belonging on campus by allowing agency over their learning, and wider university journeys wherever feasible.
- **Compassion** – an intentional commitment to recognise and modify institutional systems and practices that disadvantage minoritised students (Hamilton and Petty, 2023).
- **Co-production** – establishing trust and communication with neurodivergent members of the university community to allow collaborative decision-making; sharing responsibility for inclusive practice across the institution (Cumming et al., 2023).
- **Value-neutral communication** – auditing university communications for stigmatising use of language in relation to diversity, including minority neurotypes and respecting personal language preferences.
- **Training and upskilling** – ensuring that staff and, where possible, student communities have access to high-quality neurodiversity training that combines insights from lived experience with research evidence.
- **Strategic inclusion** – including neurodiversity as a dimension in institutional equality, diversity and inclusion (EDI) risk assessments, audits and strategies; incorporating neurodivergent first-person perspectives in the development of EDI strategy (Dwyer et al., 2023).

These principles signal changes to practice that are relatively minimal in terms of cost, time, and resources. The primary requirement is a willingness to question the way that things have always been done and to identify and implement small steps towards more neurodiversity-affirming practice. This approach might then better enable the increasingly neurodiverse student population to actualise their potential at university and into the workplace.

The following sections consider how these principles might be enacted within three aspects of the university ecosystem. Using a bioecological lens, the scenarios described draw on research literature; personal reflection on pedagogical practice, including first-hand accounts from neurodivergent students; and insights from an ongoing cross-campus participatory action research project (Hamilton, Williams and Petty, 2024).

The Learning and Teaching Microsystem

Physical and virtual learning environments provide the context for proximal processes that support students' acquisition of new knowledge and skills. Pervasive barriers to inclusion and participation for neurodivergent students within traditional classroom environments at all levels of education have been well documented (e.g. Clouder et al., 2020; Leifler, Borg and Bölte, 2024) and are summarised briefly here. Miscommunications (staff to student or student to student) can be underpinned by the 'double empathy problem', that is, barriers to reciprocal interaction between people who have widely different dispositions and experiences of the world (Milton, Gurbuz and López, 2022). Neurodivergent students report that their behaviours are often misconstrued as rude or disengaged. For example, closing eyes, directing gaze away from an instructor or wearing headphones might facilitate a student's focus and engagement with class content but can be interpreted by others as displaying a lack of interest (Spaeth and Pearson, 2023). Participation in group-work, *if implemented inflexibly*, can reduce engagement and inhibit learning for some students. Virtual learning environments are not always designed to the highest standards of accessibility. While assessment types have diversified in higher education over recent years, traditional assignments such as essays still dominate, with a near total reliance on written formats in many degree programmes. At the mesosystem level, accommodations set out in learning adjustment plans may be inconsistently implemented in the classroom. Within the exosystem, sensory differences may not have been considered in the design of learning spaces, meaning that lights might be uncomfortably bright with no dimmer option, or seats in lecture theatres are packed closely together. From the macrosystem, outdated stereotypes based on diagnostic category (e.g. 'Autistic students can't understand counterfactual perspectives') may lead educators to hold lower expectations of neurodivergent learners and prompt generic accommodations rather than responsive, personalised approaches. Within the chronosystem, negative experiences at earlier stages of education, perhaps including experiences of exclusion, school distress or a punitive approach to neurodivergent behaviours at school, can mean that students hold a negative academic self-concept – and find it difficult to trust those in positions of authority (Hummerstone and Parsons, 2021; Hamilton, 2024). Thus, layers of exclusion embedded within the university ecology can interact with neurodivergent characteristics to limit learning and well-being.

Moving on from a pedagogical status quo that can exclude students who think differently requires an intentional and compassionate approach, but there are many useful frameworks to draw upon. Universal Design for Learning (UDL) anticipates learner variability from the point of curriculum design, through delivery to assessment of learning, without reducing this variability to simplistic 'learning styles' (CAST, 2024). Providing multiple means of engagement, representation of information and expression affords students agency in how they navigate their learning. For example, flexible participation in class activities (e.g. working silently and independently, joining small-group discussions and/or posting comments on a live online noticeboard) accommodates diverse social communication preferences, which can – perhaps counterintuitively – result in increased participation and engagement (Hamilton and Knight, 2025). This in turn allows the instructor opportunities to formatively assess and scaffold students' understanding of instructional content. Flexible, strength-based assessment allows students choice over topics and, where possible, format of delivery, so that for example a presentation could be delivered orally, recorded or formatted as a detailed infographic. While there is, of course, good pedagogic rationale for retaining traditional, standardised academic assessments for certain learning outcomes, integrating some scaffolded, flexible assessment through programme design allows students with diverse cognitive profiles to demonstrate their learning in a way that harnesses strengths.

A growing body of research indicates that UDL can improve learning process and outcomes for all students (e.g. Kings-Sears et al., 2023) and is preferred by neurodivergent learners specifically (Barrera Ciurana and Moliner García, 2024). (It is important also to note critiques of UDL, commonly relating to an underdeveloped evidence base or underspecified theoretical foundations [Boysen, 2024]). UDL offers a framework for inclusive pedagogical design but needs to be combined with responsive teaching and a reflective approach to student progress in context. Inclusive pedagogical approaches more broadly have been critiqued for compromising rigour. Educators sometimes argue embedding flexibility and choice may deprive students of practising work-relevant, transferable skills, such as groupwork or presentation in front of an audience (Hills, Overend and Hildbrandt, 2022). However, with constructive alignment to learning objectives and clarity of expectations for different forms of engagement, rigour can be maintained. Moreover, many modern workplaces offer flexibility, and employers that embrace neurodivergent ways of working are gradually becoming more commonplace (Austin and Pisano, 2017). Ideally, students select career paths that allow them to play to their strengths, and universities can play an important role in facilitating the recognition and development of those strengths (i.e. metacognition). Most seriously, instances where a pedagogical approach has been inflexibly enforced have occasionally been associated with psychological harm, as in the tragic case of Natasha Abrahart in 2018 (Burin and Atrey, 2024). Academic staff, faced with demanding and complex workloads, may feel ill-equipped to respond to increasingly diverse student needs in their teaching practice. However, planning in flexibility and choice at the curriculum design stage can mitigate the need for multiple reactive accommodations.

Giving students a greater degree of control over their learning can feel uncomfortable for educators, but it can also produce a higher standard of work, boost engagement, and have a meaningful impact on the inclusion of neurodivergent students and other minoritised groups. This is illustrated in a testimonial from an Autistic final-year psychology undergraduate participating in a module incorporating UDL and strength-based assessment techniques:

I struggled socially in my first year at university, which was made worse by COVID restrictions. In contrast to others, I enjoyed online learning. Learning at my own pace, online in my own home, was ideal for me. This comfort did not extend to my second year. I found the lights in the lectures too bright, I felt unable to ask for help within large groups, and I often struggled with fatigue resulting in me missing lectures. The structure of this module comes from a place of understanding about neurodivergent brains, which has massively helped me to feel comfortable. I get to follow what I'm interested in and complete the assignment in the best way for me, which I believe has improved the quality of my work. I still struggle with noises from inside and outside the building and the lights still hurt my eyes, but I know that I am not going to be chastised or singled out for wearing my headphones or looking away from the board, which allows me to do the things I need to do to keep learning and stay engaged.

Navigating the Mesosystem: Professional Support Services

Beyond the classroom, professional and support services have a crucial role to play in students' university experience. These services typically include disability, well-being and study support, library and information technology, accommodation and facilities, admissions, student records, and career guidance. In a whole-system approach, proximal processes within and between these contexts are also expected to contribute to psychological outcomes for neurodivergent students.

Eliminating sensory stressors entirely from a physical campus that hosts thousands of people each day is unfeasible. However, adopting a flexible approach wherever possible, anticipating need, and prioritising consultation and accessibility in the design of new buildings and virtual systems can go a long way to improve neurodivergent inclusion (Fabri and Andrews, 2016). An example of technological infrastructure that supports the needs of neurodivergent students is lecture capture. Many universities globally now use lecture capture software, although the practice of recording lectures remains controversial among academic staff partly due to concerns about its impact on student attendance. However, a recent study indicated the high value of lecture capture for neurodivergent and disabled students both as an inclusive learning tool (e.g. so that taught material could be replayed at a pace appropriate for the individual's processing speed, or listened to while moving) and as a 'flexible safety net' for the occasions when on-campus attendance was not possible due to health or self-care concerns (Horlin, Hronska and Nordmann, 2024). Factoring these perspectives into decisions about budgetary spend and campus-wide academic practice demonstrates a systemic inclusive approach. Likewise, paying close attention to access to natural light, uncluttered space, and the layout of seating in the design of new physical spaces, or renovation of older ones, indicates that neurodivergent members of the university community are seen and prioritised (Hope, 2022).

Communication differences extend to the university information ecosystem beyond the classroom. For example, a study with Autistic university students in the United States illustrated how double empathy barriers, such as misaligned processing speed or inaccurately assumed common ground, can prevent access to crucial information about academic courses, resources, and extracurricular opportunities (Stockwell et al., 2024). When key information is transmitted informally via social interaction, especially in large gatherings such as freshers' fairs, neurodivergent students are placed at further disadvantage. Clear, accessible information about university services and processes provided in accessible formats in easily located online spaces is paramount. One-way communications from parts of the university that exist in the student's exosystem (e.g. the student records directorate) can be formal and difficult to parse. Students who are at risk of academic failure receive written communications that might refer to 'termination of studies' or 'enforced suspension'. Auditing and revising standard university email templates in line with principles of compassionate communication can minimise unnecessary distress for a student recipient who may already be struggling.

Disability services are particularly salient to the success of neurodivergent students (although importantly not all would self-describe as disabled). The traditional model of university disability services has been retrofitting accommodations to standard practice in response to confirmed clinical diagnoses. For example, a dyslexic or dyscalculic student might be awarded extra time in examinations if proof of diagnosis can be obtained. As the number of neurodivergent students in universities continues to rise, this model seems increasingly untenable. New students may have to wait for long periods until a learning adjustment plan can be agreed and disability support funding accessed. In the interim, some may drop out as their learning and non-academic needs are not met (Nuske et al., 2019). Universal design in campus space and teaching practice should reduce the need for individual accommodations but, where still required, a more inclusive approach to disability support is to provide adjustments on the basis of need rather than diagnosis.

Case Study: Implementing Universal Design in a Disability Service – Jenny Anderton

I have worked in various disability services in Higher Education for 17 years, mostly in services operating a diagnosis-dependent model. This means that resources are provided to students through a single pathway, with the emphasis on the student to justify why they need support, adaptation or access to a resource. Barriers such as the cost of diagnosis, wait-times for healthcare services, the administrative burden of sourcing paperwork and disparity of medical provision have prevented students from accessing resources in a timely way, sometimes blocking access entirely. The impact on an individual student of not being able to access support and resources can be the difference between academic success and failure. The use of a diagnosis-dependent model further reinforces the perspective that there is one 'correct' way to access resources, and anyone who sits outside that ideal must justify their access needs, and therefore their value in a space.

In our setting, a recent move towards universal design in disability support embraces the natural differences in our student population and enables everyone to access resources in a way which suits their needs, processing preferences and tools, without having to draw on a deficit-focused model. Designing resources in a way that embeds choice and flexibility allows everyone to work to their individual strengths, empowers and increases independence, reduces administration for the student, academic and support staff, and fosters an inclusive culture, which embraces differences in working styles and boosts effective collaboration.

Although there is a still a long way to go, the impact of this shift so far is that disabled and neurodivergent students feel more valued at university. Having a resource or space made accessible to them without having to specifically request it makes them feel that they belong in the university community, and less like an outsider trying to fit into a world where previously they were an afterthought.

Universal design of services, in combination with personalised support through trusted relationships with key members of university staff (e.g. disability support workers, academic tutors), is a more promising approach to inclusive practice than retrofitting generic accommodations.

Changing Discourses of Neurodiversity: The Macrosystem and Chronosystem

At a more distal level, changes in scientific and lay understanding of neurodiversity indirectly impact the experiences of neurodivergent students at university. As content related to autism and ADHD in particular proliferates on social media platforms, discourse rooted in the neurodiversity paradigm is more accessible to young people, with implications for adolescent identity construction and community building (Akhmedova et al., 2024; Leveille, 2024). Thus, neurodivergent students entering higher education now are more likely to view neurodivergence as an integral part of their identities, advocate for their needs and those of their peers, and form epistemic communities in physical and digital spaces. If universities can embrace neurodivergent advocacy, meaningful co-production of initiatives to promote inclusion and belonging at university is possible (Kat, 2024).

Case Study: Establishing and Running a Neurodivergent Study Group – Milo Kat

In 2023, another neurodivergent student and I set up our university's Disabled Students' Network, because we felt misunderstood as neurodivergent students and wanted to connect with others having similar experiences. We felt that raising awareness, running events and having an online forum could help. I'm interested in neurodivergent wellbeing and was eager to set up a neuro-divergent study group to facilitate a healthier relationship between students and their work.

We booked a computer room in a familiar place on campus, which students would have been to previously and could visit before the study group. It ran as a regular weekly 7-hour drop-in window, so students felt no pressure if they turned up 'late', or to stay for the whole session. We released information about the study sessions on the online forum Discord, which was already popular with neurodivergent students, and via on-campus posters.

We made effort to talk like a friend and not to look 'in charge' (e.g. wearing informal clothing), which increased trust. We used non-judgmental language when asking about assignments and told people to take time off when needed (regardless of deadlines) to help ease burnout. Letting people discuss previous negative experiences in education or work helped them understand their work behaviours better and see that they could sometimes self-sabotage. They could then start to address this. As a student committee, we collaborated with other universities' networks, and external agencies. This helped us feel that we were part of a wider movement, as the workload involved in running the group could be isolating. These connections also helped us to conceptualise what we wanted the group to achieve, and how it could draw from wider systems of support and research in neurodiversity.

While holding open conversations about experiences in education was helpful and built trust, some students started to use the group as therapy. Our group was always about defusing work-related stress, guilt and shame and we became trusted sources of support because we were friendly and understood the challenges. However, some group members needed mental health support from neurodiversity-aware staff, but demand unfortunately outweighed supply at the time. The university provided our committee members 'distressed students' training, which was somewhat helpful, but wider structures need to change too. I felt that our committee needed input from practitioners, who understood the issues and had more experience than us, to reflect on our group's activities. We are disabled students ourselves after all, still developing our understanding of, and approach towards, these issues.

Peer support networks, as illustrated here, can make the difference between a student staying in university and dropping out; there is immense value in finding others with similar experiences and having the opportunity to tackle problems collaboratively. However, neurodivergent student networks need to operate within safe boundaries, with clear communication lines to wider university support systems in place. Peers cannot and should not replace institutional accommodations and pastoral support.

Achieving a sense of belonging at university is key to student retention and satisfaction. For neurodivergent students, barriers to belonging are often rooted in negative past experiences of education. The perceived accessibility of programmes and campuses is also key to feelings of belonging (Edgar, Pownall and Harris, 2024). For any minoritised group, representation matters for inclusion and belonging. Historically, neurodivergence has predominantly been represented through a deficit-focused lens in university curricula in psychology, health sciences, and other disciplines, which serves to marginalise neurodivergent students studying those curricula (Botha, 2021). As discourses rooted in the neurodiversity paradigm become increasingly commonplace in communities and across media, universities can anticipate tensions by auditing curricula for narrowly pathologising and outdated content. Further, given the growing recognition of the advantages of a neurodiverse workforce, universities should seek to be at the vanguard of neurodiversity affirming hiring and employment practices (Petty et al., 2025). If university staff members feel enabled to disclose their own neurodivergence safely, within a working culture that allows flexibility and welcomes difference, there are knock-on benefits for neurodivergent students in terms of representation and positive models for future employment.

Conclusion

Over the last two decades, both the science of neurodiversity and the higher education landscape have shifted dramatically. The growing numbers of neurodivergent students accessing higher education prompt a reframing of inclusive practice at the whole-university level, moving away from accommodations underpinned by a narrow, deficit-focused understanding of neurodivergence. Bronfenbrenner's bioecological systems theory, and particularly the person-process-context-time model, offers a useful theoretical lens through which to conceptualise this work.

The responsibility for actualising neurodivergent potential within and beyond higher education should be shared across the university ecosystem. Students who feel that they belong on campus and who have a sense of agency in their learning are more likely to develop metacognitive understanding of their own strengths and challenges and to enjoy positive well-being while at university. These 'intrinsic' factors are likely to facilitate successful completion of degree programmes and progression to preferred employment after graduation. In this chapter, I have argued that universities can intentionally promote neurodivergent belonging on campus, enacting neurodiversity-affirming practice by design. There is much left to do to achieve these goals, however.

High-quality evidence on trajectories and outcomes for neurodivergent students is scarce; for example, in the United Kingdom, higher education data do not routinely disaggregate neurodivergence from disability. Many neurodivergent students are not captured within these data because they choose not to disclose and/or do not view themselves as disabled. A data-driven characterisation of the 'problem' is an important first step in designing evidence-informed solutions. University staff are not routinely trained in neurodiversity and the quality of training that exists is unknown. Channels for dialogue and collaboration between neurodivergent student communities and staff across university systems are often absent, unclear or compromised by lack of trust. Nonetheless, much can be achieved by embedding and enacting principles of universal design, compassion and co-production, and by allowing flexibility and choice across systems to disrupt practices that are 'neuro-normative by default'. By enhancing the quality of proximal processes and environmental contexts in this way, universities can transform life trajectories for people who think differently.

References

Akhmedova, A., Sutcliffe, J., Greenhow, C., Fisher, M. H., and Sung, C. (2024) 'Social media use among neurodivergent college students: Benefits, harms and implications for education', *Information and Learning Sciences*, 125(10), 850–876.

Aitken, D., and Fletcher-Watson, S. (2022) 'Neurodiversity-affirmative education: Why and how?', *The Psychologist*. www.bps.org.uk/psychologist/neurodiversity-affirmative-education-why-and-how (accessed: 12 November 2024).

Anderson, L.K. (2023) 'Autistic experiences of applied behavior analysis', *Autism*, 27(3), 737–750.

Anderson, A.H., Carter, M., and Stephenson, J. (2018) 'Perspectives of university students with autism spectrum disorder', *Journal of Autism and Developmental Disorders*, 48, 651–665.

Astle, D.E., Holmes, J., Kievit, R., and Gathercole, S.E. (2022) 'Annual research review: The transdiagnostic revolution in neurodevelopmental disorders', *Journal of Child Psychology and Psychiatry*, 63(4), 397–417.

Austin, R.D., and Pisano, G.P. (2017) 'Neurodiversity as a competitive advantage', *Harvard Business Review*, 95(3), 96–103.

Barrera Ciurana, M., and Moliner García, O. (2024) ' "How does universal design for learning help me to learn?": Students with autism spectrum disorder voices in higher education', *Studies in Higher Education*, 49(6), 899–912.

Botha, M. (2021) 'Academic, activist or advocate? Angry, entangled and emerging: A critical reflection on autism knowledge production', *Frontiers in Psychology*, 12, 727542.

Boysen, G. (2024) 'A critical analysis of the research evidence behind CAST's universal design for learning guidelines', *Policy Futures in Education*, 22(7), 1219–1238.

Bronfenbrenner, U. (2005) *Making human beings human: Bioecological perspectives on human development*. Thousand Oaks, CA: Sage.

Bronfenbrenner, U., and Ceci, S.J. (1994) 'Nature-nurture reconceptualized in developmental perspective: A bioecological model', *Psychological Review*, 101(4), 568–186.

Bronfenbrenner, U., and Morris, P. A. (2006) 'The bioecological model of human development'. In W. Damon (Series Ed.) and R. M. Lerner (Vol. Ed.), *Handbook of child psychology: Theoretical models of human development* (pp. 793–828). New York, NY: Wiley.

Burgstahler, S.E., and Cory, R.C., eds. (2010) *Universal design in higher education: From principles to practice*. Harvard: Harvard Education Press.

Burin, A.K., and Atrey, S. (2024) 'Unleashing the anticipatory reasonable adjustment duty: *University of Bristol v Abrahart (EHRC intervening)* [2024] EWHC 299 (KB)', *International Journal of Discrimination and the Law*, 24(1), 7–18.

CAST. (2024) 'Universal design for learning guidelines, version 3.0 [graphic organiser]'. https://udlguidelines.cast.org/static/udlg3-graphicorganizer-digital-numbers-a11y.pdf

Chapman, R. (2021) 'Neurodiversity and the social ecology of mental functions', *Perspectives on Psychological Science*, 16(6), 1360–1372.

Clouder, L., Karakus, M., Cinotti, A., Ferreyra, M.V., Fierros, G.A., and Rojo, P. (2020) 'Neurodiversity in higher education: A narrative synthesis'. *Higher Education*, 80(4), 757–778.

Cook, A., and Ogden, J. (2022) 'Challenges, strategies and self-efficacy of teachers supporting Autistic pupils in contrasting school settings: A qualitative study', *European Journal of Special Needs Education*, 37(3), 371–385.

Cumming, T.M., Bugge, A.S.J., Kriss, K., McArthur, I., Watson, K., and Jiang, Z. (2023) 'Diversified: Promoting co-production in course design and delivery', *Frontiers in Education*, 8, 1329810.

Dwyer, P., Mineo, E., Mifsud, K., Lindholm, C., Gurba, A., and Waisman, T.C. (2023) 'Building neurodiversity-inclusive postsecondary campuses: Recommendations for leaders in higher education', *Autism in Adulthood*, 5(1), 1–14.

Edgar, E., Pownall, M., and Harris, R. (2024) 'Perceptions of university accessibility predicts feelings of belongingness in students with disabilities', *International Journal of Disability, Development and Education*, 1–12.

Fabri, M., and Andrews, P.C.S. (2016) 'Human-centered design with Autistic university students: Interface, interaction and information preferences'. In *Design, user experience, and usability: Novel user experiences: 5th international conference, DUXU 2016, held as part of HCI International 2016, Toronto, Canada, July 17–22, 2016, proceedings, Part II 5* (pp. 157–166). Springer International Publishing.

Hamilton, L.G. (2024) 'Emotionally based school avoidance in the aftermath of the COVID-19 pandemic: Neurodiversity, agency and belonging in school', *Education Sciences*, 14(2), 156.

Hamilton, L.G., and Knight, R. (2025) 'Bridging double empathy gaps in the higher education classroom'. In D. Milton (Ed.), *The double empathy reader*. London: Pavilion.

Hamilton, L. G., and Petty, S. (2023) 'Compassionate pedagogy for neurodiversity in higher education: A conceptual analysis', *Frontiers in Psychology*, 14, 1093290.

Hamilton, L.G., Williams, J., and Petty, S. (2024). *Inclusive neurodiverse campuses*. York St John University.

Hewett, R., Douglas, G., McLinden, M., and Keil, S. (2019) 'Developing an inclusive learning environment for students with visual impairment in higher education: Progressive mutual accommodation and learner experiences in the United Kingdom'. In *Postsecondary educational opportunities for students with special education needs* (pp. 90–109). Abingdon, Oxfordshire: Routledge.

Hewett, R., Douglas, G., McLinden, M., and Keil, S. (2020) 'Balancing inclusive design, adjustments and personal agency: Progressive mutual accommodations and the experiences of university students with vision impairment in the United Kingdom', *International Journal of Inclusive Education*, 24(7), 754–770.

Hills, M., Overend, A., and Hildebrandt, S. (2022) 'Faculty perspectives on UDL: Exploring bridges and barriers for broader adoption in higher education', *Canadian Journal for the Scholarship of Teaching and Learning*, 13(1), 1–18.

Hope, J. (2022) 'Make neurodiversity central to design decisions', *Disability Compliance for Higher Education*, 28(2), 5.

Horlin, C., Hronska. B., and Nordmann, E. (2024) 'I can be a "normal student": The role of lecture capture in supporting disabled and neurodivergent students' participation in higher education', *Higher Education*, 88, 2075–2092.

Hummerstone, H., and Parsons, S. (2021) 'What makes a good teacher? Comparing the perspectives of students on the autism spectrum and staff', *European Journal of Special Needs Education*, 36(4), 610–624.

Kat, M. (2024) 'Running a neurodivergent study group', *The Psychologist*. www.bps. org.uk/psychologist/running-neurodivergent-study-group (accessed: 1 December 2024).

Kings-Sears, M.E., Stefanidis, A., Evmenova, A.S., Rao, K., Mergen, R.L., Owen, L.S., and Strimel, M.M. (2023) 'Achievement of learners receiving UDL instruction: A meta-analysis', *Teaching and Teacher Education*, 122, 103956.

Leifler, E., Borg, A., and Bölte, S. (2024) 'A multi-perspective study of perceived inclusive education for students with neurodevelopmental disorders', *Journal of Autism and Developmental Disorders*, 54(4), 1611–1617.

Leveille, A.D. (2024) '"Tell me you have ADHD without telling me you have ADHD": Neurodivergent identity performance on TikTok', *Social Media and Society*, 10(3), 20563051241269260.

Milton, D., Gurbuz, E., and López, B. (2022) 'The "double empathy problem": Ten years on. *Autism*, 26(8), 1901–1903.

Mulisa, F. (2019) 'Application of bioecological systems theory to higher education: Best evidence review', *Journal of Pedagogical Sociology and Psychology*, 1(2), 104–115.

Nuske, A. (2019) 'Transition to higher education for students with autism: A systematic literature review', *Journal of Diversity in Higher Education*, 12(3), 280–195.

Pellicano, E., and den Houting, J. (2022) 'Annual research review: Shifting from "normal science" to neurodiversity in autism science', *Journal of Child Psychology and Psychiatry*, 63(4), 381–396.

Petty, S., Hanser, C.H., Williams, J.A., and Hamilton, L.G. (2025) 'Sharing an example of neurodiversity affirmative hiring', *Autism in Adulthood*. https://doi.org/10.1089/aut.2024.0134

Snowling, M.J., Hulme, C., and Nation, K. (2020) 'Defining and understanding dyslexia: Past, present and future', *Oxford Review of Education*, 46(4), 501–513.

Sonuga-Barke, E., and Thapar, A. (2021) 'The neurodiversity concept: Is it helpful for clinicians and scientists?', *The Lancet Psychiatry*, 8(7), 559–561.

Spaeth, E., and Pearson, A. (2023) 'A reflective analysis on neurodiversity and student wellbeing: Conceptualising practical strategies for inclusive practice', *Journal of Perspectives in Applied Academic Practice*, 11(2), 109–120.

Stockwell, K.M., Robertson, Z.S., Lampi, A.J., Steinmann, T., Morgan, E., and Jaswal, V.K. (2024) '"A system that wasn't really optimized for me": Factors influencing Autistic university students' access to information', *Autism in Adulthood*, early online view.

Thapar, A., Cooper, M., and Rutter, M. (2017) 'Neurodevelopmental disorders', *The Lancet Psychiatry*, 4(4), 339–346.

Unite Students. (2023). *An asset, not a problem: Meeting the needs of neurodivergent students.* www.unitegroup.com/wp-content/uploads/2023/03/Neurodivergent-students_report_Unite-Students.pdf

Chapter 2

ADHD in Higher Education
Key Issues and Future Directions

Jane Sedgwick-Müller

Introduction

This chapter explores attention deficit hyperactivity disorder (ADHD) in higher education (HE), focusing on the experiences and challenges faced by university students with ADHD in the United Kingdom (UK). It begins by defining and contextualising ADHD within the framework of educational transitions then provides a historical overview that traces the evolution of ADHD within the educational system, and how over time it came to be categorised as a specific learning difference (SpLD). Categorising ADHD in this way arguably diminishes its visibility in UK higher education institutions (HEIs) as a distinct neurodivergence with unique strengths and needs. Key topics to be discussed are the prevalence of ADHD in UK HEIs, the impact of ADHD on academic functioning in HE, and management strategies for promoting positive learning experiences. The chapter emphasises the importance of inclusive and equitable practices in HEIs and accessible healthcare for university students with ADHD. It concludes with recommendations to tackle the urgent need for timely access to medical treatment and tailored academic support for university students with ADHD. Strengthening partnerships between disability services in HEIs and healthcare providers, both on and off campus, is identified as a critical next step in achieving this goal.

ADHD and Educational Transitions

Transitioning into or returning to HE can be an exciting yet stressful experience for many students. Leaving home – often for the first time – while managing academic pressures, including adapting to learning environments that demand personal motivation and initiative, building new relationships and becoming self-sufficient can strain the mental health and well-being of university students, especially emerging adults with ADHD. Emerging adulthood is a pivotal developmental phase marked by identity exploration, greater independence and increased responsibility (Arnett, 2016). This phase is also associated with increased experimentation, including with drug and alcohol use,

DOI: 10.4324/9781003495925-4

high-risk sexual or other behaviours, and with the onset or exacerbation of mental health issues (MacLeod and Brownlie, 2014). Certain student groups, such as neurodiverse individuals with ADHD and/or autism are particularly vulnerable to mental health challenges during periods of transition and change (Bolton and Lewis, 2024).

ADHD is a neurodevelopmental disorder that begins in childhood and often persists into adulthood. ADHD is characterised by symptoms of inattention and/or hyperactivity and impulsivity that impair functioning across multiple domains of daily life (American Psychiatric Association/APA, 2022; World Health Organization/WHO, 2019). Table 2.1 lists typical traits and behaviours seen in students with ADHD. These students can also present with co-occurring SpLD (i.e. dyslexia), developmental co-ordination disorder

Table 2.1 Typical traits and behaviours in adults (incl. university students) with ADHD (adapted from Sedgwick-Müller et al., 2020, p. 3)

Typical traits	Associated behaviours
Inattention (or attention deficits)	Easily losing focus, concentration, absent-mindedness
	Being distracted by low-priority activities
	Spontaneous mind-wandering, 'zoning out' or daydreaming
	Overlooking details which can lead to careless mistakes or incomplete work
	Quietly getting bored, especially when the novelty wears off
Hyper-focusing	Tuning out and becoming totally absorbed in self-interesting, stimulating, or rewarding tasks and activities
Disorganisation and forgetfulness	Poor organisational skills such as planning, goal setting, decision-making, keeping track of tasks/ responsibilities.
	Procrastination, forgetting commitments, appointments, or deadlines
	Frequently losing or misplacing things (keys, wallet, phone, documents)
Hyperactivity, restlessness, or having lots of energy	Inner restlessness, always 'on the go' as if driven by a motor, talking excessively, trouble being still, fidgetiness
	Craving excitement or stimulation
	Engaging in high-intensity sports which may involve speed, height, a high level of physical exertion
Impulsivity	Interrupting others or talking over them; blurting out thoughts or saying things without thinking
	Engaging in reckless or risk behaviours (e.g. spontaneous sexual 'hook-ups', gambling, Internet overuse, binge drinking or drug taking, driving too fast)
Emotional lability/ Dysregulation	Often feeling irritable, unable to cope; having a short or explosive temper; easily flustered and/or stressed; hypersensitive to criticism
	Low self-esteem, sense of underachievement, constantly worrying about making the same mistakes, fatigue or burn-out, finding it hard to stay motivated

(DCD, or dyspraxia), autism, anxiety, depression, personality, substance use, or eating disorders (Sedgwick-Müller et al., 2022). However, ADHD can also come with positive attributes including creativity, 'thinking outside the box', high energy levels that can be channelled into productivity, enthusiasm for engaging tasks, hyperfocus, and resilience (Sedgwick et al., 2019).

Historical Context

The history of ADHD in education reflects evolving perceptions and understandings of the condition. In UK HEIs, ADHD is categorised as a SpLD, yet it's described in medical classification systems, the DSM-5-TR and ICD-11, respectively, as 'the most common mental health disorder in childhood that often persists in adulthood' (APA, 2022; WHO, 2019). For authors such as Hinshaw and Scheffler (2014), the inception of compulsory education in the late 19th century, rather than advances in medicine, was the environmental trigger for transforming ADHD into a salient societal concern. In the UK, when compulsory education was first introduced, government funding for schools and teachers' salaries hinged on children attending school for 100 days and passing tests in the 3Rs – [r]eading, w[r]iting and a[r]ithmetic. This system, called 'payment by results' incentivised teachers to raise concerns about children failing their 3Rs tests and eventually they were deemed ineducable in mainstream schools (Midgley, 2016; Potts, 1983). Some children were described as 'hyperactive, distractible, unruly, and unmanageable in school ... frequently disturbing the whole class ... quarrelsome and impulsive ... often leaving the school building during class time without permission' (Ross and Ross, 1976, p. 15).

The Egerton Royal Commission (1889) was first to examine the problem of ineducable pupils in mainstream schools and they introduced the term 'feebleminded' to categorise pupils needing special education. This marked the beginning of medicalising poor scholastic performance and failure (Petrina, 2006). In the early 20th century new research on the heritability of intelligence roused a relentless eugenics enterprise to eradicate feeblemindedness by preventing its procreation (Woodhouse, 1982). Coincidental developments in psychometric tests of intelligence then provided the means by which pupils were differentiated as either feebleminded or dull/backward (Burt, 1922). The former cohort was sent to residential colonies for care and management, while the later cohort continued to be taught in mainstream schools (Radnor Report, 1908). Financial sustainability of special education, mounting complaints from parents about their children being labelled as 'special needs' and appeals from teachers to no longer leave the assessment of 'ordinary' learning problems in pupils to medical officers, fuelled calls for reform.

The London County Council, responsible at the time for all schools in London, responded by appointing Cyril Burt [1883–1971], the UK's first school psychologist, and father of educational psychology. Burt transformed approaches to special education, emphasising intelligence between boys and girls was the same and that scholastic ability was variable (Burt, 1922, 1925). Burt's seminal work highlighted the overlap between disorders of behaviour and temperament, including traits resembling contemporary features of ADHD, and that with additional support in place, pupils identified with 'special educational needs' (SEN) could be taught in mainstream schools (Burt, 1937). In the same year, Charles Bradley in the USA reported on the effectiveness of stimulant medication in treating school children with behavioural problems akin to ADHD (Bradley, 1937). The landmark Warnock Report (1978) expanded the concept SEN and advocated for inclusion and individualised support for pupils who needed it. Despite these advances, ADHD continued to be a contentious medical diagnosis in education, possibly influenced by Burt's legacy and the Warnock Report which subsumed it under the category of SEN.

Prevalence of ADHD in Higher Education

University students with ADHD are part of a larger group of disabled students under the *widening participation strategy*, a key policy for UK HEIs. This policy also requires HE providers to collect and respond to data about disabled students. Codes provided by the Universities and Colleges Admissions Service (UCAS) are used to collect this data. As shown in Table 2.2, data about ADHD is collected using the code 'G – *Specific Learning Difference, e.g. dyslexia, dyspraxia, or AD(H)D*'. Once the data are collected, it is returned to the Higher Education Statistics Authority (HESA) for processing and publication on its website (e.g. HESA, 2022/2023, www.hesa.ac.uk/data-and-analysis/students/table-15). In Table 2.3, HESA data for 2022/23 indicates a total of 441,600 university students declared a disability (20.3% of a total of 2,175,530 students). In the

Table 2.2 Current UCAS codes and descriptors of disability

A	No disability
B	Social/Communication impairment such as Asperger's syndrome/other autism spectrum disorder
C	Blind or have a serious visual impairment uncorrected by glasses
D	Deaf or have a serious hearing impairment
E	Long standing illness or health condition such as cancer, HIV, diabetes, chronic heart disease, or epilepsy
F	Mental health condition, such as depression, schizophrenia, or anxiety disorder
G	**Specific learning difference such as dyslexia, dyspraxia, or AD(H)D**
H	Physical Impairment or mobility issues such as difficulty using your arms or using a wheelchair or crutches
I	Disability, impairment or medical condition that is not listed above
J	You have two or more impairments and/or disabling medical conditions

Source: Taken from UCAS Admissions Guide 2021, p. 84, at www.ucas.com/file/366691/download?token= 5UycyRoa

Table 2.3 HESA data for UK domiciled disabled students

Disability declared at university	UK – disabled student total	RoI – disabled student total	UK – % of disabled students	RoI – % of disabled students
Blind or have a visual impairment	3,910	323	0.9	1.6
D/deaf or have a hearing impairment	7,245	518	1.6	2.5
Mental health condition, challenge or disorder	122,760	4,412	28.0	21.7
Physical (or mobility) impairment or disability	9,955	1,210	2.0	5.9
Development condition that you have had since childhood (UK only)	545		0.1	
Neurological/Speech and language (RoI only)		1,378		6.8
Learning difference such as dyslexia, dyspraxia or AD(H)D (UK only) **ADD/ADHD (RoI only)**	**137,555**	**2,612**	**31%**	**12.8%**
Specific learning difficulty (RoI only)		7,897		38.8
DCD dyspraxia/dysgraphia (RoI only)		1,672		8.2
Long-term illness or health condition (UK only)	34,050		8.0	
Significant ongoing illness (RoI only)		2,520		12.4
Social/communication conditions such autism spectrum condition (UK only)	19,565		4.4	
Asperger/Autism (category in RoI only)		2,236		11
An impairment, health condition, or learning difference not listed (UK only)	33,090		7.5	
Multiple impairments, health conditions, or learning differences (category in UK only)	72,925		16.5	
Other (RoI only)		311		1.5
Total	**441,600**	**25,089**	**100%**	**123%**

Source: From www.hesa.ac.uk/data-and-analysis/students/table-15 & AHEAD data for the incidence of disability

Republic of Ireland (RoI), the Association for Higher Education Access and Disability (AHEAD) also collects and processes data about disabled students. In Table 2.3, AHEAD data for 2022/23 indicates that 25,089 university students declared a disability (7.4% of a total of 276,508 students). AHEAD acknowledged that some students registered multiple disabilities at university. Therefore, the total of 25,089 disabled students (rather than the actually recorded total of 20,351) shown in Table 2.3 represents the incidence of disability rather than its prevalence in RoI HEIs (AHEAD, 2024, p. 24).

There are key differences in the disability data shown in Table 2.2. AHEAD data reveals an incidence of 12.8% (n = 3,211) for ADD/ADHD. There is no similar HESA data because ADHD is subsumed under the SpLD category, resulting in a prevalence estimate of 31% (n = 136,896). The lack of data about university students with ADHD not only conflates data for SpLD but a prevalence estimate for ADHD in UK HEIs cannot be extrapolated. Without accurate data about ADHD in UK HEIs, the reported sharp rise in the number of university students with ADHD is difficult to corroborate (Williams et al., 2019). Disaggregated student data by disability categories, such as ADHD, can inform planning and budgeting for student support services. Data like these can also inform further studies to challenge stigmatising perceptions of ADHD in university students or be used to identify areas of exclusion and evaluate support services or progress towards removing systemic barriers to inclusion (Sedgwick-Müller et al., 2022).

Impact of ADHD in Higher Education

Academic functioning is significantly impaired in many university students with ADHD. Academic functioning refers to *academic engagement* (e.g. interest and active participation in learning), *academic achievement* (e.g. grades attained, knowledge and skills acquired), and *academic performance* (e.g. retention, progression, and completion rates) (Alrashidi et al., 2016; Langberg et al., 2011). Previous research about ADHD in university students has mainly originated from North America, where this topic area has been studied since the 1990s. A comprehensive review of these studies is provided by Sedgwick (2018). More recently, Doyle et al. (2024) reported that university students with ADHD in the RoI faced significant challenges, including difficulties managing academic tasks and meeting deadlines. These issues were compounded by insufficient support, a lack of awareness and understanding of ADHD, and persistent stigma. Similarly, Morley and Tyrrell (2023) found that female university students with ADHD in the UK reported challenges with masking symptoms and feeling misunderstood by faculty staff and peers due to male-centric ADHD stereotypes. Attention deficits, procrastination, and emotional dysregulation were also reported as key factors impairing academic and social functioning, contributing to low self-esteem and strained relationships.

Female university students with ADHD can be misdiagnosed with other conditions such as anxiety, mood, or personality disorders, because they are more likely to present with internalised symptoms including emotional dysregulation (Young et al., 2020). Emotional dysregulation/lability (EL) is a prominent feature of ADHD linked to low self-esteem and poor self-concept. EL is characterised by short-lived emotional outbursts, irritability, low frustration tolerance, and heightened sensitivity to criticism (Skirrow and Asherson, 2013). These traits, although typical of mood symptoms in ADHD, when severe, they can be misinterpreted as mood or personality disorders. University students with ADHD who struggle with EL are also more likely to face additional challenges in forming and maintaining academic and social relationships. If these students find it difficult to manage anger, sadness, or sensitivity to criticism, they could turn to coping mechanisms such as using tobacco, alcohol, cannabis or other drugs, sex, gambling, or gaming (Sedgwick-Müller et al., 2022).

Attention regulation problems in university students with ADHD allow them to focus during highly stimulating or interesting academic activities, but not during activities or tasks perceived as boring. Deficits in executive function (EF) are said to mediate the relationship between ADHD and impaired academic functioning. EF deficits reflect difficulties with cognitive processes essential for *goal-directed behaviour* (e.g. planning, organising, prioritising, and managing time) and *self-regulation* (e.g. regulating emotions, impulse control, and adapting to new or unexpected situations) (Dvorsky and Langberg, 2014). However, EF deficits are not observed in all people with ADHD, therefore they cannot be the sole reason why students with ADHD have learning problems in HE or why they are more likely to experience retention or academic failure (Holst and Thorell, 2019). Research about intellectual giftedness (IG) – characterised by above-average academic ability, creativity, and task-commitment (Reis and Renzulli, 2020) – offers an alternative perspective.

Evidence suggests that IG can mitigate EF deficits and enable some university students with ADHD to excel academically and go on to have successful careers (Milioni et al., 2016). Some authors argue the protective effects of IG usually diminish once a student transitions into HE (Antshel, 2008) and increased demands at university precipitate a worsening of ADHD symptoms and significant levels of impairments begin to emerge (Rommelse et al., 2017). In some cases, it can also be hard to ascertain if ADHD with or without IG, SpLD or a mental health condition are different facets of the same condition or are separate conditions. For instance, a student with undiagnosed ADHD may work really hard then perform badly academically and start to worry excessively about their performance or feel like a failure and become depressed. This student may seek help because they are feeling anxious or depressed, but their underlying condition is ADHD. IG in particular, can complicate the identification of ADHD especially in university students who achieve high grades.

IG can also be misdiagnosed as ADHD and vice versa, or IG and ADHD can present as a dual diagnosis (Milioni et al., 2016; Mullet and Rinn, 2015).

Management Strategies

Many university students in the UK face significant barriers in accessing a diagnostic assessment for ADHD. Getting an ADHD diagnosis is important because it can validate a student's lived experience, provide a reason for their struggles, and facilitate access to treatment and support. However, university students are also at risk of being dismissed by healthcare professionals, who may think they are feigning ADHD to obtain a prescription for stimulants to use or share with peers as 'study drugs', or that they are unlikely to have ADHD because they get high grades or study at an elite HEI. Stigma surrounding ADHD can complicate experiences at university. Misconceptions and stereotypes about ADHD can discourage students from seeking help or disclosing their diagnosis, exacerbating feelings of isolation, and hindering access to support systems. Gender-specific stigma, particularly affecting female students, adds another layer of complexity, as ADHD in females often presents with internalised symptoms and is less likely to be identified or understood (Young et al., 2020). Another significant barrier in the UK is the long waiting times to access specialist adult ADHD clinics in the National Health Service, which often exceeds two or more years (Adamou et al., 2024). Such delays can increase the risk of academic failure or a worsening psychopathology.

An appealing option for some students may be seeking an educational psychology diagnosis for SpLD funded through university disability services. This option can identify SpLD and indicators of ADHD if present and provide access to educational support, including via a Disabled Students Allowance (DSA); a government-funded support scheme designed to cover additional costs in HE related to a student's disability (additional detail can be found at www.gov.uk/disabled-students-allowance-dsa/eligibility). Support like this can certainly be helpful. But if core symptoms of ADHD remain untreated, learning and other difficulties can persist. In the UK, NICE (National Institute of Health and Care Excellence, 2018) recommends stimulant medication (methylphenidate or lisdexamphetamine) as the first-line treatment for ADHD. There is good evidence for the effectiveness of stimulants in treating core symptoms of ADHD and improving functioning in multiple domains, including educational. University students with ADHD who take stimulants have reported marked improvements in task management, planning, organisation, use of study skills, working memory, and academic engagement (Müller-Sedgwick and Sedgwick-Müller, 2020). In one study, young adults with ADHD taking medication attained higher scores in their university entrance examinations compared to peers with ADHD not taking medication (Lu et al., 2017).

However, some university students with ADHD may not take their medication as prescribed and instead prefer flexible use; for instance, optimising dosing when writing summative assignments or studying for examinations, then not taking any medication on days without academic work. Prescribing practitioners need to be open to discussing the benefit and drawbacks of flexible dosing with university students and offer them appropriate advice and guidance (Müller-Sedgwick and Sedgwick-Müller, 2020). Medication alone may be sufficient for some university students with ADHD. But combining medication with psychosocial interventions tends to offer the greatest benefits, underscoring the importance of a multimodal approach. Psychosocial interventions usually begin with post-diagnosis psychoeducation. This is about having a conversation about ADHD – its positive attributes and functional impairments, whether or not to disclose a diagnosis of ADHD at university or to future employers, the effects of medication including side-effects and options for non-pharmacological interventions including environmental modifications (NICE, 2018).

In UK HEIs, environmental modifications often involve reasonable adjustments (RAs) implemented through an inclusion plan. However, support via an inclusion plan can be inconsistent, and the 'one size fits all' approach to RAs may fail to meet individual student's needs (Clouder et al., 2020). In studies, mindfulness-based therapies, cognitive-behavioural therapy, and dialectical-behaviour therapy have shown positive results for university students with ADHD (Sedgwick-Müller et al., 2022). Academic coaching is another effective intervention that can help university students with ADHD set goals, create study plans, be more self-determined, and focus on long-term goals (Ali et al., 2024). In the UK, coaching, specialist mentoring, and specialist study-skills support can be funded through DSA. Peer support and mentorship programmes also play a pivotal role, fostering belonging and resilience by connecting university students with ADHD to peers who share a similar diagnosis and lived experiences (Anastopoulos and King, 2015).

Conclusion

The impact of ADHD in HE can have long-term negative effects on the mental health, well-being, and socioeconomic outcomes of university students. Rapid access care pathways for a diagnosis and treatment remain a critical issue. This can be addressed through partnership working between HEIs and healthcare providers on and off campus. The Health Service Executive (HSE) Clinical Pathway for ADHD in the RoI (HSE, 2021) offers an example of how care can be integrated, with recommendations for 'larger third-level colleges to include a psychiatrist as part of their health service provision for students. Given the age group the psychiatrists are providing for, the ability to screen and treat ADHD is necessary. Equally, each institution must ensure it funds sufficient sessions of psychiatry time in order to ensure that this service is available for both students known to have symptomatic ADHD and those requiring assessment' (HSE, 2021, p. 69).

In UK HEIs, the categorisation of ADHD as a SpLD, arguably, diminishes its visibility and misrepresents its unique neurodivergence. Introducing a separate UCAS code for ADHD, as seen in the RoI, can improve data collection, enabling a better understanding of the prevalence of ADHD in HE. This data could also be used to inform targeted support initiatives, policy development, staff training to raise awareness and challenge stigma. Without visible data about ADHD in UK HEIs, the challenges and needs of university students with ADHD risk being overlooked. However, practices in HE that incorporate a neurodiversity perspective (Singer, 1999), such as universal design for learning (UDL), offer a promising framework for fostering inclusivity and equity (Rose and Meyer, 2002). According to Martin (2021) though, a lack of staff development and senior management support hinders the widespread adoption of UDL across the sector. Resource constraints – whether financial, time, or staff capacity – can derail efforts to redesign programmes of study in line with UDL principles. There is also scepticism about whether scarce resources should be redirected towards implementing UDL due to insufficient empirical evidence supporting its core claims (Murphy, 2021).

ADHD in HE is an under-recognised yet impactful neurodevelopmental difference. Raising awareness and understanding, addressing stigma, providing tailored support to university students with ADHD, including timely access to a diagnostic assessment and treatment, is essential. HEIs can certainly create more inclusive and supportive learning environments that unlock the potential of university students with ADHD, enabling them to thrive personally and academically. The path forward requires HEIs to support diversity in all its forms, to recognise the unique strengths and challenges of neurodivergent students and embrace a vision where all students, including students with ADHD, have opportunities to achieve their full potential.

References

Adamou, M., Arif, M., Asherson, P., Sedgwick-Müller, J., et al. (2024) 'The adult ADHD assessment quality assurance standard', *Frontiers in Psychiatry*, 15, 1380410.

AHEAD. (2024) *Students with Disabilities Engaged with Support Services in Higher Education in Ireland 2022/23*, Dublin: The Association for Higher Education Access and Disability (AHEAD).

Ali, A., Collier, K., and Mayomi, T. (2024) 'Navigating ADHD in higher education: Evaluating psychosocial interventions for student self-esteem, well-being, and quality of life', *BJPsych Open*, 10(S1), S17–S18.

Alrashidi, O., Phan, H.P., and Ngu, B.H. (2016) 'Academic engagement: An overview of its definitions, dimensions, and major conceptualizations', *International Education Studies*, 9(12), 41–52.

American Psychiatric Association (APA). (2022) *Diagnostic and statistical manual of mental disorders-TR* (5th ed.), Washington, DC: American Psychiatric Association.

Anastopoulos, A.D., and King, K.A. (2015) 'A cognitive-behavior therapy and mentoring program for college students with ADHD', *Cognitive and Behavioral Practice*, 22(2), 141–151.

Antshel, K. (2008) 'Attention deficit hyperactivity disorder in the context of a high intellectual quotient/giftedness', *Developmental Disabilities Research Reviews*, 14(4), 293–299.

Arnett, J.J. (2016) 'College students as emerging adults: The developmental implications of the college context', *Emerging Adulthood*, 4(3), 219–222.

Bolton, P., and Lewis, J. (2024) *Equality of access and outcomes in higher education in England*, Research Briefing 9195, London: House of Commons Library.

Bradley, C. (1937) 'The behaviour of children receiving benzedrine', *American Journal of Psychiatry*, 94(3), 577–585.

Burt, C. (1922) *Mental and scholastic tests*, London: P.S. King & Son.

Burt, C. (1925) *The young delinquent* (1st ed.), London: University of London Press.

Burt, C. (1937) *The backward child*, London: University of London Press.

Clouder, L., Karakus, M., Cinotti, A., et al. (2020) 'Neurodiversity in higher education: A narrative synthesis', *Higher Education*, 80, 757–778.

Doyle, A., Healy, O., Paterson, J., et al. (2024) 'What does an ADHD-friendly university look like? A case study from Ireland', *International Journal of Educational Research Open*, 7, 100345.

Dvorsky, M.R., and Langberg, J.M. (2014) 'Predicting impairment in college students with ADHD: The role of executive functions', *Journal of Attention Disorders*, 23(13), 1624–1636.

Health Service Executive (HSE). (2021) *ADHD in adults national clinical programme: Model of care for Ireland.* Dublin: Clinical Design and Innovation, Health Service Executive.

Higher Education Statistical Agency (HESA). (2022/2023) *UK-domiciled student enrolments by disability and sex, for the academic years 2022/23.* www.hesa.ac.uk/data-and-analysis/students/table-15 (accessed: 10 January 2025).

Hinshaw, S.P., and Scheffler, R.M. (2014) *The ADHD explosion: Myths, medication, and today's push for performance.* New York: Oxford University Press.

Holst, Y., and Thorell, L.B. (2019) 'Functional impairments among adults with ADHD: A comparison with adults with other psychiatric disorders and links to executive deficits', *Applied Neuropsychology: Adult*, 27(3), 243–255.

Langberg, J.M., Molina, B.S.G., Arnold, L.E., et al. (2011) 'Patterns and predictors of adolescent academic achievement and performance in a sample of children with attention deficit/hyperactivity disorder', *Journal of Clinical Child and Adolescence Psychology*, 40(4), 519–531.

Lu, Y., Sjolander, A., Cederlof, M.D., et al. (2017) 'Association between medication use and performance on higher education entrance tests in individuals with attention-deficit/hyperactivity disorder', *JAMA Psychiatry*, 74(8), 815–822.

MacLeod, K.B., and Brownlie, E.B. (2014) 'Mental health and transitions from adolescence to emerging adulthood: Developmental and diversity considerations', *Canadian Journal of Community Mental Health*, 33(1), 77–86.

Martin, N. (2021) 'Universal design for learning (UDL) in higher education: A UK, USA comparison', *Journal of Inclusive Practice in Further and Higher Education*, 13(1).

Midgley, H. (2016) 'Payment by results in nineteenth-century British education: A study in how priorities change', *Journal of Policy History*, 28(4), 680–706.

Milioni, A.L.V., Chaim, T.M., Cavallet, M., et al. (2016) 'High IQ may "mask" the diagnosis of ADHD by compensating for deficits in executive functions in treatment-Naive adults with ADHD', *Journal of Attention Disorders*, 21(6), 455–464.

Morley, S., and Tyrrell, L. (2023) 'Female university students with ADHD: A qualitative study', *Journal of Gender and Education*, 35(3), 312–329.

Mullet, D.R., and Rinn, A.N. (2015) 'Giftedness and ADHD: identification, misdiagnosis, and dual diagnosis', *Roeper Review*, 37(4), 195–207.

Müller-Sedgwick, U., and Sedgwick-Müller, J.A. (2020) 'Drugs to treat attention deficit hyperactivity disorder (ADHD)'. In P.M. Haddad and D.J. Nutt, eds., *Seminars in clinical psychopharmacology* (pp. 392–432). College Seminars Series, Cambridge University Press.

Murphy, M.P. (2021) 'Belief without evidence? A policy research note on Universal Design for Learning', *Policy Futures in Education*, 19(1), 7–12.

NICE (National Institute for Health and Care Excellence). (2018) *Attention deficit hyperactivity disorder: diagnosis and management*, London: NICE. www.nice.org. uk/ guidance/ng87

Petrina, S. (2006) 'The medicalization of education: A historiographic synthesis', *History of Education Quarterly*, 46(4), 503–531.

Potts, P. (1983) 'Medicine, morals and mental deficiency: The contribution of doctors to the development of special education in England', *Oxford Review of Education*, 9(3), 181–196.

Radnor Report. (1908) *Report of the Royal Commission on the care and control of the feeble-minded, VIII, cd 4202*. London: HMSO.

Reis, S.M., and Renzulli, J.S. (2020) 'Intellectual giftedness'. In R.J. Stenberg, ed. *The Cambridge handbook of intelligence* (pp. 291–316). Cambridge: Cambridge University Press.

Rommelse, N., Antshel, K., Smeets, S., et al. (2017) 'High intelligence and the risk of ADHD and other psychopathology', *British Journal of Psychiatry*, 211(6), 359–364.

Rose, D.H., and Meyer, A. (2002) *Teaching every student in the digital age: universal design for learning*. Alexandria, VA: Association for Supervision and Curriculum Development.

Ross, D.M., and Ross, S.A. (1976) *Hyperactivity: Research, theory, and action*, Hoboken, NJ: John Wiley & Sons.

Sedgwick, J.A. (2018) 'University students with attention deficit hyperactivity disorder (ADHD): A literature review', *Irish Journal of Psychological Medicine*, 35(3), 221–235.

Sedgwick, J.A., Merwood, A., Asherson, P. (2019) 'The positive aspects of attention deficit hyperactivity disorder: A qualitative investigation of successful adults with ADHD', *Attention Deficit Hyperactivity Disorder*, 11(3), 241–253.

Sedgwick-Müller, J.A., Müller-Sedgwick, U., Adamou, M., Catani, M., Asherson, P., et al. (2022) 'University students with attention deficit hyperactivity disorder (ADHD): A consensus statement from the UK Adult ADHD Network (UKAAN)', *BMC Psychiatry*, 22(1), 292.

Skirrow, C., and Asherson, P. (2013) 'Emotional lability, comorbidity and impairment in adults with attention-deficit hyperactivity disorder', *Journal of Affective Disorders*, 147(1–3), 80–86.

Singer, J. (1999) 'Neurodiversity and its implications for educational policy', *Disability Studies Quarterly*, 19(2), 23–38.

The Egerton Royal Commission. (1889) *Report of the Royal Commission on the blind, the deaf and dumb & c., of the United Kingdom*. London: HMSO.

Warnock Report. (1978) *Special Educational Needs: Recommendations for Reform.* London: HMSO.

Williams, M., Pollard, E., Takala, H., et al. (2019) *Review of support for disabled students in higher education in England.* Brighton: Office for Students.

Woodhouse, J. (1982) 'Eugenics and the feeble-minded: The parliamentary debates of 1912–14', *History of Education,* 11, 127–137.

World Health Organization (WHO). (2019) *International classification of diseases* (11th ed.), Geneva: WHO Publishing.

Young, S., Adamo, N., Asgeirsdottir, B.B., Sedgwick, J., et al. (2020) 'Females with ADHD: An expert consensus statement taking a lifespan approach providing guidance for the identification and treatment of attention-deficit/hyperactivity disorder in girls and women', *BMC Psychiatry,* 20, 404.

Chapter 3

Dyslexia in Higher Education

The Australian Story

Shae Wissell, Judith Hudson, Steve Edwards and Claire Davill

Introduction

In the context of this chapter, the term 'higher education' is used to describe the tertiary education setting within Australia, principally post-secondary schooling such as university and vocational training that sits under the umbrella of Technical and Further Education (TAFE) institutions. In this chapter, the terms used to describe dyslexia will include dyslexia, dyslexic, neurodevelopment condition(s) (NDC) and disability. We understand these terms and language are not all aligned with the neuroaffirming framework; however, these are the common terms used within Australian Acts, legislation and policies, as well as the ongoing use of the medical model (Wissell et al., 2025). When reading this chapter, you will note Australia has a long way to go in effectively supporting, understanding, and working with dyslexic students in higher education within a neuroaffirming framework.

The number of students in Higher Education (HE) in Australia, with a known disability, has steadily increased over time with about 12.7% of undergraduates now identifying as having a disability (Cadby et al., 2024), yet students with a disability remain an under-represented group. The most common types of reported disabilities come under the neurodivergent label, which includes but is not limited to, specific learning disabilities/difficulties (SpLD), autism, attention deficit hyperactivity disorder (ADHD), Tourette syndrome, and developmental language disorder. Within this group, the largest faction is those with SpLD, which includes dyslexia, dysgraphia, dyscalculia and dyspraxia/development coordination disorder (Gregory, 2021). The pathway of students with dyslexia in further and higher education is the focus of this chapter.

In Western countries, there has been an increase in the number of students with dyslexia participating in vocational and university settings (Gregory, 2021). In Australia, recent data from the Students with Disability in Australian Higher Education report (Cadby et al., 2024) highlighted that 13.3% of students participating in undergraduate degrees identified as having a specific learning disability (Cadby et al., 2024). Students with disabilities have some of

DOI: 10.4324/9781003495925-5

the worst attainment outcomes (Moojen et al., 2020), and those with dyslexia are less likely to complete their course compared to students without disability (Hubble and Bolton, 2021).

Dyslexia is recognised as a disability across several countries, and those with dyslexia are protected under the United Nations Convention of the Rights of Persons with Disability (UNCRPD) (United Nations, 2006) and several country-based Disability and Anti-Discrimination Acts and legislation (Commonwealth of Australia, 1992, 2009). As such, in Australia, those with dyslexia are legally entitled to 'reasonable adjustments' within education, higher education, and employment settings. However, educators first need to be aware of what dyslexia is, and how it can and does impact the student, particularly in the higher education setting. In most Global North nations, dyslexia has been known about for well over a century (Hudson, 2014); however, awareness is greater in some countries than in others.

Dyslexia Diagnosis, Terminology, and Identity

Dyslexia is diagnosed according to criteria for a specific learning disorder (SpLD), one of the neurodevelopmental conditions such as autism and ADHD (American Psychiatric Association, 2022). It affects one in 10 people, although countries such as America and the UK state it affects one in five of the population (Yang et al., 2022; Kita et al., 2020; Wagner et al., 2020). Like other neurodevelopmental conditions, the prevalence rates of individuals with dyslexia in Australia are likely to be significantly higher than reflected in the UK and USA. This discrepancy can be attributed to various factors, including methods of diagnosis (Wissell et al., 2025), costs associated with obtaining a diagnosis, lengthy wait times for assessments (discussed later in this chapter) and personal beliefs about the appropriateness of pursuing a diagnosis (American Psychiatric Association, 2022).

Like autism and ADHD, dyslexia is usually identifiable early in an individual's developmental period, it presents in varying degrees, is not related to intelligence, is highly genetic and lifelong and can be disabling in academic and work settings (American Psychiatric Association, 2022). In Australia, dyslexia makes up the largest percentage of the neurodivergent population (dyslexia 10%, dysgraphia 7%, dyscalculia 5%, ADHD 5–7% and autism 1% (Wissell, 2024; Australian Government, 2024a; The Senate, 2023; Kalenjuk et al., 2022; Williams, 2013) and globally is potentially the current leading NDC. Dyslexia affects a person's phonological processing ability, meaning they have difficulty decoding the written word. This can then impede their reading speed, fluency, and comprehension and can have a flow-on effect with challenges across spelling, grammar, numeracy, and executive function (Snowling et al., 2020; Snowling, 2019; Wissell, 2024). Beyond reading and writing, it can also impact the social determinants of health including education attainment, employment outcomes, relationships, and social and emotional well-being.

Dyslexia co-occurs with other SpLDs (dysgraphia, dyscalculia, and dyspraxia) and other NDCs, particularly with other SpLDs, ADHD (40%) and autism (20–30%) (Wissell, 2023; Brimo et al., 2021; O'Donnell and Colvin, 2019). However, the prevalence rates of autism and ADHD and the co-occurring rates are increasing globally, particularly for women (Wilson et al., 2023; Attoe and Climie, 2023; Mitchelson, 2024). This is due to growing awareness and understanding of these conditions, specifically with improved childhood screening, yet there is still a lack of understanding of dyslexia in adulthood compared to other NDCs (Wissell, 2023). Those with dyslexia have also been found to be at greater risk of low levels of mental health and well-being when compared to the general population (Wissell et al., 2021; Wilmot et al., 2023; Livingston et al., 2018). They are twice as likely to experience depression and anxiety, are 46% more likely to attempt suicide or have ideational thoughts about suicide, and experience high levels of mental fatigue and overall lower levels of mental health and well-being (Wissell et al., 2022; Alexander-Passe, 2012; Wilson et al., 2009; Wilmot et al., 2023; Fuller-Thomson et al., 2018). Poor mental health and well-being can be due to the need to manage their dyslexia within an unsupportive environment and increased experience of social exclusion (Morgan et al., 2007), which heightens their difficulties.

Prevalence Rates in Higher Education

Accurately establishing the prevalence of dyslexic students in HE is difficult, as identification at the university level relies on self-disclosure and at a national level, specific NDCs are not delineated within the disability categories (Cadby et al., 2024; Australian Government, 2024b). International studies are similarly hampered and of course, dyslexia may not be the primary diagnosis for some (Brunswick et al., 2024). Available Australian data suggest that dyslexic students may be substantially under-represented in proportion to their population prevalence and relative to the proportions of other NDCs. For example, in a Victorian university-wide survey, 524 past and present, neurotypical and neurodivergent students responded to questions about whether they identified as SpLD, ADHD, or Autistic. While those with (at least) autism ($n = 208/30\%$) were nearly as common as ADHD ($n = 230/44\%$), those identifying with SpLD were much less common ($n = 136/26\%$) (Edwards et al., 2025a). This may be due to several barriers dyslexic students face including self-disclosure and lack of diagnostic access in childhood. A number of factors probably contribute to this under-representation including poor access to diagnosis in childhood and reluctance to disclose as adults. It might also be that dyslexia and the other SpLDs are proportionally more disabling than other NDCs in an academic environment.

Dyslexic Student Profile

Students with dyslexia represent a significant portion of individuals with disabilities in HE (Thompson, 2021). Yet they face unique challenges in the educational environment that impinge on academic performance and the overall learning experience. Dyslexia manifests in various ways for each individual, with challenges that extend beyond reading and writing. These can include difficulties in executive functioning, such as time management, organisational skills, and meeting deadlines. Additionally, individuals may experience challenges with numerical information, completing online forms, navigating online learning management systems and accessing support services.

Research that has explored the lived experiences of students with dyslexia in higher and further education within the Australian context has found that to complete their courses, students reported a personal need for emotional and financial support from family and friends (Davill, 2024). There was also a reported heavy reliance on their peers or family for academic support, such as proofreading essays for spelling and grammatical errors, having a partner read textbooks and journal papers to them and peer support to help with assignments (Wissell, 2024). Students with dyslexia may also struggle to keep up with the workload, compared to their peers, and manage competing priorities of work, relationships, and socialising (Wissell, 2024).

Emphasised again, dyslexia is not related to an individual's overall intelligence, yet students reported being made to feel stupid, not bright enough to be studying at a higher level, accused of laziness, stigmatised and labelled dumb, lacking effort, and not living up to their potential (Tanner, 2009). These labels can lead to feelings of marginalisation and social isolation as dyslexic students try to navigate the many competing demands that are placed upon them (Thompson, 2021). Some of the noted psychosocial challenges experienced by dyslexic students include anxiety and/or depression, stress, feelings of low self-worth, imposter syndrome, and developing a negative self-image (Cotton, 2009; Schabmann et al., 2020). The stigma associated with having to disclose their disability can prevent some students from seeking and accessing the support that they are entitled to, legally, but also need if they are to succeed (Kuriakose and Amaresha, 2024). All these difficulties can create barriers to academic progress, highlighting the need for tailored support and understanding within the higher educational environment (Kuriakose and Amaresha, 2024).

In a paper recently published by Davill (2024), several striking insights are offered from both dyslexic students and educators' perspectives. Some have reported that dyslexic students have difficulties keeping up and/or catching up in subject areas if they enter a course of study from a low literacy and/or numeracy base. However, reading errors with dyslexia may be a question of misreading rather than being unable to read, as one student demonstrated '...*I remember I misread the assignment question and wrote a completely wrong response, and I failed...*'. Some educators had low opinions of dyslexic students' abilities to achieve successfully; one tutor raised this point: '...*there is no way with all these years of failure that they are going to grasp the theory straight away...*'(Davill, 2024).

Despite the challenges they face in an academic environment, many dyslexic students continue to achieve success (Thompson, 2021). Research indicates that dyslexic students bring many coping strategies (Thompson, 2021) and strengths into the HE system not solely linked to academic success but include attributes such as resilience, perseverance, different ways of thinking and seeing visual-spatial problems, strong interpersonal skills, collaboration strengths, self-awareness, leadership skills, and empathy (Dyslexia, 2024; Rappolt-Schlichtmann et al., 2018; Brunswick, 2012). Empowering dyslexic students to draw upon their strengths is imperative as such attributes are intuitive skills that enable them to succeed, are equally useful in supporting good mental health and well-being, and later, within a workplace setting (Rappolt-Schlichtmann et al., 2018; Wissell, 2024). Although individuals with dyslexia may have several strengths that can contribute to their success, both strengths and difficulties need to be considered when identifying what type of support and how often they may need it to complete their studies or education.

Disclosure of Dyslexia

Formal diagnosis can unlock access to disability support services and reasonable adjustments (Brunswick et al., 2024), yet it has traditionally cast a pathologising shadow over other aspects of a person's identity when viewed simply as a deficit (Griffin and Pollak, 2009). Indeed, some students cite fear of being labelled or stereotyped as a barrier to disclosing their diagnosis to disability support units (Clouder et al., 2020; Edwards et al., 2025b). However, as more students participate in, HE and self-advocate, explanatory models and terminology evolve within the ND communities (Brunswick et al., 2024; Wissell et al., 2025). Divergent patterns of ability are increasingly accepted as simply different neurotypes, that bestow strengths as well as weaknesses, within a neurodiverse world (Butcher and Lane, 2024). It follows that a dyslexic neurotype may result in disability, in ways that are specific to the neurotype in a setting like higher education but not necessarily in others. International studies show that dyslexic students are reluctant to disclose their diagnosis due to fear of stigmatisation, being singled out and academic failure (Clouder et al., 2020).

In Australia, once a young or mature student enters HE, if they have a formal diagnosis of dyslexia, they have an entitlement to access disability support services. However, they must be able to self-advocate, express their needs succinctly, and know where to go to access such services. If a person does *not* wish to disclose their disability, then they cannot access support.

If the student with a diagnosis *does* disclose, they are entitled to have their needs supported with 'reasonable adjustments' to ensure they can complete their course to conclusion (Commonwealth of Australia, 1992). There are a limited number of studies undertaken in Australia that have looked at this issue, but international research has highlighted that those with dyslexia experienced discrimination within higher education programs due to a lack of awareness and understanding by educators (Kuriakose and Amaresha, 2024; Aloka, 2023; Gregory, 2021). In their survey of past and present students of a regional/rural university in Australia, Edwards et al. (2025b) found that 52% of neurodivergent students were not even aware of the support services available. Although 62% lacked confidence to ask for help and 66% feared stigmatising, being accustomed to complete self-reliance (75%) was the most commonly endorsed barrier to disclosure (Edwards et al., 2025b).

Access to Support Services and Accommodations

Requirements to Access Support Services

Although learning support policies in HE are varied in Australia, one commonality across *all* institutions is the requirement for specific diagnostic documentation for students with dyslexia when registering for and qualifying for support. In many universities, dyslexia or SpLDs are the only permanent, non-fluctuating conditions that require recent documentation or diagnosis.

TAFE institutions generally only require confirmation of diagnosis from a registered medical practitioner, whereas most universities in Australia require a recent copy of a full psychometric assessment. Often, dyslexia and other SpLDs require specific documentation. However, other conditions, such as medical conditions and disabilities, do not. Such other conditions require only a standard form filled out by a medical practitioner (Davill, 2024).

In 53% of university institutions, eligibility carries a further caveat with the requirement that the psychometric assessment must be recent. This can include a requirement that a diagnosis be given:

- within the last three years
- post-secondary school (15–18 years of age)
- as an adult (aged 18 or higher)
- from a practitioner specialising in, and with significant experience in, diagnosing specific learning disabilities (Davill, 2024)

Most TAFE websites do not mention the requirement of a recent diagnosis, and the websites of the two TAFEs that required a recent diagnosis do not mention a timeframe. In contrast, university websites do not, in general, give the reasoning for a recent diagnosis, and where a reason is proffered, it is given as '*because student needs may have changed since a childhood diagnosis*' (Davill, 2024).

In a group of recently interviewed university students with dyslexia, eight of the eleven participants interviewed (73%) were diagnosed in primary school, most commonly around the age of seven (Davill, 2024). Similarly, the respondents of an online questionnaire of higher education students reported that they received a diagnosis during primary school (62%) or high school (27%) (Davill, 2024). However, many are falling through the cracks, with up to 58% of those with dyslexia not being diagnosed until adulthood including while at university (Wissell et al., 2021). Some universities offer referrals to in-house psychology clinics for low-cost diagnosis options. However, only one Australian university website explicitly mentions this option. Some participants mentioned only finding out about in-house diagnostic services at their institution after talking to fellow students. Disability support staff did not mention the option during consultations when exploring support options (Davill, 2024). Considering dyslexia is a lifelong disability, it is hard to understand why ongoing evidence is required when this is not the case for other NDCs or other disabilities. This requirement for recent documentation creates a significant barrier to accessing support for adult students, as many students entering university undergo assessment and are diagnosed as young children.

The cost of seeking a diagnosis and the lead time in securing an appointment (often over three months) means that some students cannot obtain the documentation required to qualify for support services at their HE institution. Questionnaire responses confirm this, with 33% of respondents reporting that the reason they did not receive assistance was because they did not qualify and a further 17% reporting that the process of seeking assistance was too onerous (Davill, 2024).

In Australia, students in HE report that disability support services were inadequate in the type of support they provided, and students experienced negative attitudes from disability support officers, educators and other staff. They expressed frustration at the need to self-advocate to access appropriate services and resources when this should be the role of the disability officer (Maccullagh, 2014; Tanner, 2009; Caskey et al., 2018). Other students have voiced concerns about being segregated into special classes with students with intellectual disabilities (Tanner, 2009; Maccullagh, 2014). This was usually due to educators not having a good understanding of dyslexia (Tanner, 2009; Caskey et al., 2018).

Further barriers to accessing support while studying in HE includes:

- awareness of support available
- attitudes of educators in secondary school, '*University is the real world; you won't receive accommodations*'. One student was told:

  ...She doesn't believe that children should receive any diagnosis because the world is tough and they should learn to navigate and not use it as an excuse. And I thought, what? The poor child!...

- Information regarding available support is not always advertised to new students or is hard to find on websites. Multiple students reported not finding out about available supports until they had spent significant time studying in their degree programs, as evidenced in one student example:

  ...I've had other people who say, you know, they've gotten, like, part way through their second year at uni before somebody else said...
  Ohh but like this is available and they're like, nobody told me that....

Financial Barriers in Higher Education

When an individual, regardless of age, enters higher education, they may have a diagnosis of dyslexia and have previously accessed accommodations. Alternatively, they may have a diagnosis but have not yet received accommodations, or they may not have had the opportunity to obtain a diagnosis despite displaying developmental characteristics of dyslexia.

Yet there is a significant financial barrier to accessing a diagnosis. The cost of an adult dyslexia diagnosis in Australia is often between $A1,500 and $A2,000 (Wissell, 2023; Davill, 2024). The diagnostic, financial, and effort-based barriers to accessing support and the suitability of support options have resulted in some students deciding not to register for support. Some students view pursuing support at university through a cost-benefit analysis and decide that the effort required is not worth the assistance they would receive. As one student stated:

> ...If I did register ... what it would take to get to register and then if I didn't do it, what am I losing out on? And I think it just became that I wouldn't ... What was provided was just pretty much extra time on assignments ....
>
> ...I just sort of found that there was no real point in me having a few extra days to finish an assignment or extra 10 minutes in a test because I just won't utilise that time to probably the best extent, uh, if there was more support, then I might have done it, but there just wasn't enough to ... really push to get my diagnosis like redone and signed off by the psychologist ....

The lack of meaningful support options makes pursuing accommodations seem unnecessary, illustrating a common perception that current systems may inadequately meet the needs of students with dyslexia.

Societal Attitudes towards Dyslexia in Higher Education

International and local research (Černickaja and Sokolová, 2024; Tanner, 2009; Caskey et al., 2018), which has examined the experiences of dyslexic TAFE and university students, highlights that the attitudes, beliefs about dyslexia, knowledge, and practices of university educators and disability support workers significantly influence student experiences. Australian HE students have expressed that societal attitudes towards dyslexia impact their studies, family and peer relationships, and experiences in the workplace (Davill, 2024; Caskey et al., 2018). Australian research undertaken by Caskey et al. (2018) found that adult students in TAFE felt *different* compared to their non-dyslexic peers within the learning context. HE students also expressed a general lack of understanding and awareness of the nature of dyslexia, which can impact their ability to access effective study support. This can also lead to internalised guilt for seeking help and profoundly impact their sense of a negative social identity (Caskey et al., 2018).

Dyslexic students face barriers to inclusion and success that are unique to their NDC, but they hold similar views to other ND students about what would enhance social inclusion and academic success in HE. The groups were not statistically different on the three highest-ranked strategies for social inclusion (professional development for staff, access to sensory spaces, and case management support) or on the highest three for teaching and learning supports (clear communication, professional development for staff, and automatic recording of lectures) (Edwards et al., 2025a). Students are often reluctant to seek support due to embarrassment or feeling they don't deserve support. Many students report that they feel they are asking for too much, particularly when denied support, as one student reported:

>...Like asking for something and them going .... Oh no, you can't have that. That's not valid, and you're like oh I feel terrible. Like lots of my peers, the people that were with me, though, they said the same thing. That like, I feel like I was like asking for too much and I was being terrible....

Another student explained:

>...I felt so guilty trying to organise it, and they made me feel so bad about having to ask for it....

Students were frequently told they weren't eligible for basic support options, and the attitudes displayed by disability support staff made them feel that they were asking for too much or that they didn't need support.

>...I was just like, hey, do you know anyone that does like editing like this? And, or does the school do this? And it's just like, oh no, that'd be prejudicial. You, you're not allowed to have that extra help....

Attitudes from peers and staff also suggested to dyslexic students that they were making excuses/being lazy/using dyslexia as a crutch:

>...Yeah, there was a lot of misunderstanding in school, like in school and also in university. You know people have said, oh people with specific learning disorders. They're just like, like freeloading....

Disability support staff misunderstanding dyslexia and the type of support required were commonly reported (Davill, 2024). Many students found that disability support staff had a poor understanding of dyslexia and did not offer appropriate support options as a result. One student reported:

>...I was talking to the accessibility person in my first year of the PhD and she said OK, so ... you ... have ... dyslexia. And she started speaking to me really slowly. And I was like, this woman does not know what dyslexia is.

And so ... then I actually, I didn't bother for like a whole year after that whole meeting because I was just so like this woman, she didn't even know what it was, like. How the hell is she going to help me?...

The availability and nature of support can also impact the student university experience. Interviewed students commonly expressed frustration with the suitability and effectiveness of accommodations received, particularly postgraduate students, for whom basic examination accommodations no longer apply. Postgraduate students interviewed expressed frustration when offered exam concessions by university disability services, like extra time, when studying in a program with few, if any, exams. The support offered was rarely suitable for studying a program with research-based assessment at the Master's and PhD levels (Davill, 2024).

Students also reported difficulties accessing assistive software such as text-to-speech and speech-to-text software. When offered, students' options were limited to specific software programs provided by the university, even if they had experience with already uploaded alternative programs. Often, no follow-up support was available, either when installing or learning to use the software provided, and many students reported embarrassment at being unable to install the offered software on their own successfully and did not seek further help.

Many students had found success in sourcing their own assistive software, such as Grammarly, but in most cases, were required to self-fund their subscription costs as the university would not cover it. One interviewed student noted: '*...So there's things like that, that just, you know, you have to pay for like, my Grammarly is $55 a month. I pay for that myself...*'. In some isolated cases, students reported that their university had banned the use of *Grammarly* due to artificial intelligence components of the software viewed by some institutions as 'cheating'. This resulted in them being unable to use the software that they had previously found so helpful to write the components of their studies. Students also described having to self-funding additional supports, such as private tutoring and editing services, when they were unable to obtain these supports through the university: '*...I think for honours I paid for it [editing] myself. That was around $700. Umm, because it was very long...*'.

Strategies to Increase the Participation of Dyslexic Learners in Higher Education

The utilisation of university support services is positively associated with academic satisfaction, self-efficacy, and self-regulated learning strategies, particularly when students can access tailored accommodations (Pellegrino et al., 2023). This section examines how HE institutions can create more inclusive learning environments for dyslexic students. It is a starting point for considering approaches that enable success and mitigate barriers so that every student can thrive.

Recent Diagnosis Requirements

Requiring a recent diagnosis of dyslexia creates an economic and effort barrier to students pursuing HE studies. To reduce these barriers the requirement for recent diagnoses and extensive documentation for dyslexic students seeking support should be removed. In Australia, the Nationally Consistent Collection of Data (NCCD) acknowledges learning difficulties and disabilities, including 'imputed disabilities', which are undiagnosed conditions recognised by professionals. For instance, imputed dyslexia' can be used to describe students exhibiting traits and learning challenges aligned with dyslexia, as identified by educators.

Adult learners who have struggled with dyslexic-type difficulties throughout their education, even without a formal diagnosis, could provide reasonable evidence of lifelong challenges to qualify for support. Allowing these students to declare 'imputed dyslexia' would offer equitable access to support without creating unfair advantages. After all, who would claim this except for genuine cases?

In many cases, SpLDs are the only ongoing conditions requiring stringent comprehensive documentation of recent evidence of a diagnosis and to provide what exactly? The evidence would suggest extraordinarily little. If dyslexic students were required to provide a standard form confirming the diagnosis from a medical practitioner such as a General Practitioner (as needed for other ongoing conditions), this would allow access to available support or advice removing unnecessary barriers to academic success.

Another key improvement would be enhancing HE institution website pathways, making information more accessible, and displaying what is available to potential students. A review of university and TAFE websites showed that disability support information is not always easy to find for potential students (Davill, 2024) and some websites do not meet Website Content Accessibility Guidelines standards for the use of screen readers (Davill, 2024). This lends itself to the earlier section on entry into HE, which highlights some of the barriers preventing students from accessing these opportunities to attend in the first place.

Training of Educators and Support Staff

Academic success hinges on the commitment and understanding of staff and the provision of appropriate accommodations (Thompson, 2021). To ensure the success of students, which in turn brings in revenue for HE institutions, dyslexia awareness training, including what constitutes reasonable adjustments for a dyslexic student from undergraduate through to PhDs, is required for both educators and support staff. Work by Edwards et al. (2025a) found that 31 % of staff responding to their survey had formal education regarding SpLD, whereas 34% had education about ADHD and 43% about autism. Again, considering dyslexia is the largest neurodivergent cohort more SpLD training is needed. Training should also include information on co-occurring difficulties that include executive functions such as maintaining attention, working memory and information processing mechanisms. Recognition of these interconnected challenges would ensure successful outcomes enabling dyslexic students to achieve their full potential.

Educators should be aware that non-compliant behaviour in students, particularly in a TAFE setting, may stem from difficulties with specific tasks rather than defiance. This awareness can prompt teachers to explore whether students need additional support, or adjustments, to succeed. It is crucial to view dyslexia as a disability, like any other, and to recognise that students with dyslexia are entitled to these reasonable adjustments. Educators must be equipped to identify and implement supportive strategies that are bound to 'reasonable adjustments' and help the student thrive, while also being aware of what 'reasonable adjustments' can look like. Ensuring that dyslexia is formally recognised as a disability and that students' legal rights are upheld is crucial to creating fair and supportive educational experiences. Asking the student 'what works for you' would also be a good place to start.

Additionally, students must have access to trained disability support officers and a disability team (Caskey et al., 2018) and be offered 'reasonable adjustments' when required to undertake assessment tasks. Many students expressed that disability support officers had a poor understanding of dyslexia and were unable to provide the right study support as a result. This significantly impacts whether a student will be able to complete their course and transition to a successful career. Appropriate training should include:

- Understanding of the strengths and challenges a dyslexic student may face
- The variety of reasonable adjustments that can support the learner
- Additional support and resources that can help the learner

Equally important is understanding the unique strengths students with dyslexia bring to the classroom. There are higher rates of twice-exceptional students with dyslexia, and many can excel in creative thinking, problem-solving and visual-spatial reasoning (Kranz et al., 2024; Dyslexia, 2024; von Károlyi et al., 2003; Majeed et al., 2021). Educators can foster an environment that values diverse talents and learning styles by focusing on the challenges and strengths.

Reasonable Adjustments

The Parliamentary Inquiry of the Victorian Government in Australia into 'Access to TAFE for learners with disability' (September 2021), as well as international research, have found that there is a significant lack of awareness and understanding of dyslexia across all HE settings. This lack of understanding, and old style of thinking, view accommodations as offering an unfair advantage and accommodations are 'cheating' (Little et al., 2023). There is also a perception that dyslexics cannot reach higher academic study, such as a PhD, and this needs to change. However, two of the authors (Wissell and Hudson) run a Dyslexic PhD researcher and student online network, a global community offering peer support and mentoring from those with lived experience from a wide range of academic disciplines. Since the inaugural meeting three years ago, many have graduated, in the fields of science, arts, and humanities.

Reasonable adjustments come in many forms. Extensions of time for assignments, alternative mediums for assessing work, the right use of assistive technology in exams, and recordings of lectures or seminars, can make all the difference and involve low, or no, cost to the university. We propose several strategies below that, if available, could increase participation and enhance the learning experience for students with dyslexia.

Access to technology that supports reading and writing skills is essential for dyslexic students if they are to reach their full potential and effectively demonstrate their abilities. Utilising assistive tools is not cheating but rather can provide an equitable way to address the challenges these students face. However, students have reported several barriers to using such technology. These include difficulties installing assistive software due to limited technical support, the need to self-fund software subscriptions when universities fail to provide funding for tools suited to the needs of the individual and/or compatibility issues arising between assistive software and online assessment platforms.

As AI tools become more prevalent, higher education institutions must see these technologies as valuable aids and not view them as threats to academic integrity. For example, tools like *Grammarly* have proven highly effective in supporting students with dyslexia, underscoring the potential for AI to enhance the structure of writing, accessibility, and learning outcomes. Yet some universities are now restricting the use of these tools which may limit students with dyslexia to succeed.

Dyslexia-Friendly Practices

Promoting greater inclusion of learners with dyslexia in HE requires implementing effective strategies that aim to remove barriers, enhance accessibility, and create supportive learning environments that enable all students to thrive academically. Dyslexia related difficulties are not restricted to reading, spelling, and writing but may be experienced across various tasks that students encounter in higher education (Mortimore and Crozier, 2006). To ensure students are well supported, they need to be in a setting that will provide them with a positive, nurturing, and safe learning environment and that helps develop a strong self-identity through both social and learning support.

Dyslexic-friendly practices play a crucial role in improving the effectiveness of educational and support strategies for learners with dyslexia. These approaches are grounded in a deep understanding of the unique challenges and strengths associated with dyslexia, ensuring that each learner's individual experiences are acknowledged and valued. By adopting these practices, educators, and support providers can critically evaluate whether existing instructional methods adequately meet the needs of learners with dyslexia. When gaps are identified, alternative strategies can be explored and implemented to offer more tailored and meaningful support (Ross, 2023).

Such practices may include the use of multisensory learning techniques, which engage multiple senses to reinforce understanding, or incorporating assistive technologies like text-to-speech and speech-to-text tools to reduce barriers to learning. Providing structured, clear, and consistent instructions, along with regular feedback, ensures that learners feel confident and supported in their educational journey. Additionally, creating an inclusive environment that celebrates diverse learning styles fosters a sense of belonging and encourages learners with dyslexia to thrive academically and personally (Ross, 2023).

Awareness training should be available for all personnel, to give them the tools to recognise, and understand, dyslexia-friendly practices. Staff cannot do what they don't know how to do or know and understand why it is important. Giving all staff the knowledge of how to create a 'dyslexia-friendly' learning environment will create a safer space and enhance outcomes for the student. Dyslexic learners tend to be 'big-picture thinkers' but may be less adept at processing and remembering details. Tutors are advised to give an overview of what is to be taught/learned at the commencement of a module or training program, and at the start of any new training section.

When creating dyslexic-friendly resources, it is best practice to ensure they are accessible to *all* learners. Using universal design principles will ensure that all students benefit, bringing equity to all, and not just providing additional support to those students with dyslexia. Dyslexic-friendly resources are best developed using methods confirmed as effective through research, and it is important to note a one-size-fits-all solution is rarely available. It is also useful to ask the student what strategies are effective for them and what is a help or a hindrance to their learning. Resources need to be learning, and not just assessment-focused, and it is also no use providing a student with an adjustment for an allowance of extra time, or negotiated assignment submission times, if the student has not been provided with the learning experience that allowed for them to access, acquire, or familiarise themselves with such supports, or absorb information through learning.

Finally, very few universities or TAFE institutions in Australia offer mentoring, or peer support programs specifically targeted at students with dyslexia or specific learning disabilities. Work by Davill (2024) and Edwards et al. (2025a) found that students often had to find peer support themselves or become advocates for other students, who were not receiving support or were struggling. Students frequently learn about available support options through peer connections rather than through the promotion of the university's disability support services, even though these services can provide various benefits, including reducing social isolation and enhancing mental health and well-being.

Conclusion

Dyslexia is by no means incompatible with a successful outcome, given an appropriate level of commitment on the part of the student and an appropriate level of resources on the part of their education institution.

(L. MacCullagh, 2014)

Dyslexia does not need to be a barrier to accessing and succeeding in an academic environment where dyslexic students have the reasonable adjustments and support needed. In Australia, much more research must be undertaken to identify the prevalence rates of dyslexia in HE settings and how to make it safe for the dyslexic student to disclose, while enabling them to be better equipped to support dyslexic students' success. Societal attitudes need to be addressed, including pre-conceived biases of what dyslexic students in HE are capable of, and what they can, and do, achieve. This can only be achieved through training and development of all staff who work with dyslexic students. Most importantly, removing diagnostic barriers that prevent students from accessing the support they need is a first, very simple change that could be easily implemented.

A change in mindset is required, which is in the financial interest of all HE institutions. Outdated views, subconscious bias, limiting beliefs, and the idea that those with dyslexia cannot participate and succeed in an academic environment must be changed. Universities also need to ensure that dyslexic students have the same opportunities as students who are not dyslexic. This is not just crucial for their education but also for their future success, including their careers, financial security, and overall well-being.

References

Alexander-Passe, N. (2012) *Dyslexia and depression: The hidden sorrow: An investigation of cause and effect.* New York, NY: Novinka/Nova Science Publishers.

Aloka, P. (2023) *Emotional wellbeing of students in higher education institutions.* Hershey, PA: IGI Global.

American Psychiatric Association. (2022) *Diagnostic and statistical manual of mental disorders: DSM-5-TR.* Washington, DC: American Psychiatric Association Publishing.

Attoe, D.E., and Climie, E.A. (2023) 'Miss. diagnosis: A systematic review of ADHD in adult women', *Journal of Attention Disorders,* 27, 645–657.

Australian Government. (2024a) Draft National Autism Strategy. Canberra: Australian Government.

Australian Government. (2024b) *D.o.E. 2023 – Section 16 Equity performance data.* Canberra: Australian Government. www.education.gov.au/higher-educat

ion-statistics/resources/2023-section-16-equity-performance-data (accessed: 23 December 2024).

Brimo, K., Dinkler, L., Gillberg, C., Lichtenstein, P., Lundström, S., and Åsberg Johnels, J. (2021) 'The co-occurrence of neurodevelopmental problems in dyslexia', *Dyslexia*, 27, 277–293.

Brunswick, N. (2012) *Supporting dyslexic adults in higher education and the workplace*, Chichester, West Sussex: Wiley-Blackwell.

Brunswick, N., Wilson, N.J., Kruger, I., Chamberlain, R., and Mcmanus, I.C. (2024) 'The prevalence of specific learning difficulties in higher education: A study of UK universities across 12 academic years', *Journal of Learning Disabilities*, 222194241281479.

Butcher, L., and Lane, S. (2024) 'Neurodivergent (autism and ADHD) student experiences of access and inclusion in higher education: an ecological systems theory perspective', *Higher Education*. https://doi.org/10.1007/s10734-024-01319-6

Cadby, G., Pitman, T., and Koshy, P. (2024) *Students with disability in Australian higher education (Nov. 2024 update)*. Perth: Australian Centre for Student Equity and Success (ACSES).

Caskey, J., Innes, P., and Lovell, G.P. (2018) 'Making a difference: Dyslexia and social identity in educational contexts', *Support for Learning*, 33, 73–88.

Černickaja, K., and Sokolová, L. (2024) 'Dyslexia in higher education – Teacher's perspective: scoping review', *Frontiers in Education (Lausanne)*, 9.

Clouder, L., Karakus, M., Cinotti, A., Ferreyra, M.V., Fierros, G.A., and Rojo, P. (2020) 'Neurodiversity in higher education: A narrative synthesis', *Higher Education*, 80, 757–778.

Commonwealth of Australia. (1992) *Australia: Act No. 135 of 1992, Disability Discrimination Act 1992*. Canberra: National Legislative Bodies/National Authorities.

Commonwealth of Australia. (2009) *Fair work act 28* Canberra: Commonwealth of Australia.

Cotton, S.M. (2009) *Breaking down the barriers: Strategies to assist apprentices with a learning disability*, In: Department of Education, E.A.W.R. (ed.). Canberra: National Vocational Education and Training Research and Evaluation.

Davill, C. (2024) Accessibility and effectiveness of support programs for students with dyslexia in Australian higher education [Unpublished doctoral thesis]. Adelaide: Flinders University.

Dyslexia, M.B. (2024) *The Intelligence 5.0, a new school of thought rethinking the intelligence needed in the Industry 5 U.K.*

Edwards, S., Kennedy, G., Debney, B., Frost-Camilleri, L., Dowling, M., Thorpe, K., De Gracia, R., Burns, D., Bilney, L., Moore, K., and Sawyer, N. (2025a) 'Neurodiversity, success and inclusion at Federation University survey: Descriptive Results', *Federation University Australia report*. https://doi.org/10.25955/28300 937.v2

Edwards, S., Kennedy, G., Dowling, M., Frost-Camilleri, L., Thorpe, K., De Gracia, R., Burns, D., Bilney, L., and Sawyer, N. (2025b) 'Barriers to diagnostic disclosure amongst rural and regional higher education students', Federation University Australia. https://doi.org/10.25955/28301078.v1

Fuller-Thomson, E., Carroll, S.Z., and Yang, W. (2018) 'Suicide attempts among individuals with specific learning disorders: An underrecognized issue', *Journal of Learning Disabilities*, 51, 283–292.

Gregory, R. (2021) 'Dyslexia in higher education', *Educational Research and Reviews*, 16, 125–135.

Griffin, E., and Pollak, D. (2009) 'Student experiences of neurodiversity in higher education: Insights from the BRAINHE project', *Dyslexia*, 15, 23–41.

Hubble, S., and Bolton, P., UK Parliament, corp creator (2021) House of Commons Library: Briefing Paper Number 8716, 22 February 2021: 'Support for disabled students in higher education in England.' *House of Commons Library briefing paper.*

Hudson, J.P. (2014) 'A practical guide to congenital developmental disorders and learning difficulties.' London: Routledge.

Kalenjuk, E., Laletas, S., Subban, P., and Wilson, S. (2022) 'A scoping review to map research on children with dysgraphia, their carers, and educators', *Australian Journal of Learning Difficulties*, 27, 19–63.

Kita, Y., Ashizawa, F., and Inagaki, M. (2020) 'Prevalence estimates of neurodevelopmental disorders in Japan: A community sample questionnaire study', *Psychiatry and Clinical Neurosciences*, 74, 118–123.

Kranz, A.E., Serry, T.A., and Snow, P.C. (2024) 'Twice-exceptionality unmasked: A systematic narrative review of the literature on identifying dyslexia in the gifted child', *Dyslexia (Chichester, England)*, 30, e1763.

Kuriakose, A., and Amaresha, A.C. (2024) 'Experiences of students with learning disabilities in higher education: A scoping review', *Indian Journal of Psychological Medicine*, 46, 196–207.

Little, C., Pearson, A., and Gimblett, K. (2023) 'Reasonable adjustment, unfair advantage or optional extra? Teaching staff attitudes towards reasonable adjustments for students with disabilities', *Journal of Perspectives in Applied Academic Practice*, 11, 12.

Livingston, E.M., Siegel, L.S., and Ribary, U. (2018) 'Developmental dyslexia: Emotional impact and consequences', *Australian Journal of Learning Difficulties*, 23, 107–135.

Maccullagh, L. (2014) 'Participation and experiences of students with dyslexia in higher education: A literature review with an Australian focus', *Australian Journal of Learning Difficulties*, 19, 93–111.

Majeed, N.M., Hartanto, A., and Tan, J.J.X. (2021) 'Developmental dyslexia and creativity: A meta-analysis', *Dyslexia*, 27, 187–203.

Mitchelson, M. (2024) 'Autism & ADHD in girls and women: Using neurodiversity affirming therapy throughout the lifespan.' Chatswood: PESIau.

Moojen, S.M.P., Goncalves, H.A., Bassoa, A., Navas, A.L., De Jou, G., and Miguel, E.S. (2020) 'Adults with dyslexia: How can they achieve academic success despite impairments in basic reading and writing abilities? The role of text structure sensitivity as a compensatory skill', *Annals of Dyslexia*, 2020

Morgan, C., Burns, T., Fitzpatrick, R., Pinfold, V., and Priebe, S. (2007) 'Social exclusion and mental health', *British Journal of Psychiatry*, 191, 477–483.

Mortimore, T., and Crozier, W. R. (2006) 'Dyslexia and difficulties with study skills in higher education.' *Studies in Higher Education*, 31(2), 235–251. https://doi.org/10.1080/03075070600572173

O'Donnell, E.H., and Colvin, M.K. (2019) 'Disorders of written expression', In H.K. Wilson & E.B. Braaten (Eds.). *The Massachusetts general hospital guide to learning disabilities: Assessing learning needs of children and adolescents* Massachusetts, Cham: Springer International Publishing.

Pellegrino, G., Casali, N., Meneghetti, C., Tinti, C., Re, A.M., Sini, B., Passolunghi, M.C., Valenti, A., Montesano, L., and Carretti, B. (2023) 'Universal and specific services for university students with specific learning disabilities: The Relation to study approach, academic achievement, and satisfaction', *Learning Disabilities Research & Practice*, 38, 274–284.

Rappolt-Schlichtmann, G., Boucher, A.R., and Evans, M. (2018) 'From deficit remediation to capacity building: Learning to enable rather than disable students with dyslexia', *Language, Speech & Hearing Services in Schools*, 49, 864–874.

Ross, H. (2023) *The British Dyslexia Association – Teaching dyslexic students: Theory and practice*. London: Jessica Kingsley Publishers.

Schabmann, A., Eichert, H.-C., Schmidt, B.M., Hennes, A.-K., and Ramacher-Faasen, N. (2020) 'Knowledge, awareness of problems, and support: university instructors' perspectives on dyslexia in higher education', *European Journal of Special Needs Education*, 35, 273–282.

The Senate. (2023) 'Assessment and support services for people with ADHD', In: Committee, C.A.R. (ed.). Canberra: The Senate.

Snowling, M.J. (2019) *Dyslexia: a very short introduction*, Oxford: Oxford University Press.

Snowling, M.J., Hulme, C.T., and Nation, K. (2020) 'Defining and understanding dyslexia: past, present and future', *Oxford Review of Education*, 46, 501–513.

Tanner, K. (2009) 'Adult dyslexia and the "conundrum of failure"', *Disability & Society*, 24, 785–797.

Thompson, L.S. (2021) 'The dyslexic student's experience of education', *South African Journal of Higher Education*, 35, 204–221.

United Nations. (2006) 'Convention on the rights of persons with disability', In: United Nations (ed.), *Work and employment*. Switzerland: United Nations.

von Károlyi, C., Winner, E., Gray, W., and Sherman, G.F. (2003) 'Dyslexia linked to talent: Global visual-spatial ability', *Brain Language*, 85, 427–431.

Wagner, R.K., Zirps, F.A., Edwards, A.A., Wood, S.G., Joyner, R.E., Becker, B.J., Liu, G., and Beal, B. (2020) 'The prevalence of dyslexia: A new approach to its estimation', *Journal of Learning Disabilities*, 22219420920377.

Williams, A. (2013) 'A teacher's perspective of dyscalculia: Who counts? An interdisciplinary overview', *Australian Journal of Learning Difficulties*, 18, 1–16.

Wilmot, A., Pizzey, H., Leitão, S., Hasking, P., and Boyes, M. (2023) 'Growing up with dyslexia: Child and parent perspectives on school struggles, self-esteem, and mental health', *Dyslexia (Chichester, England)*, 29, 40–54.

Wilson, A., Deri Armstrong, C., Furrie, A., and Walcot, E. (2009) 'The mental health of Canadians with self-reported learning disabilities', *Journal of Learning Disabilities*, 42, 24–40.

Wilson, R.B., Thompson, A.R., Rowse, G., Smith, R., Dugdale, A.-S., and Freeth, M. (2023) 'Autistic women's experiences of self-compassion after receiving their diagnosis in adulthood', *Autism: The International Journal of Research and Practice*, 27, 1336–1347.

Wissell, S. (2023) *Dyslexia—The hidden disability in the workplace*. Doctor of Public Health La Trobe.

Wissell, S. (2024) *Dyslexia: Insights into the hidden disability in and out of the workplace*, Melbourne: KMD Books.

Wissell, S., Hudson, J., Flowers, R., and Goh, W. (2025) '"I hate calling it a disability": Exploring how labels impact adults with dyslexia through an intersectional lens', *Neurodiversity Journal*, 3. https://doi.org/10.1177/27546330241308540

Wissell, S., Karimi, L., and Serry, T. (2021) 'Adults with dyslexia: A snapshot of the demands on adulthood in Australia', *Australian Journal of Learning Difficulties*, 1–14.

Wissell, S., Karimi, L., Serry, T., Furlong, L., and Hudson, J. (2022) '"You Don't Look dyslexic": Using the job demands-resource model of burnout to explore employment experiences of Australian adults with dyslexia', *International Journal of Environmental Research and Public Health*, 19, 10719.

Yang, L., Li, C., Li, X., Zhai, M., An, Q., Zhang, Y., Zhao, J., and Weng, X. (2022) 'Prevalence of developmental dyslexia in primary school children: A systematic review and meta-analysis', *Brain Sciences*, 12, 240.

Chapter 4

Creating Inclusive Learning Environments

The Role of Library Design in Supporting Neurodivergent Students in Higher Education

Sonja Duric, Emil Jonescu, Winnie Dunn, Jessica Green, Talia Uylaki and Jessika Hames

Introduction

University libraries are the nexus of academic program, research activities and resources, and student services. It is a place where students congregate to complete coursework, prepare for examinations, attend tutoring sessions, browse research resources, seek student support services, use computers, printers, and photocopiers, grab a coffee or snack, socialise, and relax. The architectural design of a library is essential to consider for it determines how users access the library and interact with its resources.

Extant research on library accessibility and inclusivity has typically focused on people with disabilities, either as a homogenous population or single disability groups like visual impairment and mobility impairment (Pionke, 2017). Neurodiversity, a term coined by Australian sociologist Judy Singer to foster equality and inclusion of neurological conditions that cause the brain to function in ways not considered neurotypical, is not the same as disability (Stanton, 2023). Therefore, what may be considered best practice for designing for disabilities may not be equitable for neurodivergent library patrons. Around one in five people are neurodivergent (Neurodiversity Hub, n.d.), with more people in the general population who also prefer various adaptations. Neurodivergent variations include attention deficit hyperactivity disorder (ADHD), autism, dyspraxia, dyslexia, and obsessive-compulsive disorder. It is important to make university facilities, such as the academic library, accessible, and supportive to neurodivergent students to improve their academic outcomes. This is because neurodivergent students may face unique challenges regarding academia compared to neurotypical students. For example, in Australia, less than 10% of Autistic people successfully complete a bachelor's degree and students with dyslexia report feeling unsupported in tertiary education (Radulski and Jaworowski, 2022).

Many neurodivergent individuals have differences in how they process sensory input throughout their days, which can make them misinterpret everyday sensory information such as touch, sound, and movement (SPD Australia.

DOI: 10.4324/9781003495925-6

(n.d.)). Individuals with differences in sensory processing may experience their world as either hypersensitive (over-reactive, sensory avoidant) or hyposensitive (under-reactive, sensory seeking) (SPD Australia, n.d.). Their interactions with the sensory environment can lead to uncomfortable reactions such as anxiety and stress (Jonescu et al., 2024). It is not uncommon that when a library is available, many neurodivergent individuals seek the library as a place of calm, privacy, and refuge to recover from sensory overloads (Anderson, 2021; Bahrampour and deCourcy Hinds, 2022; Birkett, McGrath and Tucker, 2022). The library can also be sought out as a place for social inclusion (Bahrampour and deCourcy Hinds, 2022). Conversely, for other neurodivergent individuals, the library can be a source of anxiety due to crowds, noise, inadequate lighting, poor wayfinding, and a lack of privacy (Boyer and El-Chidiac, 2023).

An inclusive library design approach is essential for addressing the needs of all patrons, especially neurodivergent users. True inclusivity, however, extends beyond basic accessibility standards. Participatory and co-design approaches, which actively involve users in the design process, are increasingly recognised as crucial for understanding and meeting neurodivergent needs.

To assist understanding of how people interact with sensory information, Dunn (2009) developed a Model of Sensory Processing, and a validated instrument that measures individual's responses to everyday sensory experiences. Dunn (2009, 2014) describes how people with high brain thresholds need a lot of sensory input to notice what is going on around them, whereas people with low thresholds notice sensory input very quickly. Dunn (2009, 2014) identified four types of sensory patterns (see Figure 4.1) based on research with thousands of people across the lifespan. *Seekers* actively seek out sensory stimulation, they like to control the amount and type of sensory input they are around; *bystanders* are generally passive to sensory stimuli and will not be distracted by sensory information, therefore they need a lot of sensory information to be engaged; *avoiders* actively try to control and reduce the amount of sensory information around them; and *sensors* are very attuned to sensory information and can be easily distracted by the details of sensory input (Dunn, 2009, 2014). The Adolescent/Adult Sensory Profile evaluates people's responses to sensory experiences in everyday life using Dunn's

Neurological thresholds	Self-regulation	
	Passive	Active
High threshold	Bystander	Seeker
Low threshold	Sensor	Avoider

Figure 4.1 Dunn's model of sensory processing, showing how the concepts fit together. Source: Dunn (2009).

sensory processing framework (SPF) (Brown et al., 2001; Dunn, 2014). The SPF offers a comprehensive way to understand how individuals react to their sensory environment and can be utilised as a methodology in design projects to help determine the sensory profiles of a building's users – thereby informing design choices. For example, applying the SPF to the patrons of an academic library could help determine the percentage of floorspace zoned to active, sensory-stimulating spaces (such as Maker Space rooms, circulation pathways, shared study spaces etc.), and passive, low-stimulation spaces (such as private study pods or reading nooks).

It is worth noting that although sensory processing differences are a significant aspect of neurodiversity, fully inclusive design must also consider other factors that may affect neurodivergent users, such as wayfinding, spatial layout, social zoning, and technological integration. Acknowledging sensory adaptation as a critical yet preliminary focus, this study underscores the need for expanding research to develop comprehensive design frameworks that cater to a wide range of needs within neurodivergent populations.

Extant studies on neurodivergent library users have typically focused on how accessibility affects Autistic persons (Anderson, 2021; Birkett, McGrath and Tucker, 2022; Mustey, 2019; Shea and Derry, 2022; Svaler, 2023; Walton and McMullin, 2021). While Autistic individuals and those with ADHD have received considerable research attention, these groups alone do not represent the full spectrum of neurodiversity. This chapter advances the understanding of architectural design for neurodivergent library patrons by addressing a broader diversity of sensory experiences (Brown et al., 2001; Dunn, 2001, 2009), including those of both neurodivergent and neurotypical users.

A scoping review was conducted across five databases to identify design interventions to support the sensory comfort of neurodivergent library users. The Findings and Discussion sections of this chapter explore how the research data intersects with practical design applications to create library spaces that support neurodivergent students. The chapter highlights how design strategies can enhance accessibility, comfort, and sensory well-being for neurodivergent individuals. Drawing on a case study, empirical research, and emerging trends, the Discussion underscores the role of libraries as inclusive learning hubs within the higher education environment.

The chapter also emphasises the importance of collaboration among librarians, academic institutions, built environments professionals, researchers and neurodivergent communities, and the role of co-design in library planning illustrating how such partnerships can drive innovation in library design. While Universal Design offers a foundational framework, co-design brings essential insights often overlooked in standard applications.

This approach aims to promote environments that accommodate and actively support diverse learning needs and preferences. The Conclusion synthesises the key findings, demonstrating a comprehensive understanding of the research problem, discussing the broader implications for inclusive design in educational spaces, and suggesting potential avenues for future research. While this research focuses primarily on sensory experiences, inclusive library design encompasses a broader range of adaptations that extend beyond sensory considerations. Sensory adaptations offer a tangible entry point into neurodivergent-inclusive design but do not represent the entirety of user needs.

Background

The design of modern university libraries is increasingly informed by key trends and insights that address the evolving needs of students and the broader academic community. While the traditional model of the academic library was a building to facilitate the consumption of knowledge, the role of the modern library is to support and facilitate learning and assist students in the creation of knowledge (Oliveira, 2018). This includes an increasing focus on the social and technological dimensions of learning as libraries transition into 'learning commons' through communal, informal spaces that cater for both group and individual study, facilitate social interaction, provide technology integration, and provide spaces for collaboration (Cox, 2018; Oliveria, 2018). Cox (2023) identified evolving pedagogies as the primary force for change in a library's architectural design and functionality. Other dominant and emerging factors that affect how people interact with, and design spaces within, an academic library include efficiency; student experience; brand and marketing; equality, diversity, and inclusion policies; sustainability; big data and artificial intelligence (AI); mental health and well-being; and student governance and co-design (Cox, 2023).

This section outlines significant considerations in the iterative design of case study university libraries, with a particular focus on student engagement, technological integration, multifunctional spaces, spatial standards, and inclusivity for neurodivergent individuals.

Student Engagement and Usage Patterns

Time spent and frequency of visits: Research indicates that university libraries remain central to student life, with significant time spent within these spaces. Findings from Edith Cowan University's Library of the Future Report (Johnston, 2021) reveal that students typically spend over two hours per visit, with nearly half visiting multiple times a week. This highlights the ongoing relevance of physical library spaces as vital hubs for both solitary and group study activities. To meet these usage patterns, libraries must be designed to accommodate frequent, extended visits comfortably, ensuring that spaces are conducive to prolonged periods of study.

Resource preferences: The most utilised resources in university libraries include individual study spaces, online resources, access to computers, group study areas, and bookable rooms (Johnston, 2021). This diverse range of preferences underscores the need for libraries to balance digital access with physical spaces that cater to various modes of study, from quiet individual work to collaborative group activities.

Technological Integration and Innovation

Emerging technologies: The integration of advanced technologies such as augmented reality, extended reality, virtual reality, AI, and machine learning is becoming increasingly prevalent in university libraries (Pinfield, Cox and Rutter, 2017). These technologies enhance learning experiences by providing interactive and immersive environments that support innovative research. The successful incorporation of such technologies must be seamless and aligned with the library's educational mission, facilitating not only access to information but also the development of digital literacy skills.

Makerspaces and innovation hubs: The emergence of makerspaces and innovation hubs within libraries reflects a broader trend towards experiential learning. Libraries are transitioning from being merely repositories of information to becoming dynamic spaces for creation and innovation. This transformation aligns with the idea of the library as a 'community kitchen', a space where ideas are shared, developed, and brought to fruition through collaboration (Landgraf, 2014).

Learning Commons and Multifunctional Spaces

Evolution of learning commons: As libraries evolve, they are increasingly transforming into comprehensive learning centres that combine a variety of student services. According to Oliveira (2018), modern libraries now often feature tutoring centres, multimedia workstations, and adaptable collaborative spaces, all designed to support diverse learning preferences and facilitate both individual and group study.

Integration with academic services: Embedding library services within the broader context of academic support and student success initiatives is increasingly common. Libraries now frequently host services such as writing centres, counselling, and career development offices (Oliveria, 2018). This integration not only aligns libraries with institutional missions but also enhances student engagement and retention by making a broad range of services readily accessible within a central, familiar space.

Spatial Considerations and Standards

Seat and space ratios: Effective space planning is critical for accommodating the needs of a diverse student body – including housing physical collections, staff service operations, intuitive wayfinding, diverse learning styles, multifunctional areas, and technology and furnishings (MBLC and Sasaki, 2020). The overall provision for a university campus library space is between 0.5 m² and 1.5 m² useable floor area per equivalent full-time student load (TEFMA Inc., 2009). Meeting or exceeding these standards ensures that library spaces can effectively support learning and research activities, accommodating both current and future demands.

Flexibility and zoning: The design of library spaces must prioritise flexibility to allow for the easy reconfiguration of spaces to support various learning activities (MBLC and Sasaki, 2020). Clearly defined zones for quiet study and collaborative work are essential to meet the differing needs and preferences of students. This adaptability ensures that libraries can respond dynamically to changing usage patterns, library services, and educational practices.

Neurodiversity Considerations

Inclusive design for neurodivergent students: The inclusion of design elements that consider the needs of neurodivergent individuals is becoming a key focus in library design. The Australian Library and Information Association (ALIA) recommends universal design principles, guidelines, and standards to ensure that library services, collections, equipment, and facilities meet the identified needs of all users (ALIA, 2019). This may involve providing a range of environments, from quiet, low-stimulation areas for those who may be sensitive to sensory overload, to more dynamic, interactive spaces that facilitate collaborative work and social interaction (Downey, Muszkiewicz and Muskin-Press, 2024). These considerations ensure that library spaces are accessible and welcoming to all university members, regardless of their neurological profiles.

Flexible and adaptive spaces: The availability of flexible spaces that can be adapted to meet different sensory needs is crucial. Features such as adjustable lighting, soundproof rooms and noise-cancelling headphones contribute to creating environments that are more accessible to neurodivergent students (Boyer and El-Chidiac, 2023). These adaptive elements allow for personalised learning experiences that support the well-being and academic success of students.

Training and awareness: Equipping library staff with training on neurodiversity and the specific needs of neurodivergent students is essential for fostering an inclusive environment. Libraries might also collaborate with neurodivergent student support programs designed to assist neurodivergent students in navigating academic challenges, further supporting their success and integration within the university community (Anderson, 2021).

Alignment with Case Study

These key trends and considerations have been systematically applied to the design of the case study library, ensuring alignment with current and future developments in library design. The focus on inclusivity, flexibility, and technological integration supports a diverse student population, reflecting the broader shift towards creating equitable and supportive academic environments. The TL Robertson Library at Curtin University serves as a pertinent example of these principles in action, demonstrating how design can contribute to an inclusive and enriching educational experience.

By integrating these elements, the case study not only meets contemporary educational needs but also anticipates future challenges, reinforcing its significance in the academic landscape.

Methodology

Scoping Database and Literature Review

A scoping review was carried out across five databases using keyword searches to find extant research on how libraries can be designed to accommodate neurodivergent students. In the context of this research, exploring how neurodivergent people interact with sensory environments, databases were selected based on their focus on psychology as a research subject. For this reason, APA PsychINFO and ProQuest Psychology Database were selected. To then expand the potential number of papers for review, Science Direct, PubMed, and Google Scholar were also selected. For each keyword search, 'neuro*' AND 'library' were the two main words in each search, combined with the following words 'design', 'architecture', 'space', 'trends', 'guideline', 'standard', 'future', 'university', and 'students'. Inclusion and exclusion criteria were used to refine the results: published between 2014 and 2024, English language and articles from peer-reviewed scholarly journals.

An initial review of the databases was conducted. Science Direct did not allow for the use of a wildcard (*) in searches and so was excluded from the database searches. The number of results for database searches was tabulated (refer Appendix – Table A.1). Titles and abstracts of the results were scanned to select papers for further review and summarisation. Most results were irrelevant to the research aim of the study. This was most likely due to the use of a wildcard (*) in the keyword 'neuro' which brought up, mainly, research papers on medical and pharmaceutical interventions, or other biomedical-focused research, on neurological conditions. As such, only two papers were identified for further review.

Due to the limited number of selected papers, a second series of keyword searches were conducted. This time the keyword 'neuro*' was replaced with 'neurodiverse', with the hypothesis that this may refine the results to enable more papers (relevant to the aim of exploring how neurodivergent people interact with built spaces) to be selected for further review. The number of results for the second database review was tabulated (refer Appendix – Table A.2). Titles and abstracts of the results were scanned to select papers for further review and summarisation; five more papers were selected.

Finally, the bibliographies of the seven selected papers from the database reviews were scanned and, using the pearl harvesting technique, four final papers were selected for review and summarisation (refer Appendix – Table A.3). This technique involved iteratively examining the references of the initial selection to identify additional, high-value papers that aligned closely with the research objectives (Mostert, 2012). Criteria for inclusion focused on relevance, methodological rigour and the potential to fill gaps or enhance the understanding of key themes. By refining the pool of literature through this targeted approach, the study ensured that the final selection represented the most pertinent contributions to the topic.

Case Study Development: Case Study Overview and Application in Practice

The refurbishment of the TL Robertson Library (20,000 m²) at Curtin University, Perth, Western Australia, represents a transformative project that redefines the role of the campus library. This initiative is a collaborative design effort between Schmidt Hammer Lassen (SHL), a Danish architecture firm based in Aarhus, and Hames Sharley (HS), an Australian multidisciplinary design practice. HS engaged SHL for their extensive international library design experience, which includes notable projects such as the Christchurch Library in New Zealand and the State Library of Victoria in Australia. Together, they worked to enhance the TL Robertson Library's functionality, accessibility, and inclusivity, creating a landmark facility at the heart of Curtin University's Bentley campus.

Originally constructed in 1972, the TL Robertson Library is a prominent example of brutalist architecture, characterised by its off-form concrete structure and minimal fenestration (see Figure 4.2). The building's design prioritised the protection of the university's book collection, resulting in small windows and limited natural light, giving the library its distinctive brutalist appearance. In 1992, an extension was added to the east of the building, during which time the main entry on Level 3 was closed, complicating internal navigation and contributing to the library's transformation into an 'impenetrable island' at the centre of the campus.

The interior layout, featuring low ceilings, poor sightlines, and dark colour scheme (see Figure 4.3), was dominated by a large book collection that had seen diminishing use over time, further detracting from the building's usability and appeal. This case study demonstrates how evidenced-based design concepts in research can be successfully applied to real-world scenarios.

Master Planning and Design Objectives

The refurbishment of the TL Robertson Library was driven by Curtin University's strategic vision to become the 'most accessible campus in Australia

Figure 4.2 TL Robertson Library at time of opening, 1971. Source: Curtin University (2020).

Figure 4.3 TL Robertson Library before refurbishment. Source: Authors (2018).

by 2030', as outlined in the University's Disability Access and Inclusion Plan. The project was briefed to align with the Curtin University Design Guidelines, which surpass current standards for accessibility, ensuring that the library not only meets but exceeds the National Construction Code (Australian Building

Codes Board [ABCB], 2022) and AS1428 requirements (Standards Australia Limited, 2009). The refurbishment sought to reimagine the library's purpose, transitioning from a focus on book preservation to prioritising social connection, community engagement, and inclusivity from a neurotypical perspective.

Key interventions were made to increase natural light into the building and enhance the public realm with views to landscape around the library, making it more legible, safe, accessible, and improving connection between the building's interior, hardscape, and natural elements. Accessibility to all entries was significantly improved, particularly at the northern entry, where previously a management plan had been necessary to accommodate accessibility challenges. The refurbishment also addressed poor wayfinding, creating a more intuitive and welcoming experience for all users. Additionally, service areas (see Figure 4.4) that previously closed off the library's connection to the main Sir Charles Court Promenade were reconfigured to enhance visual and physical connectivity, reinforcing the library's role as a central hub on campus.

Inclusivity and Neurodiversity

A central component of the TL Robertson Library refurbishment is its commitment to inclusivity, with a particular focus on accommodating neurodivergent individuals. The library incorporates a range of flexible, adaptive spaces (outlined below) designed to meet the diverse sensory and cognitive needs of its users. This approach aligns with the principles of universal design, which emphasises creating environments accessible to all, regardless of ability. However, while Universal Design for Learning (UDL) frameworks advocate broad inclusivity, they may not

Figure 4.4 Refurbished TL Robertson Library, render emphasising open spaces, clear wayfinding, natural light, access to views of external landscaping and soft furnishings. Source: Authors (2024).

inherently address the specific and varied needs of neurodivergent users. In this case, additional considerations – particularly around sensory regulation, spatial zoning, and low-stimulation environments – were integrated into the design to enhance accessibility for neurodivergent individuals. These include:

EQUITY SPACES AND ASSISTIVE TECHNOLOGIES

Equity spaces are a significant feature of the library's design, providing dedicated areas that support students and staff within the Curtin community. Equity spaces embody UDL principles, but here they are tailored with specific assistive technologies to meet neurodivergent cognitive and sensory needs. The quiet and structured environment, coupled with ergonomic features and adaptive tools like screen readers and visual aids, ensures that neurodivergent users can effectively access library resources in a way that minimises sensory discomfort. The equity room on Level 2, for instance, offers a quiet study area equipped with specialised facilities such as ergonomic chairs, motorised adjustable desks, angled workboards and document holders. Assistive technologies available in the Equity Room include the JAWS screen reader program, Window Eyes, NV Access, and Fire Vox, which cater to students with visual or cognitive impairments, ensuring neurodivergent students can effectively access and engage with library resources.

RESTING AND CHANGING PLACES ROOMS

To further support inclusivity, the library includes a resting room on Level 2, which provides a low-stimulation environment with comfortable seating, offers students a space to relax and take breaks as needed. Rest pods on Level 2, and comfortable more intimate small group seating (see Figures 4.5 and 4.6) furthers the library's comfort offering, providing students with the ability to 'break-away' to lower stimulation spaces with varying light penetration, sources, and intensities. This adaptation acknowledges that while UDL encourages spaces accessible to all, neurodivergent students may benefit from designated areas that allow for breaks from sensory input, supporting self-regulation and mental well-being.

The inclusion of a changing places facility on Level 3 (see Figure 4.12 later in this section), featuring a full-sized change table and hoist, accommodates individuals with high support needs, demonstrating the library's commitment to providing accessible and dignified facilities for all.

WAYFINDING AND ZONING

The refurbishment introduced clear and effective wayfinding strategies to guide users through the library (see Figures 4.7 and 4.8). These measures include dual language naming, signalling inclusion, and enhancing the overall user experience. Zoning within the library clearly demarcates quiet study areas from

Figure 4.5 Refurbished TL Robertson Library, example of individual rest pods, orientated towards views to landscape. Source: Authors (2024).

collaborative zones, catering to different student needs and preferences. This thoughtful and intuitive approach to spatial organisation supports neurodivergent students by reducing sensory overload and providing environments that are conducive to both individual and group work. The library's wayfinding and zoning strategies take UDL principles further by tailoring the environment to reduce sensory overload and facilitate ease of navigation for neurodivergent users. Features like dual language naming and clear demarcations between quiet and collaborative areas aid in minimising confusion and sensory strain, offering an improved experience that aligns with neurodivergent preferences.

Findings and Discussion

Database Literature Review: Overview of Application in Practice in Case Study

The comprehensive review of the literature highlights a range of design interventions and strategies that can make library spaces more welcoming, comfortable, and sensory-friendly for neurodivergent users.

Figure 4.6 Refurbished TL Robertson Library, example of rest areas, orientated towards views to landscape and natural light. Source: Joel Barbitta (2023).

Figure 4.7 Refurbished TL Robertson Library, example of clear signage for lifts and different floor levels. Source: Authors (2024).

Figure 4.8 Refurbished TL Robertson Library, render example of demarcation of different exhibition (public) and study (private) zones, lighting control, connection to external promenade, and views to landscape. Source: Authors (2024).

Key findings from the reviewed studies align with the design outcomes observed in the Curtin University TL Robertson Library case study, demonstrating a significant overlap between theoretical recommendations and practical implementations. These findings underscore the importance of designing library environments that cater to the sensory and spatial needs of neurodivergent individuals, particularly Autistic individuals, who are often the primary focus of such studies. Furthermore, this chapter builds upon extant research by positioning real-world design considerations within existing scholarly theory on how architectural design choices influence the functionality and comfort of spaces for neurodivergent individuals. Finally, design choices in the refurbishment of TL Robertson Library were also informed by the research of Professor Winnie Dunn (2009) and Brown et al. (2001) on how people process sensory information and the diverse sensory profiles of individuals (seekers, bystanders, sensors, and avoiders).

Quiet Zones and Sensory-Friendly Spaces

A recurring theme across multiple studies is the creation of designated quiet zones that provide respite from sensory overload. Such spaces are essential for neurodivergent individuals who may find the hustle and bustle of typical library environments overwhelming. Anderson (2021) emphasises the importance of offering quiet rooms for studying and sensory escape, as well as clear information about busy times to help students avoid crowds. Similarly, the study by Walton and McMullin (2021) at West Chester University, USA, highlighted the success of implementing an autism-friendly study room, positioned on a quiet floor with flexible lighting and seating options. These findings align with the design outcomes at Curtin University, where the incorporation of quiet, low-stimulation areas supports the sensory well-being of neurodivergent users (see Figure 4.9).

Flexible Lighting and Natural Light

The preference for natural lighting and adjustable lighting options is consistently noted in the literature as beneficial for neurodivergent individuals. Harsh fluorescent lighting can be a trigger for sensory discomfort, as noted by Bahrampour and deCourcy Hinds (2022). Their participatory design approach at Bard High School Early Colleges led to the inclusion of dimmable lights and reduced use of fluorescent lighting, reflecting the importance of flexible lighting solutions. Moreover, 'active' lighting control ensures that internal lighting intensity automatically adjusts to account for changing external lighting. This aligns with the Curtin University library, where careful consideration was given to lighting design to create an inviting and calming atmosphere. The use of natural light and the option to adjust lighting conditions (see Figure 4.10a and b) helps accommodate different sensory preferences, providing a more inclusive environment.

Figure 4.9 Refurbished TL Roberston Library, example of private, sound-dampening, and visual screening study pods, bright reflective up lighting and wide circulation paths. Source: Joel Barbitta (2023).

Figure 4.10a and 4.10b Refurbished TL Robertson Library: (a: top) taking advantage of natural daylight, (b) controlled light penetration with focused views to landscape. Source: Joel Barbitta (2023).

Figure 4.11 Refurbished TL Robertson Library, render of soft lighting and furnishings, and provision of different seating options. Source: Authors (2024).

Seating Options and Flexible Furnishings

The need for various seating options and flexible, adjustable workstations is another critical finding that resonates with neurodiverse needs. Boyer and El-Chidiac (2023) discuss the provision of wobble stools, bean bags, and adjustable desks in Susquehanna University's library to create more inclusive spaces. These furniture choices allow neurodivergent users to select seating that meets their comfort and sensory needs, enhancing their ability to focus and feel at ease. The Curtin University library also incorporated a variety of seating arrangements, including private study nooks, collaborative spaces, and comfortable lounge areas, with a range of seating types accommodating diverse preferences and promoting a sense of belonging and control over one's environment (see Figure 4.11).

Sensory Items and Tools

The inclusion of sensory items such as fidget toys, weighted blankets, and noise-cancelling headphones is another design intervention that supports neurodivergent users. Boyer and El-Chidiac (2023) highlighted the availability of such items in designated 'chill out study rooms' at Susquehanna University,

USA, which were specifically designed for stress relief and sensory regulation. Providing these items not only supports the sensory needs of neurodivergent users but also normalises their presence in the library environment, fostering inclusivity. Similarly, Curtin University's library offers sensory tools and quiet spaces equipped with calming elements, demonstrating a commitment to creating an environment conducive to neurodivergent students' needs.

Universal Design and Inclusivity

Implementing Universal Design principles from the outset is widely advocated in the literature as a strategy for creating inclusive spaces that cater to a broad range of users. However, while UDL frameworks emphasise inclusivity, they may not fully address the complex, varied needs of neurodivergent students, highlighting the value of co-design. Neurodivergent stakeholders bring unique perspectives that can refine and adapt UDL applications, ensuring inclusivity goes beyond compliance and becomes truly experiential. While Pionke (2017) emphasises the importance of broad-based accessibility, a co-design approach acknowledges that neurodivergent users require additional accommodations, such as sensory-friendly zoning and adaptive technologies, which may otherwise be overlooked.

At Curtin University, the library's approach reflects this understanding, with targeted adjustments to Universal Design principles, including sensory-friendly zoning, specialised assistive technology, and participatory design. These elements were implemented with neurodivergent users' needs in mind, providing a level of inclusivity that goes beyond the general scope of UDL (see Figure 4.12).

Student Input and Co-design

Engaging neurodivergent users in the design process through participatory approaches is highlighted as a key factor in creating spaces that genuinely meet their needs. Co-design allows stakeholders to communicate their requirements directly to designers, a process essential for achieving inclusivity that standard frameworks, such as UDL, may not cover in sufficient detail. Bahrampour and deCourcy Hinds (2022) illustrate the value of involving students in the design process, enabling them to voice their preferences and directly influence the outcome. This approach recognises that neurodivergent students may have distinct, often underrepresented perspectives that are not fully accounted for in standard UDL frameworks. This participatory approach is echoed in the Curtin University case study, where stakeholder engagement and feedback played a crucial role in shaping the library's design. Incorporating user input ensured that the spaces created are not only functional but also resonate with the users' lived experiences and needs.

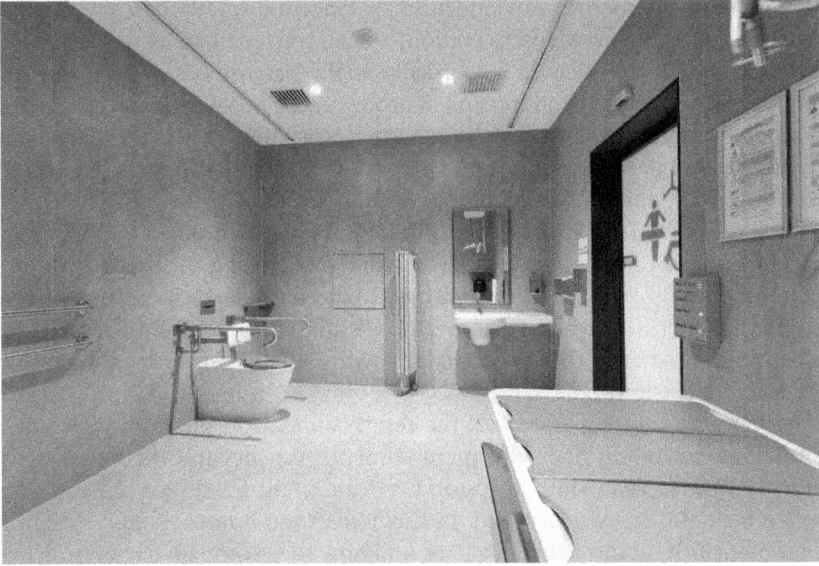

Figure 4.12 Refurbished TL Robertson Library, example of accessible facilities. Source: Joel Barbitta (2023).

Impact on Well-Being and Success

The studies reviewed provide compelling evidence that well-designed library environments contribute to the overall well-being and academic success of neurodivergent students, but the effectiveness of these designs is strongly linked to co-design efforts that directly involve neurodivergent users. Downey, Muszkiewicz and Muskin-Press (2024) report that the creation of wellness spaces in Valparaiso University's library positively impacted students' mood, relaxation, and stress levels. Such spaces not only support mental health but also enhance the students' sense of belonging and connection to the campus community. The Curtin University library design reflects this understanding, with wellness areas and sensory-friendly environments that foster both academic engagement and emotional well-being.

Conclusion

The changing functionality and design of library spaces are being largely driven by evolving pedagogies, but an increased societal focus on diversity, inclusion, and equality is also transforming how people interact with the built environment, including academic facilities.

Contemporary libraries no longer solely prioritise knowledge preservation but actively foster knowledge creation, social engagement, and accessibility. However, as UDL principles are broadly applied across educational environments, their limitations in addressing neurodivergent needs underscore the need for careful adaptation. By prioritising participatory design, Curtin University's TL Robertson Library serves as a model for how academic buildings can become more attuned to the specific requirements of neurodivergent users.

The TL Robertson Library's refurbishment serves as a model for reimagining academic spaces to prioritise inclusivity while recognising the specific requirements of neurodivergent users. Through targeted adaptations to Universal Design, evidence-based design research, and neurodivergent-focused participatory approaches, the project aligns with Curtin University's mission of equity and inclusion.

Evaluating the direct impact of the refurbishment on the lived experiences of students, including neurodivergent students, was beyond the scope of this study. However, this would be a good starting point for future research. The focus was on the design interventions themselves and how they align with principles of inclusivity and neurodiversity, and how they compare to best practices identified in the literature. Nevertheless, assessing the real-world impact of these interventions is a critical next step. Future research incorporating post-occupancy evaluations, user feedback, and sensory processing models (such as Dunn's Model of Sensory Processing) would provide valuable insights into how these design changes affect student experiences and engagement.

References

Anderson, A. (2021) 'From mutual awareness to collaboration: Academic libraries and autism support programs', *Journal of Librarianship and Information Science*, 53(1). https://doi.org/10.1177/0961000620918628

Australian Building Codes Board [ABCB]. (2022) *National construction code, volume one – Building code of Australia class 2 to 9 buildings*. Canberra, ACT: Commonwealth of Australia.

Australian Library and Information Association (ALIA). (2019) 'Guidelines on library and information services for people with disabilities', *read.alia.org.au* [online]. https://read.alia.org.au/guidelines-library-and-information-services-people-disabilities (accessed: 2 September 2024).

Bahrampour, N., and deCourcy Hinds, J. (2022) 'Neurodiverse navigation and disability equity in a NYC DoE Early College Library', *Urban Library Journal*, 28(2). https://academicworks.cuny.edu/ulj/vol28/iss2/1 (accessed: 21 August 2024).

Birkett, L., McGrath, L., and Tucker, I. (2022) 'Muting, filtering and transforming space: Autistic children's sensory "tactics" for navigating mainstream school space following transition to secondary school', *Emotion, Space and Society*, 42. https://doi.org/10.1016/j.emospa.2022.100872

Boyer, A., and El-Chidiac, A. (2023) 'Come chill out at the library: Creating soothing spaces for neurodiverse students', *Journal of New Librarianship*, 8(1), 41–47. https://doi.org/10.33011/newlibs/13/5

Brown, C., Tollefson, N., Dunn, W., Cromwell, R., and Filion, D. (2001) 'The adult sensory profile: Measuring patterns of sensory processing', *American Journal of Occupational Therapy*, 55(1), 75–82 [online]. https://doi.org/10.5014/ajot.55.1.75

Cox, A. (2018) 'Space and embodiment in informal learning', *Higher Education*, 75(6), 1077–1090. https://doi.org/10.1007/s10734-017-0186-1

Cox, A. (2023) 'Factors shaping future use and design of academic library space', *New Review of Academic Librarianship*, 29(1), 1–18. https://doi.org/10.1080/13614 533.2022.2039244

Curtin University. (2020) *WAIT's main library, the TL Robertson Library, opens, along with another vital student service, the computer centre* [online image]. www.curtin. edu.au/about/history-facts/history/ (accessed: 26 September 2024).

Downey, A., Muszkiewicz, R., and Muskin-Press, N. (2024) 'The library cares about me: Creating distinct spaces to support student wellness and mental health', *Humboldt Journal of Social Relations*, 1(46). https://doi.org/10.55671/0160-4341.1236

Dunn, W. (2001) 'The 2001 Eleanor Clarke Slagle Lecture. The sensations of everyday life: empirical, theoretical, and pragmatic considerations', American Journal of Occupational Therapy, 55(6), 608-620.

Dunn, W. (2009) *Living sensationally: Understanding your senses*. London: Jessica Kingsley Publishers.

Dunn, W. (2014) *The Sensory profile 2*. San Antonio: Pearson Publishing.

Johnston, N. (2021) 'Library of the future', *Ecu.edu.au*. Joondalup, WA: Edith Cowan University. www.ecu.edu.au/__data/assets/pdf_file/0004/961276/Library-of-the-Future-Report.pdf

Jonescu, E., Olatunji, O., Uylaki, T., and Duric, S. (2024) 'Understanding the principles and safety implications of neurodiversity in the design of professional construction workplaces', In: N. Umeokafor, F. Emuze, C.K.I.C. Ibrahim, R. Sunindijo, Tariq Umar, A. Windapo and J. Teizer, eds., *Handbook of drivers of continuous improvement in construction health, safety, and wellbeing* (pp. 281–294). London: Routledge eBooks [online]. https://doi.org/10.1201/9781032614069-28

Landgraf, G. (2014) *Making room for informal learning* [online]. https://americ anlibrariesmagazine.org/2014/02/26/making-room-for-informal-learning/ (accessed: 2 September 2024).

Massachusetts Board of Library Commissioners (MBLC) and Sasaki. (2020) *Library space: A planning resource for librarians* [online]. Massachusetts: Massachusetts Libraries. https://issuu.com/sasakiassociates/docs/library-space-planning-resou rce (accessed: 2 September 2024).

Mostert, M.P. (2012) 'Facilitated communication: The empirical imperative to prevent further professional malpractice', *Evidence-Based Communication Assessment and Intervention*, 6(1), 18–27. https://doi.org/10.1080/17489539.2012.693840

Mustey, J. (2019) 'A destination of choice for all', *International Information & Library Review*, 51(1), 83–87. https://doi.org/10.1080/10572317.2019.1588503

Neurodiversity Hub. (n.d.). *Neurodiversity hub – Resources for students, employers & more* [online]. Neurodiversity Hub. www.neurodiversityhub.org/ (accessed: 10 September 2024).

Oliveira, S.M. (2018) 'Trends in academic library space: From book boxes to learning commons', *Open Information Science*, 2(1), 59–74. https://doi.org/10.1515/opis-2018-0005

Pinfield, S., Cox, A.M., and Rutter, S. (2017) *Mapping the future of academic libraries: A report for SCONUL* [online]. Society of College, National & University Libraries. https://access.sconul.ac.uk/sites/default/files/documents/SCONUL%20Report%20Mapping%20the%20Future%20of%20Academic%20Libraries.pdf (accessed: 2 September 2024).

Pionke, J. (2017) 'Toward holistic accessibility: Narratives from functionally diverse patrons', *Reference & User Services Quarterly*, 57(1), 48. https://doi.org/10.5860/rusq.57.1.6442

Radulski, B., and Jaworowski, N. (2022) *Neurodiversity as the next frontier: Celebrating 'all kinds of clever' in higher education* [online]. MyLaTrobe. www.latrobe.edu.au/mylatrobe/neurodiversity-as-the-next-frontier-part-1-celebrating-all-kinds-of-clever-in-higher-education/ (accessed: 10 September 2024).

Shea, G., and Derry, S. (2022) 'A survey of library services for Autistic college students', *Journal of Academic Librarianship*, 48(6). https://doi.org/10.1016/j.acalib.2022.102591

SPD Australia. (n.d.) *What is SPD?* [online]. SPD Australia. https://spdaustralia.com.au/what-is-spd (accessed: 9 September 2024).

Standards Australia Limited. (2009) *AS1428.1 – 2009 (incorporating Amendments 1 and 2) design for access and mobility, Part 1: General requirements for access – New building work*. Sydney, NSW: SAI Global Limited.

Stanton, T. (2023) *Understanding neurodiversity and disability: A comprehensive guide* [online]. www.neurodiversity.guru/is-neurodiversity-a-disability

Svaler, T.B. (2023) 'On making libraries and museums more accessible for Autistic people', *IFLA Journal*, 50(1). https://doi.org/10.1177/03400352231202516

Tertiary Education Facilities Management Association (TEFMA) Incorporated. (2009) Space *planning guidelines*: Edition 3 [online]. TEFMA Inc. https://policy.deakin.edu.au/download.php?id=377&version=1&associated (accessed: 2 September 2024).

Walton, K., and McMullin, R. (2021) 'Welcoming Autistic students to academic libraries through innovative space utilization', *Pennsylvania Libraries: Research & Practice*, 9(2), 83–100. https://doi.org/10.5195/palrap.2021.259

Appendix

Table A.1 First keyword searches: tabulation of keyword search results across four databases: APA PyschINFO, ProQuest Psychology Database, PubMed, and Google Scholar. Science Direct excluded as search does not support wildcards (*)

Keywords	APA PsychINFO	ProQuest Psychology Database	PubMed	Google Scholar
'neuro*' AND 'library'	2,356	18,079	18,131	18,100+
'neuro*' AND 'library' AND 'design'	314	11,881	3,604	18,000+
'neuro*' AND 'library' AND 'architecture'	22	3,538	154	19,700+
'neuro*' AND 'library' AND 'space' AND 'design'	4	4,577	72	18,900+
'neuro*' AND 'library' AND 'space' AND 'architecture'	2	2,061	15	17,900+
'neuro*' AND 'library' AND 'trends' AND 'design'	8	5,544	104	19,500+
'neuro*' AND 'library' AND 'trends' AND 'architecture'	0	1,944	5	18,500+
'neuro*' AND 'library' AND 'future' AND 'design'	82	8,734	763	18,200+
'neuro*' AND 'library' AND 'future' AND 'architecture'	6	2,591	19	18,300+
'neuro*' AND 'library' AND 'guideline' AND 'design'	52	5,967	87	18,200+
'neuro*' AND 'library' AND 'guideline' AND 'architecture'	2	1,278	1	18,000+
'neuro*' AND 'library' AND 'standard' AND 'design'	33	9,551	733	18,400+
'neuro*' AND 'library' AND 'standard' AND 'architecture'	2	2,952	18	18,000+
'neuro*' AND 'library' AND 'university' AND 'students' AND 'design'	8	3,184	66	19,400+
'neuro*' AND 'library AND 'university' AND 'students' AND 'architecture'	0	816	1	17,700+

Table A.2 Second keyword searches: tabulation of keyword search results across five databases: APA PyschINFO, ProQuest Psychology Database, PubMed, Science Direct, and Google Scholar. The keyword 'neuro*' replaced with 'neurodiverse'

Keywords	APA PsychINFO	ProQuest Psychology Database	PubMed	Science Direct	Google Scholar
'neurodiverse' AND 'library'	1	21	5	23	16,300+
'neurodiverse' AND 'library' AND 'design'	0	15	2	22	11,800+
'neurodiverse' AND 'library' AND 'architecture'	0	5	0	5	3,170+
'neurodiverse' AND 'library' AND 'space' AND 'design'	0	10	0	13	8,990+
'neurodiverse' AND 'library' AND 'space' AND 'architecture'	0	4	0	4	2,810+
'neurodiverse' AND 'library' AND 'trends' AND 'design'	0	6	0	4	5,670+
'neurodiverse' AND 'library' AND 'trends' AND 'architecture'	0	3	0	2	1,670+
'neurodiverse' AND 'library' AND 'future' AND 'design'	0	15	1	20	10,500
'neurodiverse' AND 'library' AND 'future' AND 'architecture'	0	5	0	5	2,820+
'neurodiverse' AND 'library' AND 'guideline' AND 'design'	0	8	0	20	9,680+
'neurodiverse' AND 'library' AND 'guideline' AND 'architecture'	0	2	0	0	2,540+
'neurodiverse' AND 'library' AND 'standard' AND 'design'	0	8	0	15	8,610+
'neurodiverse' AND 'library' AND 'standard' AND 'architecture'	0	3	0	4	2,370+
'neurodiverse' AND 'library' AND 'university' AND 'students' AND 'design'	0	12	1	15	9,600+
'neurodiverse' AND 'library AND 'university' AND 'students' AND 'architecture'	0	4	0	4	2,540+

Table A.3 First and second keyword searches: papers selected for further review (see Findings section)

Source	Authors (date)	Title
Selected from first database review	Shea and Derry (2022)	A survey of library services for Autistic college students
	Birkett, McGrath, and Tucker (2022)	Muting, filtering, and transforming space: Autistic children's sensory 'tactics' for navigating mainstream school space following transition to secondary school
Selected from second database review	Walton and McMullin (2021)	Welcoming Autistic Students to Academic Libraries through innovative space utilisation
	Bahrampour and deCourcy Hinds (2022)	Neurodiverse navigation and disability equity in a NYC DoE Early College Library
	Downey, Muszkiewicz, and Muskin-Press (2024)	The library cares about me: Creating distinct spaces to support student wellness and mental health
	Svaler (2023)	On making libraries and museums more accessible for Autistic people
	Boyer and El-Chidiac (2023)	Come chill out at the library: Creating soothing spaces for neurodiverse students
Pearl harvested from bibliography lists	Mustey (2019)	A destination of choice for all
	Pionke (2017)	Toward Holistic Accessibility: Narratives from Functionally Diverse Patrons
	Anderson (2021)	From mutual awareness to collaboration: Academic libraries and autism support programs
	Cox (2023)	Factors shaping future use and design of academic library space

Chapter 5

Assistive Technology, Neurodiversity and Higher Education

Aoife McNicholl, Trevor Boland and Abbie Robinson

Introduction

This chapter focuses on the role of assistive technology (AT) for neurodivergent students in higher education. First, an overview of participation rates of disabled students, and neurodivergent students in particular, in higher education is outlined. Some of the broader challenges that neurodivergent students face in higher education are then discussed. The concept of AT is then introduced, followed by difficulties in accessing and procuring AT in higher education, examples of AT tools which support neurodivergent students and the educational and psychosocial impact of AT use for neurodivergent students. The chapter concludes by outlining some key recommendations and future directions in the area of AT and higher education such as tackling stigma, the intersection of AT and artificial intelligence (AI) and addressing the lack of funding for AT services.

The Context

Increasing numbers of disabled students are accessing higher education. European figures show that the percentage of students studying in higher education who indicated they had a disability or impairment was 25% or above in the Netherlands, Lithuania and Ukraine (Hauschildt et al., 2015). In the UK, participation rates have been steadily rising with disabled students comprising 17.3% of all home students (i.e. students studying in their own country) in 2019/20 which reflected an increase of 47% since 2014/15 (Hubble and Bolton, 2021). A similar trend has been observed in the USA, with undergraduate participation rates rising from 11.1% of the total undergraduate population in 2011/12 to 19.4% in 2015/16 (National Center for Education Statistics, 2018, 2022). In Ireland, disabled students represented 7.4% of the total student population in 2022/23, a 6.5% increase in the figures recorded in 2021/22 and a 110% increase in the last ten years (Association for Higher Education Access and Disability, 2024).

DOI: 10.4324/9781003495925-7

With regards to participation of neurodivergent students, those with a specific learning difficulty represented the largest proportion of students registered with a disability (38.8%) in Irish higher education institutions in 2022/23. (Editors' note: While 'disability' is the designation given for these prevalence data, this does not imply a 'disability' label is preferred. While this term may be unhelpful or even problematic in the context of the neurodiversity paradigm, it nevertheless represents how data is collected in this area.) This was followed by those with ADHD/ADD (12.8%), autism (11%) and developmental coordination disorder (8.2%) (Association for Higher Education Access and Disability, 2024). This represents a significant increase across all groups in comparison to 2021/22 data (Association for Higher Education Access and Disability, 2023). A similar trend is observed in the UK with a 6% increase for students with specific learning difficulties and a 109% increase for Autistic students from 2014/15 to 2019/20 (Hubble and Bolton, 2021). These increases in participation rates are most welcome and encouraging but must be matched with appropriate supports to ensure neurodivergent students can successfully navigate their program of study.

Challenges Neurodivergent Students Face in Higher Education

The transition to higher education involves changes in educational structure and an increase in autonomy. These changes can present an array of challenges unique to neurodivergent students across academic, social and personal dimensions.

The traditional educational structure used in higher education does not appear to align with neurodivergent learning needs. In particular, challenges with executive functioning are characteristic of neurodiversity and can include difficulty in time-planning, sustained attention, working memory and organisation needed for academic success. Varying timetables and unclear communication associated with traditional lecture-style content facilitate inattention, a lack of engagement and issues with understanding course material in neurodivergent students (Cai and Richdale, 2016; Cox, Ogle and Campbell, 2019; Davis, Watts and López, 2021). Upon entering higher education, many neurodivergent students have not been prepared with the skills needed to support their learning, such as self-organisation, self-motivation, communication and study skills (Davis, Watts and López, 2021; Wang, McCool and Wieman, 2024). These challenges are thought to contribute to the higher proportion of lower academic performance in neurodivergent populations (Arnold et al., 2020). The physical environment can also pose a challenge for neurodivergent individuals due to differences in sensory processing. Higher education environments generally are brightly lit, crowded and noisy. Neurodivergent students have reported these environments to impair their focus due to sensory sensitivity, leading to discomfort and stress (Van Hees, Moyson and Roeyers, 2015).

Higher education also presents social challenges including isolation, loneliness, bullying, rejection and anxiety (Davis, Watts and López, 2021; Pfeifer, Cordero and Stanton, 2023). Participation in active learning, such as group work, elicited contrasting evaluations among neurodivergent students, ranging from increased motivation and positive peer interactions to embarrassment and uncertainty surrounding the task instructions (Pfeifer, Cordero and Stanton, 2023). This variation illustrates the degree of diverse needs across neurodivergent populations and the lack of tailored educational support to address it. Outside the classroom, fear of stigma and the desire to belong has prevented students from disclosing their neurodivergence and accessing accommodations (Underhill et al., 2024). For those with 'hidden' differences, self-disclosure is a necessary step for accessing academic accommodations. However, anticipation of negative peer reactions appears to delay disclosure until they are no longer able to cope or discourages students from disclosing entirely (Van Hees, Moyson and Roeyers, 2015; Pfeifer, Cordero and Stanton, 2023). Those that choose to disclose report diverse consequences, including lecturer understanding and a sense of relief, but also experiences of inflexibility, poor treatment and judgement from academic staff (Van Hees, Moyson and Roeyers, 2015; Clouder et al., 2020). Some students also report issues with the quality of the accommodation provided such as inconsistency, irrelevancy and unfulfillment (Sarrett, 2018).

When such challenges are experienced, neurodivergent students are increasingly likely to withdraw from higher education (Cage, De Andres and Mahoney, 2020; DuPaul et al., 2021). Receipt of support in second-level and higher education is one of the primary protective factors for academic retention (DuPaul et al., 2021). However, late diagnosis, barriers to diagnosis, social barriers to help-seeking and dissatisfaction with current accommodations prevent the neurodivergent population from reaping the benefits of such support.

Given the rising participation rates of neurodivergent students, coupled with the multitude of challenges that these students face, it is imperative that this population are fully supported in their higher education journey to achieve their full potential. One key support is access to appropriate AT.

What is Assistive Technology?

AT can be described as any device which can help a person engage in a task more easily. It can include a range of products such as a wheelchair, hearing aid, cane and communication device, to name just a few. The World Health Organization have developed a Priority Assistive Product List, based on need and potential to transform an individual's life, which details 50 assistive products which can support a person (World Health Organization, 2016).

Within the literature, there are a number of different definitions of AT. When it comes to conceptualising AT, some definitions are grounded in a strengths-based approach. These definitions focus on how AT can support an individual to carry out tasks to the best of their ability and reach their potential. AT is seen as an enabler and tool of empowerment rather than an alleviator of burden. These include definitions such as the one in the Assistive Technology Act of 2004, defining an AT device as 'any item, piece of equipment, or product system, whether acquired commercially, modified, or customised, that is used to increase, maintain, or improve functional capabilities of individuals of disabilities' (U.S. Government, 2004, p. 1710). Similarly, other definitions focus on the positive outcomes that AT can afford an individual; AT is defined as 'assistive products and related systems and services developed for people to maintain or improve functioning and thereby promote well-being. It enables people with difficulties in functioning to live healthy, productive, independent and dignified lives, participating in education, the labour market and social life' (World Health Organization, 2018, p. 1).

Other definitions are grounded in a deficit or in a medical model approach. AT viewed from this lens functions as a device which can prevent restrictions, compensate for loss of function and alleviate strain associated with an impairment. An example of this would be the definition by the International Organization for Standardization (ISO) (2016) who define an assistive product as 'any product (including devices, equipment, instruments and software), especially produced or generally available, used by or for persons with disability for participation, to protect, support, train, measure or substitute for body functions/structures and activities, or to prevent impairments, activity limitations or participation restrictions' (International Organization for Standardization, 2016, p. 1). This definition by the ISO has since been updated to align more closely with the International Classification of Functioning, Disability and Health indicating that an assistive product both 'optimizes an individual's functioning and reduces disability' (International Organization for Standardization, 2022).

Some definitions specifically refer to AT within the educational context. The Ministry of Education in New Zealand defines AT as 'the specialised equipment and technology that assists students to access and participate in learning' (*What Is Assistive Technology*, 2020). In Ireland, the National Council for Special Education defines AT as 'any item of equipment that can be used to improve the functional capability of a student with special educational needs and is of direct educational benefit to them' (National Council for Special Education, 2013, p. 121).

It is becoming more apparent over recent years that AT is diversifying and no longer being viewed as products solely for disabled people. This is evident through the universal design of mainstream products such as Apple iPhones which are incorporating many assistive features which all users can access and use (Apple Support, 2024). The increasing availability of mainstream products with assistive features is becoming an emerging trend and as a result, the distinction between AT and mainstream technology is becoming blurred (World Health Organization and United Nations Children's Fund, 2022). In addition, research papers are increasingly examining and exploring the utility of mainstream devices as AT rather than focusing exclusively on devices designed and developed for disabled people (McNicholl et al., 2021). The mainstreaming of AT could have many benefits for users such as reduced cost, wider availability and reduced visibility/stigma. This could be instrumental in closing the gap between need and access to AT on a global level as at present, one in three people worldwide require AT and access is as low as 3% in certain countries (World Health Organization and United Nations Children's Fund, 2022). This is despite access to AT being identified as a human right in the United Nations Convention of the Rights of Persons with Disabilities (United Nations General Assembly, 2006).

Institutional Challenges for AT Procurement

The procurement processes in universities, while essential for ensuring transparency and accountability, can often become a barrier to effectively supporting students. These processes are typically designed to ensure that public funds are spent wisely and that purchases are made in a fair and competitive manner. However, the complexity and rigidity of these procedures can sometimes hinder the timely acquisition of resources and services that directly impact student support.

One significant issue is the lengthy approval times. Procurement in universities often involves multiple layers of approval, from departmental requests to central procurement offices (McLeod et al., 2015). This can lead to delays in acquiring essential AT resources (Lazar, 2022), such as updated technology and educational materials needed for student activities and projects. For students, these delays can mean a lack of timely access to AT (Potnis and Mallary, 2021), missed opportunities and a less effective learning experience.

Additionally, the strict adherence to budgetary constraints may limit the flexibility needed to address urgent or unforeseen student needs. Universities operate within tight budgets (Lazar, 2022), and procurement processes are designed to ensure that spending stays within these limits. However, this can make it difficult to respond quickly to emerging needs to accommodate a growing and diverse student population.

The bureaucratic nature of procurement processes can also stifle innovation. Institutions can get locked into specific vendors for technology, as a result of tenders, so a technology type, for example, a laptop model used by a blind student in secondary school, may have to be reviewed. The limited number of vendors available may mean the blind student has to compromise the long-standing relationship they have with a particular laptop model and instead accept a similar model from an approved vendor of the institution.

Questions can arise like is it 'reasonable' for a blind student to have to change laptop models due to procurement restrictions? Can a reasonable argument be made for institutions seeking technologies from non-tendered vendors so a student can continue using a brand of laptop/device that they have a long-standing familiarity with? This issue has been raised by disabled students who highlight the need for procurement processes to be inclusive, ensuring input and consultation with students regarding selection of ATs for procurement (Macheque, Kadyamatimba and Ochara, 2024).

While procurement processes are necessary for maintaining financial integrity and accountability, their complexity and rigidity can pose significant barriers to effectively supporting students. Streamlining these processes and allowing for more flexibility could help universities better meet the AT needs of their students and enhance their overall educational experience. Examining what are reasonable accommodations and how educational institutions for disability services can have flexible procurement process, that is, seek technology devices from tendered vendors to accommodate device model continuity, would greatly help the transition of students from school to college but also help them acculturate faster to college if processes could be in place for this accommodation.

AT Tools Which Support Neurodivergent Students

Types of challenges for neurodivergent students can involve working within a rigid curriculum that does not allow for accommodations or modifications, which can hinder academic progress. Flexibility and choice are essential as these students can experience a range of challenges that can affect their learning experiences in higher education. These can include difficulty sustaining attention, being easily distracted and forgetfulness. Others can include excessive fidgeting and impulse control, difficulties with social interactions and challenges with reading speeds and spelling, writing structures, difficulty with fine and gross motor coordination and organisational approaches.

Access to appropriate AT or awareness of AT in digital ecosystems, like Google and Microsoft for Education as well as specialised AT devices, is crucial for neurodivergent students. These students may struggle with technology skills which can be an integral part of academic work like group assignments.

Technology can offer ways to accommodate these students if there are flexible teaching approaches. This can include a video instead of a written assignment. A student can use PowerPoint to create a video of their slides, add narration and then be assessed on their knowledge. Alternative types of assessment like this can support the learning styles of neurodivergent students.

The demands of reading can be high in universities so tools like Immersive Reader in Word give students choice so the document can be read aloud, and the content can be heard instead of reading. This allows the student to listen to the content as they walk so the act of reading can now be kinaesthetic.

Similarly, immersive reader is available in Google Docs through downloading the helperbird extension (www.helperbird.com/).

Lessening distractions, especially on a laptop when reading, can be achieved through Immersive Reader with an in 'focus mode' to read out the document and fill the whole screen so browser tabs and applications in the background can be pushed aside. This allows students to better focus on the task at hand.

In-person presentations can be a part of continuous assessment and pose a challenge as standing in front of peers can activate social anxiety. Options like converting the slides into video are a possibility or encouraging students to use the inbuilt presentation practising tool in PowerPoint so a student can rehearse their presentation and get feedback from PowerPoint about their talking speed and use of language. This provides an opportunity to practice the presentation in a safe environment, get constructive feedback and to pre-pare for the final presentation.

Group work is a key component in a student's studies so using a Google Doc, for example, can offer choices to a neurodivergent student. These choices can include contributing to the document online both synchronously and asynchronously with the student group. Choice about how to approach writing can allow the student to use the dictation tool in the Google Doc instead of typing. This means the student can type with their voice as some students articulate ideas better through speaking and others are faster typing with their voice instead of their hands.

Specialised software has become so dynamic now that it can cater for a number of different challenges for these students. One example is a note-taking tool called 'Glean' that has a simple user interface that allows students to upload slides, type notes and record audio from class and automatically index the notes and audio to the slide displayed. It can also transcribe the audio so information can be listened back to and/or read. Additional features include adding relevant images, definitions and terminologies within the tool to supplement the lecture content. Tasks can be created throughout the recorded class that are centrally gathered so they can be managed easily. An inbuilt pomodoro tool can help focusing the students for specific times as well as reminding them to take breaks. Finally, AI within the tool can convert the transcript of the audio into a quiz so the student can revise and evaluate their knowledge of the class content. Essentially, this tool becomes a type of one-stop shop for students as it brings slides, notes and recordings into one place so it can be easily accessed and support organisation skills. Simple to complex notes can be taken and then searched easily so this reduces cognitive work-load issues. The interface itself can be modified to reduce distraction if needed which enhances concentration. Finally, the tool can be accessed via a laptop or app so the student can access all the materials on their phone giving them options about when and how they engage with the recorded information. Information relating to the above AT tools has been collated into Table 5.1.

Table 5.1 Assistive technology types and how they support students

Ecosystem/ Provider	Name of tool	Description
Microsoft	Word (dictation)	It allows you to convert your spoken words into text which is an alternative to typing
Microsoft	Word (immersive reader)	It offers features like text-to-speech, adjustable text size, spacing and background colour, as well as a line focus tool to lessen distractions. This makes it easier for users with dyslexia, ADHD and visual impairments, or other reading difficulties to read and understand text
Microsoft	PowerPoint (video)	Converting a presentation into a video allows students to add narration to the slides which is an alternative to presenting in-person
Microsoft	PowerPoint (coach)	The coach feature in PowerPoint provides real-time feedback on your pacing, pitch, use of filler words and more, helping you become a more effective speaker. It can also boost your confidence by allowing you to rehearse and refine your presentation
Google	Docs (voice typing)	It allows the student to use their voice to create text which is an alternative to typing
Google	Docs (collaboration)	Docs allows the sharing of online documents, so a group has options to work in different ways that include in-person or online. The student can manage the ways they engage in the activity
Glean	Audio recording/ note taking/ organisation	Glean is an online tool that supports note taking – audio of the class can be recorded then linked to the notes and slides in real time. Each note has a play button so the student can access specific notes they type and listen to the lesson recording at the exact time they wrote a note. AI in Glean also allows for the audio to be converted into a text format and AI can convert the recording into a quiz to support the revision and comprehension of the lecturer's class. Finally, AI in Glean can clean up the audio; that is, background noises can be removed or lessened with filters that support focus

For further information on AT tools and how they can support learning, visit the AT Hive developed by the Association of Higher Education Access and Disability (www.ahead.ie/The-AT-Hive).

Addressing these AT challenges for neurodivergent students requires a concerted effort from all stakeholders in higher education institutions from disability service to lecturers as well as procurement and IT services. This is to ensure effective awareness and support can be delivered to create inclusive and supportive environments that recognise and accommodate the diverse needs of neurodivergent students.

Educational Impact of AT in Higher Education

AT can have significant positive impacts for disabled students in higher education from an educational perspective. AT has been associated with an increase in grades, can support students in carrying out academic tasks and ensures greater access to academic content (McNicholl et al., 2021). Within the neurodivergent community, research has predominantly focused on students with learning differences and their performance of key academic tasks such as reading and writing. These students report that text-to-speech devices enhance comprehension, improve reading rate and increase retention (Floyd and Judge, 2012; Schmitt et al., 2012; Tanners et al., 2012). Other neurodivergent students report that speech-to-text software, such as Dragon, can enhance the speed at which they can produce written text, help eliminate spelling mistakes and improve their vocabulary (Nelson and Reynolds, 2015). Other tools such as Mind Map can help dyslexic students with planning and organising their ideas for their essays (Price, 2006). In addition to reading and writing skills, AT has also been associated with an increase in performance of note-taking, test-taking and studying abilities for neurodivergent students with a variety of diagnoses (Malcolm and Roll, 2019).

AT has also been associated with positive educational outcomes for Autistic students. Receiving AT services has been shown to predict college enrolment for these students (Kim and Baker, 2022). The usefulness of technology to enhance the self-management of Autistic students has shown promise. Smartphones, smartwatches and apps have been used to provide students with a variety of prompts to serve as reminders or help initiate actions. This has supported students independently engaging in academic work and dedicating more time to these tasks (Huffman et al., 2019; O'Neill and Smyth, 2024). Successful implementation involves identifying a support person/team, clearly identifying and defining the student's goals and target behaviours, selecting appropriate, person-centred technology solutions, evaluating goals and outcomes and making adjustments as necessary (Watson, Bross and Huffman, 2024).

Psychosocial Impact of AT in Higher Education

AT can have many benefits for disabled students from a psychological and social perspective. These include an increase in self-confidence and self-esteem, greater autonomy, enhanced well-being and greater social interactions (McNicholl et al., 2021; McNicholl, Desmond and Gallagher, 2023). For neurodivergent students, AT use can increase confidence in reading and writing abilities and enhance motivation to follow career aspirations (Tanners et al., 2012; Nelson and Reynolds, 2015). Students with learning differences report a greater sense of autonomy in completing academic work while for Autistic students, AT can facilitate attending appointments and independently carrying out associated tasks (Floyd and Judge, 2012; Wright et al., 2022).

AT has also been shown to increase communication for neurodivergent students. Assistive apps can be used by students to discuss classwork with others and share notes (Fichten et al., 2022). Facilitated communication devices play a crucial role in supporting social interactions with classmates for some Autistic students (Ashby and Causton-Theoharis, 2012). Other technology solutions such as computer-aided instruction, virtual reality and robot-mediated interventions have shown promise in enhancing the social skills of Autistic individuals (Pham, Bennett and Zetina, 2019). However, these are yet to be examined within a higher education setting.

It is also important to consider the potential impacts that AT can have on one's identity. AT devices increase the visibility of one's impairment and have the potential to increase stigmatisation (Lund and Nygård, 2003; Parette and Scherer, 2004). Negative social feedback from others about AT use can draw unwanted attention to the user, highlight them as different, cause feelings of embarrassment and shame, reduce self-esteem and force them to re-evaluate self-perceptions of 'normality' (Pape, Kim and Weiner, 2002; Shinohara and Wobbrock, 2011; Ellington and Lim, 2013). The increased visibility of AT use can be particularly difficult for those with invisible disabilities who have the option of 'passing' as non-disabled if they so wish (Shinohara and Wobbrock, 2011). This is relevant for some neurodivergent students whose impairment may not be overt or obvious to others. As a result, neurodivergent students may choose not to use their AT for fear of being treated differently or because they have not disclosed their learning differences previously to others (Kendall, 2016). This highlights the importance of creating an environment in higher education where students feel comfortable and confident in using AT. Otherwise, students are potentially missing out on the far-reaching benefits that AT can afford due to identity issues.

Recommendations and Future Directions

One key concern or challenge relating to AT use in higher education is associated stigma, as highlighted above. Thus, higher education institutions need to be cognisant of this and proactive in their approach to tackle this problem. This can be achieved through initiatives which aim to normalise AT use, reduce the visibility of devices and increase understanding and awareness. A number of suggestions are listed below for higher education institutions to consider:

1. Organise technology for all sessions for staff and students which focuses on the advantages of various AT devices. This promotes the idea that AT is a tool that could benefit everyone, not just disabled people.

2. Consider the language that is being used. Is AT the most appropriate term or could alternative terms such as 'technology' or 'inclusive technology' be used instead? Some people may associate the term 'assistive technology' with tools that are only relevant or useful for disabled people. By adjusting our language, we can potentially widen the reach of AT to non-disabled people, those who are undiagnosed and those who are not comfortable identifying as disabled.

3. Facilitate the formation of a group of AT users. Encourage students who currently use AT to come together, share experiences, offer advice and guidance and share information relating to emerging technologies. This will normalise AT use among disabled students and highlight how they are not alone in their experiences.

4. Consider recruiting AT advocates. These can be students who are currently using AT and are willing to share their experiences with others at talks and events for both current and prospective students. These students should be appropriately remunerated for their time and efforts.

5. Lecturers could take a proactive approach to highlighting and raising awareness of AT in their modules and classes. They could include a page at the end of their assignment brief which details freely available AT tools which can assist in the preparation of the assignment. They could also model how AT tools such as speech-to-text software and Immersive Reader, which are freely available through Microsoft Office 365, can be used to complete academic tasks. Making this information available to all students in the classroom normalises AT use and reinforces the idea that it can be useful for all students.

6. Ensure mainstream technology solutions are available and can be funded for disabled students through the disability office. Some students are more comfortable using mainstream solutions such as iPads or assistive apps as they are less visible than traditional AT devices. Having access to these devices can mean that peers are unaware of their AT use, reducing potential stigma and feelings of embarrassment.

7. Create opportunities for increased awareness and understanding of AT. This could include organising staff training or workshops on what AT is and how it can be used. For wider awareness across the higher education institution, you could consider organising a 'technology week' where a range of events for both staff and students take place relating to AT. To increase awareness both within and external to the college/university, consider creating a short docuseries which would follow individual students and how they are using AT in different contexts.

Another emerging area which warrants consideration is the intersection of AT and AI in higher education. Some AT tools are now incorporating AI features. This can allow students to quickly summarise lecture material or create quizzes based on content for study purposes. This poses a number of questions/challenges: How is access and use of AI features in these AT products managed/controlled? Does the availability of these AI features in AT products create inequity, giving disabled students a potential advantage over their non-disabled peers? In addition, is it possible that AI can serve as AT or replace existing AT products in the future? For example, certain AI tools can produce 'alt text' for blind students. Alt text is a short description of an image or photo for someone who can't see it. Other tools such as 'Be My AI' can be used to take a photo, produce a detailed description of the photo and provide options for the user to chat and ask further questions about the image. It is clear that this is an evolving and rapidly changing field but something that higher education institutions should consider in the coming years.

Lastly, funding for AT in higher education continues to be an ongoing problem. Lack of access to sufficient and appropriate AT funding is reported within some institutions (Reed and Curtis, 2012; Mullins and Preyde, 2013) with only 11% of total funds being distributed to AT services in Irish higher education institutions in 2014/2015 (Higher Education Authority, 2017). AT funding for disabled international students is even more limited within some institutions. In addition, issues with procurement further compound these problems, delaying access to AT for students. Given the wide-reaching benefits of AT in higher education, there is a pressing need for ring-fenced funding for AT services, separate to other broader funding mechanisms for disabled students, to ensure that sufficient funds are available to support students throughout their educational journeys. Higher education institutions should also explore alternative funding mechanisms, such as philanthropic funding, to supplement funding for AT received from governmental departments.

References

Apple Support. (2024) *Get started with accessibility features on iPhone.* https://support.apple.com/en-ie/guide/iphone/iph3e2e4367/ios

Arnold, L.E., Hodgkins, P., Kahle, J., et al. (2020) 'Long-term outcomes of ADHD: Academic achievement and performance', *Journal of Attention Disorders,* 24(1), 73–85. https://doi.org/10.1177/1087054714566076

Ashby, C.E., and Causton-Theoharis, J. (2012) '"Moving quietly through the door of opportunity": Perspectives of college students who type to communicate', *Equity & Excellence in Education,* 45(2), 261–282. https://doi.org/10.1080/10665684.2012.666939

Association for Higher Education Access and Disability. (2023) *Students with disabilities engaged with support services in higher education in Ireland 2021/22.* Dublin: AHEAD Educational Press. www.ahead.ie/userfiles/files/AHEAD_Research_Report_22_Interactive.pdf

Association for Higher Education Access and Disability. (2024) *Students with disabilities engaged in support services in higher education in Ireland 2022/23.* Dublin: AHEAD

Educational Press. www.ahead.ie/userfiles/files/AHEAD_Research_Report_23_d igital_supplied.pdf

Cage, E., De Andres, M., and Mahoney, P. (2020) 'Understanding the factors that affect university completion for Autistic people', *Research in Autism Spectrum Disorders*, 72, 101519. https://doi.org/10.1016/j.rasd.2020.101519

Cai, R.Y., and Richdale, A.L. (2016) 'Educational experiences and needs of higher education students with autism spectrum disorder', *Journal of Autism and Developmental Disorders*, 46(1), 31–41. https://doi.org/10.1007/s10803-015-2535-1

Clouder, L., Karakus, M., Cinotti, A., et al. (2020) 'Neurodiversity in higher education: a narrative synthesis', *Higher Education*, 80(4), 757–778. https://doi.org/ 10.1007/s10734-020-00513-6

Cox, T.D., Ogle, B., and Campbell, L.O. (2019) *Investigating challenges and preferred instructional strategies in STEM*. US Department of Education.

Davis, M.T., Watts, G.W., and López, E.J. (2021) 'A systematic review of firsthand experiences and supports for students with autism spectrum disorder in higher education', *Research in Autism Spectrum Disorders*, 84, 101769. https://doi.org/ 10.1016/j.rasd.2021.101769

DuPaul, G.J., Gormley, M.J., Anastopoulos, A.D., et al. (2021) 'Academic trajectories of college students with and without ADHD: Predictors of four-year outcomes', *Journal of Clinical Child & Adolescent Psychology*, 50(6), 828–843. https://doi. org/10.1080/15374416.2020.1867990

Ellington, T., and Lim, S. (2013) 'Adolescents' aesthetic and functional view of hearing aids or cochlear implants and their relationship to self-esteem levels', *Fashion Practice*, 5(1), 59–80. https://doi.org/10.2752/175693813X13559997788763

Fichten, C., Jorgensen, M., Havel, A., et al. (2022) *AI-based and mobile apps: Eight studies based on post-secondary students' experiences*. US Department of Education.

Floyd, K.K., and Judge, S.L. (2012) 'The efficacy of assistive technology on reading comprehension for postsecondary students with learning disabilities', *Assistive Technology Outcomes and Benefits*, 8(1), 48–64.

Hauschildt, K., Gwosc, C., Netz, N., et al. (2015) *Social and economic conditions of student life in Europe: Synopsis of indicators eurostudent 2012–2015*. Germany: W. Bertelsmann Verlag GmbH & Co. KG. www.eurostudent.eu/download_files/doc-uments/EVSynopsisofIndicators.pdf

Higher Education Authority. (2017) *Review of the fund for students with disabilities*. https://hea.ie/assets/uploads/2017/10/HEA-Review-of-the-Fund-for-Students-with-Disabilities.pdf

Hubble, S., and Bolton, P. (2021) *Support for disabled students in higher education in England*. London: House of Commons Library. https://researchbriefings.files.par liament.uk/documents/CBP-8716/CBP-8716.pdf

Huffman, J.M., Bross, L.A., Watson, E.K., et al. (2019) 'Preliminary investigation of a self-monitoring application for a postsecondary student with autism', *Advances in Neurodevelopmental Disorders*, 3(4), 423–433. https://doi.org/10.1007/s41 252-019-00124-y

International Organization for Standardization. (2016) 'Assistive products for persons with disabilities: Classification and terminology'. www.iso.org/standard/60547.html

International Organization for Standardization. (2022) *Assistive products – Classification and terminology*. www.iso.org/standard/72464.html

Kendall, L. (2016) 'Higher education and disability: Exploring student experiences', *Cogent Education* (edited by B. Tarman), 3(1), 1256142. https://doi.org/10.1080/2331186X.2016.1256142

Kim, H., and Baker, D. (2022) 'Dreaming of college versus going to college: Expectations and enrollment among Autistic students', *Remedial and Special Education*, 43(4), 222–236. https://doi.org/10.1177/07419325211046050

Lazar, J. (2022) 'Managing digital accessibility at universities during the COVID-19 pandemic', *Universal Access in the Information Society*, 21(3), 749–765. https://doi.org/10.1007/s10209-021-00792-5

Lund, M.L., and Nygård, L. (2003) 'Incorporating or resisting assistive devices: Different approaches to achieving a desired occupational self-image', *OTJR: Occupational Therapy Journal of Research*, 23(2), 67–75. https://doi.org/10.1177/153944920302300204

Macheque, V., Kadyamatimba, A., and Ochara, N.M. (2024) 'Engineering modelling requirements for integration of assistive technology as a pathway for inclusive education in the disability unit', *International Journal of Research in Business and Social Science*, 13(6), 381–404. https://doi.org/10.20525/ijrbs.v13i6.3529

Malcolm, M.P., and Roll, M.C. (2019) 'Self-reported assistive technology outcomes and personal characteristics in college students with less-apparent disabilities', *Assistive Technology*, 31(4), 169–179. https://doi.org/10.1080/10400435.2017.1406414

McLeod, F., Cherrett, T., Bailey, G., et al. (2015) 'Sustainable procurement for greener logistics in the higher education sector'. In *Conference: Logistics Research Network*, Derby. https://doi.org/10.13140/RG.2.1.1163.0808

McNicholl, A., Casey, H., Desmond, D., et al. (2021) 'The impact of assistive technology use for students with disabilities in higher education: A systematic review', *Disability and Rehabilitation: Assistive Technology*, 16(2), 130–143. https://doi.org/10.1080/17483107.2019.1642395

McNicholl, A., Desmond, D., and Gallagher, P. (2023) 'Assistive technologies, educational engagement and psychosocial outcomes among students with disabilities in higher education', *Disability and Rehabilitation: Assistive Technology*, 18(1), 50–58. https://doi.org/10.1080/17483107.2020.1854874

Mullins, L., and Preyde, M. (2013) 'The lived experience of students with an invisible disability at a Canadian university', *Disability & Society*, 28(2), 147–160. https://doi.org/10.1080/09687599.2012.752127

National Center for Education Statistics. (2018) *Digest of education statistics 2016.* Washington, DC: U.S. Department of Education. https://nces.ed.gov/pubs2017/2017094.pdf

National Center for Education Statistics (2022) *Digest of education statistics 2020.* Washington, DC: U.S. Department of Education. https://nces.ed.gov/programs/digest/d20/tables/dt20_311.10.asp

National Council for Special Education (2013) *Supporting students with special educational needs in school.* Trim, Co. Meath: National Council for Special Education. http://ncse.ie/wp-content/uploads/2014/09/Supporting_14_05_13_web.pdf.

Nelson, L.M., and Reynolds, T.W. (2015) 'Speech recognition, disability, and college composition', *Journal of Postsecondary Education and Disability*, 28(2), 181–197.

O'Neill, S.J., and Smyth, S. (2024) 'Using off-the-shelf solutions as assistive technology to support the self-management of academic tasks for Autistic university students', *Assistive Technology*, 36(2), 173–187. https://doi.org/10.1080/10400 435.2023.2230480

Pape, T.L.-B., Kim, J., and Weiner, B. (2002) 'The shaping of individual meanings assigned to assistive technology: A review of personal factors', *Disability and Rehabilitation*, 24(1–3), 5–20. https://doi.org/10.1080/09638280110066235

Parette, P., and Scherer, M. (2004) 'Assistive technology use and stigma', *Education and Training in Developmental Disabilities*, 39(3), 217–226.

Pfeifer, M.A., Cordero, J.J., and Stanton, J.D. (2023) 'What I wish my instructor knew: How active learning influences the classroom experiences and self-advocacy of STEM majors with ADHD and specific learning disabilities', *CBE—Life Sciences Education*, 22(1), p. ar2. https://doi.org/10.1187/cbe.21-12-0329

Pham, A.V., Bennett, K.D., and Zetina, H. (2019) 'Technology-aided interventions for individuals with autism: Implications for policy and practice', *Policy Insights from the Behavioral and Brain Sciences*, 6(2), 202–209. https://doi.org/10.1177/23727 32219857750

Potnis, D., and Mallary, K. (2021) 'Analyzing service divide in academic libraries for better serving disabled patrons using assistive technologies', *College & Research Libraries*, 82(6). https://doi.org/10.5860/crl.82.6.879

Price, G.A. (2006) 'Creative solutions to making the technology work: Three case studies of dyslexic writers in higher education', *ALT-J: Research in Learning Technology*, 14(1), 21–38. https://doi.org/10.1080/09687760500479894

Reed, M., and Curtis, K. (2012) 'Experiences of students with visual impairments in Canadian higher education', *Journal of Visual Impairment & Blindness*, 106(7), 414–425. https://doi.org/10.1177/0145482X1210600704

Sarrett, J.C. (2018) 'Autism and accommodations in higher education: Insights from the autism community', *Journal of Autism and Developmental Disorders*, 48(3), 679–693. https://doi.org/10.1007/s10803-017-3353-4

Schmitt, A.J., McCallum, E., Hennessey, J., et al. (2012) 'Use of reading pen assistive technology to accommodate post-secondary students with reading disabilities', *Assistive Technology*, 24(4), 229–239. https://doi.org/10.1080/10400 435.2012.659956

Shinohara, K., and Wobbrock, J.O. (2011) 'In the shadow of misperception: Assistive technology use and social interactions', in *Proceedings of the SIGCHI conference on human factors in computing systems. CHI '11: CHI conference on human factors in computing systems*, Vancouver, BC: ACM (pp. 705–714). https://doi.org/ 10.1145/1978942.1979044

Tanners, A., McDougall, D., Skouge, J., et al. (2012) 'Comprehension and time expended for a doctoral student with a learning disability when reading with and without an accommodation', *Learning Disabilities: A Multidisciplinary Journal*, 18(1), 3–10.

Underhill, J.C., Clark, J., Hansen, R.S., et al. (2024) 'Exploring Autistic college students' perceptions and management of peer stigma: An interpretative phenomenological analysis', *Journal of Autism and Developmental Disorders*, 54(3), 1130–1142. https://doi.org/10.1007/s10803-022-05867-7

United Nations General Assembly. (2006) *Convention of the rights of persons with disabilities*. www.un.org/disabilities/documents/convention/convoptprot-e.pdf

U.S. Government. (2004) *Assistive Technology Act of 2004*. www.govinfo.gov/cont ent/pkg/PLAW-108publ364/pdf/PLAW-108publ364.pdf

Van Hees, V., Moyson, T., and Roeyers, H. (2015) 'Higher education experiences of students with autism spectrum disorder: Challenges, benefits and support needs', *Journal of Autism and Developmental Disorders*, 45(6), 1673–1688. https://doi.org/10.1007/s10803-014-2324-2

Wang, K.D., McCool, J., and Wieman, C. (2024) 'Exploring the learning experiences of neurodivergent college students in STEM courses', *Journal of Research in Special Educational Needs*, 24(3), 505–518. https://doi.org/10.1111/1471-3802.12650

Watson, E., Bross, A., and Huffman, J. (2024) 'Self-monitoring to support the goals of students with autism on college campuses', *Teaching Exceptional Children*, 56(4), 284–293.

What Is Assistive Technology. (2020) Vimeo. https://vimeo.com/432307229

World Health Organization. (2016) *Priority assistive products list.* Geneva: World Health Organization. https://iris.who.int/bitstream/handle/10665/207694/WHO_EMP_PHI_2016.01_eng.pdf?sequence=1

World Health Organization. (2018) *Improving access to assistive technology.* Geneva: World Health Organization. https://apps.who.int/gb/ebwha/pdf_files/wha71/a71_21-en.pdf

World Health Organization and United Nations Children's Fund (2022) *Global report on assistive technology.* Geneva: World Health Organization. www.unicef.org/media/120836/file/%20Global%20Report%20on%20Assistive%20Technology%20.pdf

Wright, R.E., McMahon, D.D., Cihak, D.F., et al. (2022) 'Smartwatch executive function supports for students with ID and ASD', *Journal of Special Education Technology*, 37(1), 63–73. https://doi.org/10.1177/0162643420950027

Chapter 6

Neurodiversity Inclusion in Work Integrated Learning

Neurodiversity Placements Program

Beth Radulski, Cheryl Dissanayake and Katie Wright

Introduction

The number of neurominorities entering higher educational institutions (HEIs) and workplaces in Australia is rapidly rising, with inclusivity becoming a necessity. For example, recent data suggest that one in 70 Australians are Autistic, and in 2017, 83% of Autistic Australians were under the age of 25 (Australian Institute of Health and Welfare, 2017). In Australian schools, one in ten students have a disability (AIHW, 2022). The latest report specific to the prevalence of minoritised neurotypes (Australian Bureau of Statistics (ABS), 2018) indicates 20% of Australians have a mental or behavioural condition, 13% have an anxiety-related diagnosis, and 10% have depression. The prevalence of dyslexia is around 10% (Australian Dyslexia Foundation, 2022), while ADHD is experienced by one in 20 children, making it Australia's most prevalent neurominority group (ADHD Australia, 2019). Overall, up to 20% of the general population are neurominorities (Doyle, 2020).

However, Gatto et al. (2021, p. 125) found that 40% of HEI websites do not reference career support for disabled students, and only 18% reference disability support in the context of Work Integrated Learning (WIL). WIL is a form of placement that involves students applying their academic and theoretical knowledge in a practical and professional setting, often through an internship, practicum, or fieldwork (Cooper, Orrell and Bowden, 2010). Although WIL programs increase employment outcomes for both abled and disabled students (Jackson and Dean, 2023; Dollinger et al., 2022), staff in HEIs frequently report uncertainty regarding how best to support disabled cohorts, including in WIL settings (Nolan et al., 2015; Dollinger et al., 2022).

The Medical Model of Disability conceptualises disability as inherent and biological (e.g. a disabled student will experience barriers and difficulties participating in WIL due to deficits in their functioning). However, the Social Model of Disability (Oliver, 1990, 2013) and the Minority Group Model of Disability (Hahn, 1988) challenge this view, highlighting the stigma and systemic barriers to inclusion faced by disabled people. Building on these approaches, Radulski (2022, 2024) argued that a Minority Group Model

DOI: 10.4324/9781003495925-8

of Neurodiversity could assist with identifying barriers to inclusion for Neurominority cohorts. Judith Butler (1988) argues that heterosexual people experience privilege due to the cultural dominance of heterosexuality (heterosexual hegemony). Expanding this concept into the field of neurodiversity, Radulski introduced two new concepts, neurotypical hegemony, and neurotypical privilege: defined respectively as the cultural dominance of neurotypical ('typically developing') norms throughout society; and the corresponding privilege this social group experiences because of their normativity. These concepts have been further evidenced and explored by Lewis and Arday (2023) to explore the oppression of Black Neurominorities in academia.

To address neurotypical privilege and hegemony and support student employability, Radulski (first author) developed a Neurodiversity Placements Program (NPP) at La Trobe University (LTU), Melbourne, Australia, in 2019. As detailed below, the NPP aimed to provide two key outcomes: first, an accessible placement option for neurominority and disabled students; and, second, a professional opportunity for students to develop skills and expertise that can be used to enhance neurodiversity inclusion in their future workplaces.

This chapter provides an overview of the LTU NPP. It demonstrates how the WIL model is well-suited to support neurodiversity inclusion in HEIs, as it spans both academic and employment contexts. Accordingly, using the example of the NPP, the steps that universities, placement hosts, and employers can take to enhance neurodiversity inclusion are outlined in the form of a case study. It is argued that to facilitate accessibility and inclusion in WIL and employment settings: (a) the concepts of neurotypical privilege and hegemony should be used to identify barriers to inclusion, and (b) these identified barriers should be addressed in program design through mitigating the effects of neurotypical privilege and hegemony.

The La Trobe University Neurodiversity Project and Placements Program

In late-2019, under the leadership of Radulski, a new Neurodiversity Project was launched at LTU, aimed at designing, advising on, and delivering support for neurominority staff and students. LTU is an Australian HEI founded in 1967 as Melbourne's third university in the northern suburbs, traditionally home to families from working-class and migrant backgrounds (LTU, 2023c). Melbourne's two pre-existing universities, the University of Melbourne and Monash University, are both members of the prestigious 'Group of Eight', a circle containing the eight highest-ranking universities within Australia, all within the top 150 universities globally (Group of Eight, 2023).

A key aspect of the founding vision and cultural identity of LTU involves providing educational access to underrepresented groups including First in Family (i.e. those without a family history of higher education), Indigenous and/or Torres Strait Islander, Culturally and Linguistically Diverse people, women and gender minorities, LGBTQIA+ people, Life Stage and Age Diversity (i.e. mature age students), and students living in remote areas with fewer tertiary educational opportunities (LTU, 2023b). LTU maintains campuses in Melbourne, and four regional cities across the state of Victoria, to improve university attendance rates in regional communities where participation rates are less than half those seen in Melbourne (LTU, 2020b). LTU also introduced StudyFLEX mode to increase students' freedom regarding when and where they study, including remote classes offered in several courses and majors (LTU, 2020a, p. 11). This precedent improved the capacity of the NPP to accommodate both intersectionality and flexible working options to increase diversity and inclusion.

In early 2023, a for-credit WIL placement was launched within the NPP with students deemed eligible to apply if:

• They were undertaking a degree related to neurodiversity.
• They wished to graduate into a field wherein (neuro)diversity and inclusion expertise were beneficial.
• They had lived experience as a neurominority.

Refer to Figure 6.1 for an outline of the structure and goals of the NPP.

To maximise the range of students and disciplines eligible to participate, the NPP was designed to be suitable for students taking a wide range of degrees

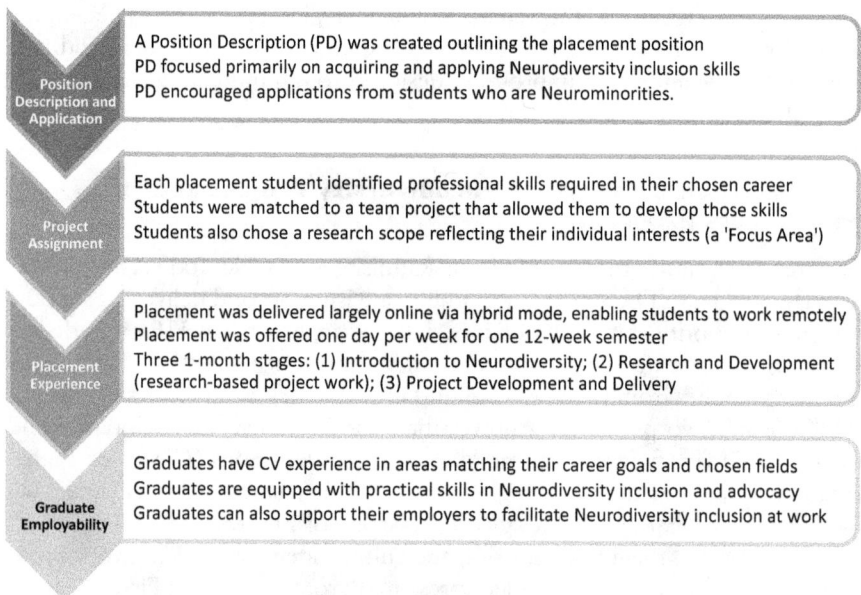

Position Description and Application
A Position Description (PD) was created outlining the placement position
PD focused primarily on acquiring and applying Neurodiversity inclusion skills
PD encouraged applications from students who are Neurominorities.

Project Assignment
Each placement student identified professional skills required in their chosen career
Students were matched to a team project that allowed them to develop those skills
Students also chose a research scope reflecting their individual interests (a 'Focus Area')

Placement Experience
Placement was delivered largely online via hybrid mode, enabling students to work remotely
Placement was offered one day per week for one 12-week semester
Three 1-month stages: (1) Introduction to Neurodiversity; (2) Research and Development (research-based project work); (3) Project Development and Delivery

Graduate Employability
Graduates have CV experience in areas matching their career goals and chosen fields
Graduates are equipped with practical skills in Neurodiversity inclusion and advocacy
Graduates can also support their employers to facilitate Neurodiversity inclusion at work

Figure 6.1 Structure and goals of the Neurodiversity Placements Program.

with broad relevance to neurodiversity inclusion. These include Arts and Social Sciences, Law, Psychology, Public Health, Business, and Sciences related to neurodiversity (neuroscience, etc.). Furthermore, the placement was open to all students – whether they identified as neurominorities, or neurotypical – who could outline the benefits of placement for their career.

Identifying Barriers to Inclusion: Contextualising Inequity

Autistic Australians face significant challenges in accessing and successfully completing higher education (Flower, Richdale and Lawson, 2020). Similarly, Dyslexic students report feeling unsupported in secondary and tertiary education (O'Byrne, Jagoe and Lawler, 2019), alongside low self-esteem in their academic pursuits prior to gaining university admission. Students who identify as ADHD – who account for up to 8% of the university student population – report difficulties in self-esteem, alongside academic performance and achievement (DuPaul et al., 2009; Kwon, Kim and Kwak, 2018).

A recent Australian study (Flower, Richdale and Lawson, 2020, p. 2) reports that young Autistic adults are:

> *less likely to be employed, more likely to attend technical and further education (TAFE) than university, more likely to enrol in higher education on a part-time basis and less likely to be engaged in both higher education and employment, compared with their non-Autistic peers.*

Indeed, over 40% of Autistic students within mainstream schools in Australia require extra support, and 46% need more support than is made available to them (ABS, 2019). While 31% of Australians with no disability hold bachelor's degrees, only 8% of Autistic people successfully complete the same level of education (ABS, 2019). Furthermore, Autistic unemployment rates are among the highest of any minority group across Australia, Canada, and the UK (Office for National Statistics, 2021; Public Health Agency of Canada, 2020; Jones et al., 2019; Amaze, 2022). These findings allowed us to identify several forms of neurotypical privilege and hegemony in educational and employment sectors.

In most Western nations, disability anti-discrimination laws state that disabled people are entitled to accessibility support in public settings including workplaces, schools, and universities. In Australia, the key pieces of legislation relevant to the NPP case study include the *Disability Discrimination Act 1992* (Australia) (Australian Government, 1992) which prohibits discrimination on the basis of disability, and the *Disability Standards for Higher Education 2005* (Victoria) (Disability Standards for Education, 2005) which outlines the obligations of HEIs in supporting disabled students. Traditionally, this involves offering reasonable adjustments for disability such as extra time to complete assignments for ADHD students, or a notetaker to assist a blind student in class (Australian Disability Clearinghouse on Education and Training, 2024). One limitation of this approach is that it relies on disabled people to disclose their disability and advocate for their support needs within a deficits-based context (i.e. I am incapable of X so the university must provide support by doing Y).

Highlighting the institutionalisation of neurotypical privilege and hegemony, reasonable adjustments involve creating ad-hoc disability inclusion options within a system built around the dominant and privileged access needs of abled and neurotypical people. Accordingly, prior to designing the NPP, research was undertaken to ensure that barriers to inclusion and success were accounted for and implemented into the design of the WIL opportunity provided to students. Moreover, the design considered the established challenges faced by neurominorities in higher education and employment and centred on a strengths-based approach.

Taking a Strengths-based Approach

The NPP focused on strengths in two key ways: institutional (i.e. LTU's strengths in programming, strategic planning, inclusive policies, and so forth); and individual (i.e. the strengths of students).

Institutional Strengths: Work Integrated Learning and Remote Work

As noted previously, LTU has a strong WIL offering, including a full Minor in Industry Placements, entailing a total of 400-hour (four 100-hour subjects) of placement. This program is resourced by a team of academics dedicated to co-ordinating several placement subjects. Through collaborating with this team, the Neurodiversity Project opted into becoming a placement host. A position description was developed, and the application process was jointly managed by the placement subject coordinators and the Manager of Neurodiversity Inclusion (Radulski).

Research on the higher education support needs of disabled students demonstrates that inaccessibility in WIL prevents many from participating in these programs (Dollinger et al., 2022; Thompson and Brewster, 2022; Langorgen and Magnus, 2020; Nolan et al., 2015). The opportunity to work remotely (e.g. from home) was one option explored to facilitate neurodiversity inclusion. For instance, sensory overstimulation is linked to anxiety and intolerance of uncertainty in Autistic people (Green et al., 2012; see also Neil, Olsson and Pellicano, 2016); the capacity to control one's sensory environment in a work or study from home setting may therefore assist in mitigating sensory triggers invoked by the physical workplace (O'Connor et al., 2022). Second, many Neurominority groups struggle with executive functioning (Doyle, 2020).

Working in an office setting places several demands on executive functioning, which involves planning, prioritising, goal-setting, and taking steps to achieve aims and objectives. For example, the expectation of commuting to work involves extensive planning and time-management skills, as does prioritising work tasks when presented with opportunities for ad-hoc socialising. Remote work may therefore reduce the demand on executive functioning by removing the mental load of planning a daily commute (Tomczak, Mpofu and Hutson, 2022), among other factors mentioned.

Drawing upon the institutional precedent for StudyFLEX – which allows for remote study – allowed the WIL placement to be offered via remote and flexible work, ensuring that environmental accessibility was accounted for. This also enhanced intersectional equity by opening access to cohorts with caring responsibilities, those living in regional areas, and so forth. Anticipating diverse accessibility needs in the design of the placement offering, and leveraging existing institutional strengths to meet these needs, allowed us to take proactive steps towards facilitating accessibility. This, in turn, reduced the pressure on placement students to self-advocate for reasonable adjustments in a 'deficits-based' manner, thereby mitigating some of the effects of Neurotypical privilege and hegemony.

Individual Strengths

The placement design also leveraged the individual strengths of students. Finn et al. (2023; see also Milton, 2012) found that the opportunity to communicate strengths in the workplace helped to mitigate challenges faced by Autistic people. Furthermore, placement and workplace supervisors report that when Neurominority students/employees work in an area they are passionate about, they are more likely to produce high-quality work (Lee et al., 2019; see also Doyle et al., 2022). Therefore, students were given the opportunity to work to their strengths in two key ways: first, they were matched to a placement project that directly drew on their disciplinary background and provided skills that they self-nominated as central to their career goals. Second, to ensure students were passionate about their work, they co-designed a focus area with their supervisor. Focus areas were developed to narrow down the scope of each placement student's contribution to their project, in line with both their strengths, career interests, and the teaching aims of the program (refer Figure 6.2). This task also equipped students with the skills needed to communicate their strengths to prospective or current employers. This strengths-based approach was used to limit the stigmatisation arising from neurotypical hegemony and privilege and reduce corresponding concerns related to stigma surrounding disclosures.

Community Engagement and Accountability

To ensure the program was able to provide the supports that students felt were necessary for their success at university, the NPP empowered leadership from

---

Focus Areas

The project I am working on is:

The Focus Area(s) I am interested in are:

These areas are related to my degree program in the following ways (1–2 sentences):

These areas are related to my career goals in the following ways (1–2 sentences):

These areas can contribute to the success of my project team in the following ways (1–3 dot points):

Figure 6.2 Focus areas template: teaching students to communicate their strengths.

within the neurominority staff and student community in two key ways. First, an Autistic staff member with research expertise in neurodiversity (Radulski, the first author of this chapter) was appointed to lead the program. Second, to empower neurominority students, research was undertaken to establish the accessibility needs of Autistic tertiary and WIL students, as evidenced in published participant studies (variously cited above). Dollinger and Vanderlelie (2021) found that co-designing with staff and student stakeholders assisted universities to solve ongoing issues by finding creative solutions. This approach has also proved helpful in co-designing peer support programs for neurodivergent high school students (Fotheringham et al., 2023). Furthermore, in the field of autism research, co-design with the lived experience community is considered a 'requirement of excellence' (Le Cunff et al., 2023; see also Pellicano, 2018; Pellicano et al., 2014), including within doctoral research (Taylor-Bower, Plaisted-Grant and Archer, 2024) as was the case with this study. Benefits of co-designing research include empowering the community to make decisions that will improve their quality of life and developing deeper understandings of accessibility and inclusion needs (Dwyer et al., 2021). Accordingly, as detailed below, the NPP engaged with students as partners, empowering the community to lead change initiatives that could effectively address neurotypical privilege and hegemony in ways that aligned with cultural and institutional norms.

Students were asked to provide significant input into determining their position descriptions and project contributions, alongside making recommendations for future initiatives in the neurodiversity space at LTU. For example, one project team worked on designing a neurodiversity-accessible event for staff and students involved in LTU's Neurodiversity Network. To ensure accountability, when organising and delivering the event, Neurodiversity Project staff asked placement students for accessibility recommendations, and supported them to implement them: including delivering the event in blended mode (i.e. having both in person and online attendance options), creating clear expectations (i.e. through materials sent to attendees before the event) and choosing a sensory-friendly location to host the in-person component. Working with students as partners allowed the NPP team to mitigate neurotypical hegemony and privilege as a core part of the programming.

Systematic Approach: The Neurodiversity Hub Model Framework

Taking a systematic approach contributed significantly to the university's steady progress in addressing neurotypical privilege. This was accomplished through partnering with Neurodiversity Hub (2023) – an organisation advocating to improve neurodiversity inclusion in business and education – and carrying out the placement work in alignment with the Neurodiversity Hub Model Framework. Each key area of the framework is outlined below, wherein we detail how these areas were implemented into both the design of the NPP, and the resulting support offered to students.

Transition to University

Many neurominority groups opt out of disclosure to avoid negative consequences such as exclusion in both university (Dollinger et al., 2022) and employment (Davidson and Henderson, 2010) settings. In the context of WIL specifically, 75% of disabled students opt out of fully disclosing their disability support needs due to a fear of experiencing stigma and discrimination (Dollinger et al., 2022). To address this issue, the position description included a statement on disclosure that framed disability as a positive factor in assessing applications (refer Figure 6.3). This was done with the aim of outlining some of the accessibility benefits of disclosure, alongside alleviating student concerns over the stigma and discrimination that may result from disclosure.

The fear of stigma and discrimination in professional and educational opportunities is a key driver of masking and camouflaging in Autistic people (Radulski, 2022; Hull et al., 2017). The placement program aimed to address this through creating positive opportunities to disclose both strengths and limitations in the workplace. As the placement supervisor, the Manager: Neurodiversity

---

Please note: We **strongly** encourage applicants who identify as a Neurominority (Autistic, ADHD, Dyslexic, or otherwise). We are very willing to work with you to ensure that your inclusion and accessibility needs are met .... We can support you with the flexibility to work from home when required, manage sensory processing differences, and work with your strengths to customise the role to you.

Figure 6.3 Excerpt from position description for the Neurodiversity Project Placement.

Inclusion, provided and filled-out a 'Work Style Preferences' template to lead by example (refer Figure 6.4). Regardless of their disability status, all students were asked to complete the template. It is important to note that, in the state of Victoria where LTU is based, a person can only be asked to disclose a disability if it is directly related to their role (Victorian Equal Opportunity and Human Rights Commission, 2023). Therefore, all students were asked to focus on describing their professional strengths and challenges, with students invited to communicate Disability support needs on a strictly voluntary basis. The goal of this activity was to give students the opportunity to practice disclosure in a safe and inviting setting, and in tandem with a strengths-based approach.

Peer Coaching/Mentoring

Peer mentorship can be helpful for Autistic tertiary students in particular (Siew et al., 2017; Merydith et al., 2019). However, often these programs are designed with a component of equipping Autistic students with 'social skills' based upon neurotypical cultural norms (e.g. Siew et al., 2017). Recent research highlights the negative well-being consequences posed by masking

I thrive with	I may need support with	Example	To support me, you can
Written communication	Verbal communication	I am very literal. I sometimes struggle with verbal processing (i.e. I can struggle to understand or use words at times). I can't 'read between the lines' or intuit things not said	Be as literal as possible. Sometimes I may ask you to repeat things you've said. If I'm not following you, please know I'm <u>not</u> disinterested – I may just need clarification
Seeing the 'big picture' of the project plan, and taking steps to ensure it is completed successfully	Smaller picture tasks and deadlines (i.e. answering e-mails in a timely fashion); and managing my Disability in this context	My role requires that I work on several projects at the same time. I often have to prioritise writing or management tasks and can fall behind in my e-mails (for context, I receive several hundred e-mails every week)	Please be patient when contacting me via e-mail; allow extra time (at least a few days) for me to respond whenever possible. If anything urgent arises, please attach a 'high importance' symbol

Figure 6.4 Excerpt of the working style preferences template provided to students in the Placement Handbook, as filled out by the placement supervisor.

and camouflaging behaviours, which involve adopting neurotypical social norms to conceal one's Autistic traits (Cage et al., 2018; Cage and Troxell-Whitman, 2019; Cage et al., 2022; Hull et al., 2017, 2019; Radulski, 2022). Therefore, the NPP offered a different style of mentorship, with several activities designed to create opportunities for peer connection. This included the creation of three small placement teams and weekly meetings wherein teams connected; the use of forums, presentations, and written tasks as opportunities to present work; and opening Microsoft Teams channels for weekly activities and chats. Offering various ways to engage with peers catered to a wide variety of accessibility needs, limiting the impacts of neurotypical hegemony and privilege.

Life Skills/Work Ready Skills Program and Work Ready Assessment

The NPP assisted students in developing a variety of professional skills. These included making individual contributions to an interdisciplinary team project; using popular professional software (Microsoft Word, PowerPoint, Excel, Outlook, and Teams), working within a diverse team, conducting research, writing a project proposal, connecting with colleagues via e-mail and video conferencing, all of which included training in how to use various accessibility features. For example, in each virtual meeting, students were invited to use closed captioning (to assist with auditory processing) and chat features (which offer an alternative to vocal participation when speaking is not possible). Each meeting plan also included an invitation for students to participate in whatever way they felt comfortable (e.g. the placement supervisor noted at the beginning of each meeting that the use of fidget toys was permitted, and cameras could be turned on or off as needed). This was done with the goal of reducing pressure on placement students to adhere to hegemonic and privileged neurotypical norms, encouraging them instead to gain confidence in setting healthy boundaries and self-advocating for support needs.

Social Media Strategy

There were several points at which social media was used to manage the impacts of neurotypical hegemony and privilege to encourage students to feel more comfortable applying for the program. First, in Neurodiversity Celebration Week (in 2022 prior to the onset of the NPP), a two-part blog series was posted on the student news webpage 'My La Trobe' (Radulski and Jaworowski, 2022a, 2022b) where a variety of neurominority staff and students were profiled through interviews in the blogs, with a focus on ensuring diverse representation across the contexts of gender, ethnicity, class, and so forth. Senior leaders at the university were asked to speak to why neurodiversity inclusion was a new priority for LTU, alongside committing the university to sustained efforts in this space. Subsequently, in Neurodiversity Celebration Week 2023, another blog was posted updating students about the launch of the program, encouraging application for 2024. To mitigate the perceived risk of stigma and discrimination for neurominority students considering applying, all three blogs highlighted how LTU was addressing neurotypical privilege, social, and institutional norms on a university-wide level.

Cultural versus Individual Change

The NPP focused on cultural change in numerous ways. First, through the research undertaken herein, it identified barriers to participation in WIL programs for Autistic and neurominority tertiary students. Then, the steps outlined above were implemented to facilitate inclusion. The students gained expertise in neurodiversity inclusion in professional settings through undertaking a curriculum focussed on cultural change. Throughout the early weeks of the placement, students engaged with a variety of materials, including the Neurodiversity Paradigm, legal protections for disabled people in universities and workplaces, disclosure and reasonable adjustments, masking and camouflaging, and intersectionality, among other resources on pertinent themes. Students then used this knowledge to shape their placement project. These projects have since influenced the university culture including through the delivery of the abovementioned neurodiversity inclusive networking event based on the placement students' research and recommendations.

The NPP also encouraged students to share their knowledge with key stakeholders across the university. For example, the Neurodiversity Project and Senior Executive Group co-hosted an event in which students had the option of presenting their projects, with senior staff responsible for student support programs across the university also attending. The event was delivered as a webinar to prevent environmental barriers to participation. The students were taught how to design and record themselves delivering a professional presentation. Each presenter was asked if they had a preference of presenting live or via video recording. Two students expressed concerns about potentially having issues with speech processing when overwhelmed, but both wanted to try to deliver their presentations live; to minimise pressure during the live presentation, the student's video recording was kept as a backup plan if deemed necessary. Students gained valuable professional skills including the ability to design, record, and deliver presentations; experience self-advocating for adjustments; and the ability to network with colleagues. Rather than focusing on individual change (e.g. through coaching students on neurotypical body language during presentations), the program aimed to make our university culture more inclusive.

Finally, there are several measures indicating the program's success on a variety of levels during its first two years of operation. In 2023, nine of the ten placement students successfully completed, with one leaving due to unforeseen personal issues. The program ran again in 2024, with a further 10 successful participants, and also secured a $A31,500 philanthropic grant which provided bursaries to support students with their accessibility and study needs. The program was also featured in *The Age* newspaper (Melbourne, Australia), bringing further awareness to the necessity of accessibility in HEIs. Finally, the NPP won a 2023 Vice-Chancellor's Cultural Qualities Award for Innovation. The Manager of Neurodiversity Inclusion, the first author, was the Team Leader, with the rest of the team comprising the two co-authors (Wright and Dissanayake) alongside two academic coordinators from the Industry Placements Minor, and the Neurodiversity Project Officer. The award description reads (LTU, 2023a):

> *The Neurodiversity Placements Program Team exemplifies innovation, by pro-moting awareness of inclusion challenges, delivering real-world impact and empowering students and communities to discover solutions to inequity.*

At LTU, 'real world impact' and 'real impact' reflect an organisational priority of translating and mobilising research for use in society (LTU, 2020a). This award demonstrates the cultural change that occurred at the university result-ing from the research undertaken herein.

Limitations

It is important to note that the case study presented here does not include par-ticipant data from student end-users. Given that the Manager: Neurodiversity Inclusion designed the placements program and supervised its students, a con-flict of interest would have been posed by the placement students acting as research participants. It was therefore crucial to ensure that potential place-ment students could access this program without becoming study participants. This case study is thereby limited to being a critical reflection of how the NPP was designed, as opposed to measuring student experiences and outcomes. However, these limitations were partly mitigated through implementing the findings of previously published participant studies wherein Neurominority groups shared their views on improving accessibility in educational and work-place settings, as outlined in the literature throughout this chapter.

Generating sustained cultural and institutional change within HEIs – along with community-based leadership – presents several challenges. A key limita-tion here is the inconsistency and unpredictability of university governance support and funding. Both businesses and universities use strategic planning to demonstrate corporate performance, with senior leaders managed via corresponding key performance indicators (KPIs) (Owolabi and Makinde, 2012). Ahmed (2012, 2015) argues that when EDI is institutionalised through such strategic plans and policies, it can become a 'brick wall' – a bureaucratic exercise that ultimately limits progress by sidelining the lived experience community's agency and leadership, in favour of ticking boxes aligned to KPIs. This theory is reflected in a late-2024 decision by LTU's academic portfolio and strategy, prevention, and education team, to create broad diversity and inclusion roles aligned with new strategic plans (LTU, 2024b), an approach which involved significant cuts to disability and neurodiversity-specific teams (see, for example, LTU, 2024a vs. LTU, 2025). This ultimately diminished LTU's ability to support lived experience leadership and co-design. At the time of submission, the NPP has been paused indefinitely – to shift the focus onto delivering new strategic action plans. These examples highlight the challenge of creating lasting cultural change, when institutional priorities are in constant flux. Future HEI initiatives should anticipate and address these structural limitations.

Conclusion

Neurominority groups experience significant cultural and systemic inequity in both universities and workplaces. As WIL programs span both academic and employment contexts, it is imperative to consider WIL program design in order to improve neurodiversity accessibility and employability for neurominority students. Key steps universities and employers can take to improve WIL accessibility include: contextualising inequity; taking a strengths-based approach; empowering the neurominority community; being accountable for implementing feedback; taking a systematic approach; and, creating cultural change. Through outlining the key features of the LTU NPP, this chapter has shown how taking this approach allows universities and employers to identify and address neurotypical privilege and hegemony as key barriers to inclusion for neurominority students and employees.

References

ADHD Australia. (2019) *ADHD in children – ADHD Australia.* www.adhdaustralia. org.au/about-adhd/adhd-in-children/ (accessed: 27 March 2023).

Ahmed, S. (2012) *On being included: Racism and diversity in institutional life.* Durham, NC: Duke University Press. http://ebookcentral.proquest.com/lib/latr obe/detail.action?docID=1173269 (accessed: 14 March 2023).

Ahmed, S. (2015, 2 February) *Institutional habits, feminist kill joys.* https://feministk illjoys.com/2015/02/02/institutional-habits/ (accessed: 26 April 2023).

Amaze. (2022) *Autism and employment in Australia.* Amaze. www.amaze.org.au/ creating-change/research/employment/ (accessed 2 August 2022).

Australian Bureau of Statistics (ABS). (2018) *Mental health, 2017–18 financial year.* Australian Bureau of Statistics, Australian Government. www.abs.gov.au/statistics/ health/mental-health/mental-health/latest-release (accessed: 27 March 2023).

Australian Bureau of Statistics (ABS). (2019) *Autism in Australia.* Australian Bureau of Statistics. www.abs.gov.au/AUSSTATS/abs@.nsf/Lookup/4430.0Main+Fea tures102018 (accessed: 14 July 2020).

Australian Disability Clearinghouse on Education and Training. (2024) *Students with disability – Reasonable adjustments: Disability specific*. ADCET. www.adcet.edu. au/students-with-disability/reasonable-adjustments-disability-specific (accessed: 16 August 2024).

Australian Dyslexia Foundation. (2022) *Dyslexia in Australia*. Australian Dyslexia Association, Dyslexia Association. https://dyslexiaassociation.org.au/dyslexia-in-australia/ (accessed: 27 March 2023).

Australian Government. (1992) *Disability Discrimination Act 1992*. www.legislat ion.gov.au/Details/C2018C00125/Html/Text, www.legislation.gov.au/Details/ C2018C00125 (accessed: 10 September 2022).

Australian Institute of Health and Welfare (AIHW). (2017) *Autism in Australia, autism*. Australian Government. www.aihw.gov.au/reports/disability/autism-in-australia/contents/autism (accessed: 27 March 2023).

Australian Institute of Health and Welfare (AIHW). (2022) *People with disability in Australia, education and skills – Australian Institute of Health and Welfare*. Australian Government. www.aihw.gov.au/reports/disability/people-with-disabil ity-in-australia/contents/education-and-skills (accessed: 27 March 2023).

Butler, J. (1988) 'Performative acts and gender constitution: An essay in phenomen-ology and feminist theory', *Theatre Journal*, 40(4), 519.

Cage, E., Di Monaco, J., and Newell, V. (2018) 'Experiences of autism acceptance and mental health in Autistic adults', *Journal of Autism and Developmental Disorders*, 48(2), 473–484.

Cage, E., and Troxell-Whitman, Z. (2020) 'Understanding the relationships between Autistic identity, disclosure and camouflaging', *Autism in Adulthood*, p. aut.2020.0016.

Cage, E., Cranney, R., and Botha, M. (2022) 'Brief report: Does Autistic community connectedness moderate the relationship between masking and wellbeing?', *Autism in Adulthood*, 4(3), 247–253.

Cooper, L., Orrell, J., and Bowden, M. (2010) *Work integrated learning: A guide to effective practice*. London: Routledge.

Davidson, J., and Henderson, V.L. (2010) '"Coming out" on the spectrum: Autism, identity and disclosure', *Social & Cultural Geography*, 11(2), 155–170.

Disability Standards for Education. (2005) *Attorney-General's Department*. www.legi slation.gov.au/Details/F2005L00767/Html/Text, www.legislation.gov.au/Deta ils/F2005L00767 (accessed: 30 October 2023).

Dollinger, M., and Vanderlelie, J. (2021) 'Closing the loop: Co-designing with stu-dents for greater market orientation', *Journal of Marketing for Higher Education*, 31(1), 41–57.

Dollinger, M., Finneran, R., and Ajjawi, R. (2022) 'Exploring the experiences of stu-dents with disabilities in work-integrated learning', *Journal of Higher Education Policy and Management*, 0(0), 1–16.

Doyle, N. (2020) 'Neurodiversity at work: A biopsychosocial model and the impact on working adults', *British Medical Bulletin*, 135(1), 108–125.

Doyle, N., McDowall, A., and Waseem, U. (2022) 'Intersectional stigma for Autistic people at work: A compound adverse impact effect on labor force participation and experiences of belonging', *Autism in Adulthood*, 4(4), 340–356.

DuPaul, G.J., Weyandt, L.L., O'Dell, S.M., and Varejao, M. (2009) 'College students with ADHD: Current status and future directions', *Journal of Attention Disorders*, 13(3), 234–250.

Dwyer, P., Acevedo, S.M., Brown, H.M., Grapel, J., Jones, S.C., Nachman, B.R., Raymaker, D.M., and Williams, Z.J. (2021) 'An expert roundtable discussion on experiences of Autistic autism researchers', *Autism in Adulthood*, 3(3), 209–220.

Finn, M., Flower, R.L., Leong, H.M., and Hedley, D. (2023) '"If I'm just me, I doubt I'd get the job": A qualitative exploration of Autistic people's experiences in job interviews', *Autism*, 27(7), 2086–2097.

Flower, R.L., Richdale, A.L., and Lawson, L.P. (2020) 'Brief report: What happens after school? Exploring post-school outcomes for a group of Autistic and non-Autistic australian youth', *Journal of Autism and Developmental Disorders*. http://link.springer.com/10.1007/s10803-020-04600-6 (accessed: 4 August 2020).

Fotheringham, F., Cebula, K., Fletcher-Watson, S., Foley, S., and Crompton, C.J. (2023) 'Co-designing a neurodivergent student-led peer support programme for neurodivergent young people in mainstream high schools', *Neurodiversity*, 1.

Gatto, L.E., Pearce, H., Antonie, L., and Plesca, M. (2021) 'Work integrated learning resources for students with disabilities: Are post-secondary institutions in Canada supporting this demographic to be career ready?', *Higher Education, Skills and Work-Based Learning*, 11(1), 125–143.

Green, S.A., Ben-Sasson, A., Soto, T.W., and Carter, A.S. (2012) 'Anxiety and sensory over-responsivity in toddlers with autism spectrum disorders: Bidirectional effects across time', *Journal of Autism and Developmental Disorders*, 42(6), 1112–1119.

Group of Eight. (2023) *About the Go8 – Group of Eight*. Group of Eight. https://go8.edu.au/about/the-go8 (accessed: 1 November 2023).

Hahn, H. (1996) 'Antidiscrimination laws and social research on disability: The minority group perspective', *Behavioral Sciences & the Law*, 14(1), 41–59.

Hull, L., Petrides, K.V., Allison, C., Smith, P., Baron-Cohen, S., Lai, M.-C., and Mandy, W. (2017) '"Putting on my best normal": Social camouflaging in adults with autism spectrum conditions', *Journal of Autism and Developmental Disorders*, 47(8), 2519–2534.

Hull, L., Mandy, W., Lai, M.-C., Baron-Cohen, S., Allison, C., Smith, P., and Petrides, K.V. (2019) 'Development and validation of the Camouflaging Autistic Traits Questionnaire (CAT-Q)', *Journal of Autism and Developmental Disorders*, 49(3), 819–833.

Jackson, D., and Dean, B.A. (2023) 'The contribution of different types of work-integrated learning to graduate employability', *Higher Education Research & Development*, 42(1), 93–110.

Jones, S., Akram, M., Murphy, N., Meyers, P., and Vickers, N. (2019) *Australia's attitudes & behaviours towards autism and experiences of Autistic people and their families*. ACU.

Kwon, S.J., Kim, Y., and Kwak, Y. (2018) 'Difficulties faced by university students with self-reported symptoms of attention-deficit hyperactivity disorder: A qualitative study', *Child and Adolescent Psychiatry and Mental Health*, 12(1), 12.

La Trobe University (LTU). (2020a) *Strategic plan 2020–2030*.

La Trobe University (LTU). (2020b) *La Trobe University Strategy for regional Victoria*.

La Trobe University (LTU). (2023a) *Staff celebrated at the 2023 Staff Awards ceremony – Intranet*. https://intranet.latrobe.edu.au/know-our-organisation/news/2023/2023-staff-award-winners?cid=edm%3Aacs%3Anan%3Astf%3Anan%3Ast f%3Anan%3Anan%3Anan%3Anan%3Anan%3Anan%3Anan%3Anan&deliveryName=DM49800 (accessed: 13 December 2023).

La Trobe University (LTU). (2023b) *Our history*. La Trobe University. www.latrobe.edu.au/about/at-a-glance/history (accessed: 3 October 2023).

La Trobe University (LTU). (2023c) *Diversity and inclusion*. La Trobe University. www.latrobe.edu.au/about/vision/diversity-and-inclusion (accessed: 3 October 2023).

La Trobe University (LTU). (2024a) *Position description: Manager, Neurodiversity Inclusion*. La Trobe University (accessed: 7 August 2024).

La Trobe University (LTU). (2024b) *Universal design and inclusion action plan*. www.latrobe.edu.au/about/at-a-glance/plans/respect-at-la-trobe/universal-design-and-disability-inclusion (accessed: 7 February 2025).

La Trobe University (LTU). (2025) *Position description: Manager, Neurodiversity and Disability*. La Trobe University (accessed: 25 January 2025).

Langorgen, E., and Magnus, E. (2020) '"I have something to contribute to working life" – Students with disabilities showcasing employability while on practical placement', *Journal of Education and Work*, 33(4), 271–284.

Le Cunff, A.-L., Logan, P.E., Ford, R., Martis, B.-L., Mousset, I., Sekibo, J., Dommett, E., and Giampietro, V. (2023) 'Co-design for participatory neurodiversity research: Collaborating with a community advisory board to design a research study', *Journal of Participatory Research Methods*, 4(1). https://jprm.scholasticahq.com/article/66184-co-design-for-participatory-neurodiversity-research-collaborating-with-a-community-advisory-board-to-design-a-research-study (accessed: 5 February 2025).

Lee, E.A.L., Black, M.H., Tan, T., Falkmer, T., and Girdler, S. (2019) '"I'm destined to ace this": Work experience placement during high school for individuals with autism spectrum disorder', *Journal of Autism and Developmental Disorders*, 49(8), 3089–3101.

Lewis, C.J., and Arday, J. (2023) 'We'll see things they'll never see: Sociological reflections on race, neurodiversity and higher education', *The Sociological Review*, 00380261231184357.

Merydith, S.P., Kulhanek, S.E., Murray, C.E., and Bradley, B.M. (2019) *Peer coaches, autism spectrum disorder, college transitions: A spectrum of supports* (p. 3).

Milton, D. (2012) *So what exactly is autism?* Autism Education Trust.

Neil, L., Olsson, N.C., and Pellicano, E. (2016) 'The relationship between intolerance of uncertainty, sensory sensitivities, and anxiety in Autistic and typically developing children', *Journal of Autism and Developmental Disorders*, 46(6), 1962–1973.

Nolan, C., Gleeson, C., Treanor, D., and Madigan, S. (2015) 'Higher education students registered with disability services and practice educators: Issues and concerns for professional placements', *International Journal of Inclusive Education*, 19(5), 487–502.

O'Byrne, C., Jagoe, C., and Lawler, M. (2019) 'Experiences of dyslexia and the transition to university: A case study of five students at different stages of study', *Higher Education Research & Development*, 38(5), 1031–1045.

O'Connor, M., Jones, S.C., Gordon, C., and Joosten, A. (2022) 'Exploring environmental barriers and facilitators to inclusion on a university campus for Autistic students', *Autism in Adulthood*. www.liebertpub.com/doi/full/10.1089/aut.2022.0053 (accessed: 19 May 2023).

Office for National Statistics. (2021) *Census 2021: Outcomes for disabled people in the UK*. www.ons.gov.uk/peoplepopulationandcommunity/healthandsocialcare/disability/articles/outcomesfordisabledpeopleintheuk/2021 (accessed 2 August 2022).

Oliver, M. (1990) *The politics of disablement*. London: Macmillan Education UK. http://link.springer.com/10.1007/978-1-349-20895-1 (accessed: 4 November 2020).

Oliver, M. (2013) 'The social model of disability: Thirty years on', *Disability & Society*, 28(7), 1024–1026.

Owolabi, S., and Makinde, O. (2012) *The effects of strategic planning on corporate performance in university education: A study of Babcock University*, vol. 2.

Pellicano, L. (2018) 'Autism advocacy and research misses the mark if Autistic people are left out', *The Conversation*. http://theconversation.com/autism-advocacy-and-research-misses-the-mark-if-autistic-people-are-left-out-94404 (accessed: 21 October 2021).

Pellicano, E., Dinsmore, A., and Charman, T. (2014) 'Views on researcher-community engagement in autism research in the United Kingdom: A mixed-methods study', *PLoS One*, 9(10), e109946.

Public Health Agency of Canada. (2020) *Infographic: Autism spectrum disorder highlights from the Canadian survey on disability*. www.canada.ca/en/public-health/services/publications/diseases-conditions/infographic-autism-spectrum-disorder-highlights-canadian-survey-disability.html (accessed 2 August 2022).

Radulski, E. (2024) 'A Sociology of Autistic masking and camouflaging: The intersectionality of neurotypical privilege and the neuroarchy' [thesis, La Trobe]. https://opal.latrobe.edu.au/articles/thesis/A_Sociology_of_Autistic_Masking_and_Camouflaging_The_Intersectionality_of_Neurotypical_Privilege_and_the_Neuroarchy/27139314/1 (accessed: 16 October 2024).

Radulski, E.M. (2022) 'Conceptualising Autistic masking, camouflaging, and neurotypical privilege: Towards a minority group model of neurodiversity', *Human Development*. www.karger.com/Article/FullText/524122 (accessed: 26 April 2022).

Radulski, R., and Jaworowski, N. (2022a, 13 May) 'Neurodiversity as the next frontier: Celebrating "all kinds of clever" in higher education', *My La Trobe*. www.latrobe.edu.au/mylatrobe/neurodiversity-as-the-next-frontier-part-1-celebrating-all-kinds-of-clever-in-higher-education/ (accessed: 27 March 2023).

Radulski, B., and Jaworowski, N. (2022b, 26 May) 'Neurodiversity as the Next Frontier: Part 2 – University, Research, and Industry Engagement', *My La Trobe*. www.latrobe.edu.au/mylatrobe/neurodiversity-as-the-next-frontier-part-2-university-research-and-industry-engagement/ (accessed: 27 March 2023).

Siew, C.T., Mazzucchelli, T.G., Rooney, R., and Girdler, S. (2017) 'A specialist peer mentoring program for university students on the autism spectrum: A pilot study', *PLoS One*, 12(7), e0180854.

Taylor-Bower, E., Plaisted-Grant, K., and Archer, S. (2024) 'Collaboration and co-creation in autism research: A reflection on the challenges and benefits of participatory approaches in doctoral research', *Educational Action Research*, 33(1), 183–189.

Thompson, D., and Brewster, S. (2022) 'Inclusive placement learning for diverse higher education students: anxiety, uncertainty and opportunity', *Educational Review*, 0(0), 1–19.

Tomczak, M.T., Mpofu, E., and Hutson, N. (2022) 'Remote work support needs of employees with autism spectrum disorder in Poland: Perspectives of individuals with autism and their coworkers', *International Journal of Environmental Research and Public Health*, 19(17), 10982.

Victorian Equal Opportunity and Human Rights Commission. (2023) *Disability and the workplace*. Victorian Equal Opportunity and Human Rights Commission. www.humanrights.vic.gov.au/for-individuals/disability-and-the-workplace/ (accessed: 21 December 2023).

Chapter 7

Towards Neurodiversity-Friendly Higher Education

Lessons from a Campus-Wide Initiative and the Case for Collaborative Evidence-Based Practice

Blánaid Gavin, Timothy Frawley and Sandra Connell

Introduction: Neurodiversity and the Need for Systemic, Evidence-Informed Practice

This chapter presents an in-depth exploration of a comprehensive institutional initiative at University College Dublin (UCD) to transform higher education through a neurodiversity-affirming lens. Drawing on findings from a five-stage research programme, the chapter synthesises qualitative, quantitative, and environmental data to propose a systems-level rethinking of inclusion. Framed within contemporary neurodiversity and higher education literature, the chapter weaves together emergent themes across policy, pedagogy, lived experience, sensory environments, and staff development to argue for a relational, co-created, and responsive model of institutional change. Ultimately, it issues a call to action for coordinated, interdisciplinary, and international research to produce the robust evidence base that neurodivergent communities deserve.

The term neurodiversity emerged from grassroots advocacy in the late 1990s, describing the natural variation in cognitive functioning across the human population, including but not limited to autism, attention-deficit hyperactivity disorder (ADHD), speech and language disorders, and specific learning difficulties, such as dyslexia and dyscalculia, dyspraxia, and Tourette syndrome. Its reframing of neurological differences as part of human diversity – rather than deficits or disorders – has slowly permeated education policy and practice. Rooted in the social model of disability and enriched by critical disability studies, this perspective affirms the value of neurodivergent cognition and insists on systemic reform to remove disabling barriers, rather than demanding conformity. Yet, despite growing rhetorical commitment to inclusion, the operationalisation of neurodiversity-friendly practices in higher education remains inconsistent, fragmented, and under-researched.

The relevance of neurodiversity in higher education is increasingly evident. Globally, more students are disclosing neurodivergent identities, and many more remain undisclosed due to stigma, lack of diagnosis, or inadequate institutional support (Brown and Leigh, 2018; Botha et al., 2022). This shift

DOI: 10.4324/9781003495925-9

has been partly driven by changing diagnostic landscapes and greater public awareness but also reflects generational change: younger cohorts are more likely to see neurodiversity as a dimension of identity. In Ireland, for example, over half of students who access disability services in higher education are neurodivergent (AHEAD, 2021).

Despite this growing presence, neurodivergent students and staff continue to face exclusionary practices, inaccessible systems, and cultural marginalisation. Research reveals widespread dissatisfaction with the adequacy and consistency of accommodations, the rigidity of academic processes and the often invisible emotional labour required to 'pass' in neurotypical settings (Cage et al., 2019; Kapp, 2020). Staff, similarly, report limited awareness from colleagues, lack of tailored supports and structural barriers to progression.

What is needed is a fundamental shift from compliance-oriented accommodation models to a proactive, affirming, and systemic approach to inclusion. Universal Design for Learning (UDL) and inclusive pedagogy offer partial answers (Rose and Meyer, 2002; Tobin and Behling, 2018), but to be fully effective, such frameworks must be informed by the lived experiences of neurodivergent people and embedded within institutional systems at every level.

Higher education institutions, in particular, have struggled to develop cohesive strategies to support neurodivergent students and staff. Many initiatives remain isolated, developed by individual champions or specific offices without a systemic mandate or sustainable resourcing. The consequence is a patchwork of supports and inconsistent student experiences – a reality repeatedly documented in both grey literature and emerging academic studies. Moreover, while neurodivergent students and staff are increasingly visible in higher education, the evidence base guiding institutions in how to support them equitably remains remarkably thin.

There is a growing awareness that high-quality, multi-institutional, and interdisciplinary research is urgently needed to underpin the development of neurodiversity-friendly practices. Much of the existing literature is limited by small sample sizes, single institution focus, and a lack of intersectional analysis. This is further compounded by chronic underfunding and the marginalisation of disability-related research agendas within institutions and research funding bodies. As a result, policymakers and practitioners often lack the robust data required to inform practice, monitor progress, or design inclusive systems change.

This chapter draws on the UCD Neurodiversity-Friendly Campus initiative as an exemplar of institution-wide change (reference to full report: UCD EDI Neurodiversity Working Group, 2024). This project represents a rare example of an integrated, participatory approach to systemic transformation. The project produced a comprehensive report detailing findings from multi-stage research and engagement with students, staff, and the wider community. In what follows, we present a summary of the methodology used across the initiative, extract, and synthesise the core findings into key themes and engage with two priority areas – disclosure and staff knowledge – in the context of broader scholarly debates. In doing so, we aim not only to highlight practical insights but to make the case for embedding neurodiversity into institutional strategy, supported by rigorous research and collaborative design.

Methodology: A Multi-Stage, Participatory Approach to Institutional Change

The UCD Neurodiversity-Friendly Campus initiative was built upon a recognition that institutional change must be grounded in both empirical data and authentic lived experience and driven by grassroots stakeholders with 'top-down' engagement. The project's methodological approach was designed accordingly: a layered, participatory model that combined desk research, stakeholder engagement, user experience data, and co-design processes. There were five stages to the initiative:

Stage 1: Scoping review
Stage 2: Mapping the journey of neurodivergent students and employees
Stage 3: Survey
Stage 4: Qualitative interviews
Stage 5: Sensory audit

The objective was not only to understand the current landscape but to co-create actionable, evidence-informed recommendations that could serve both UCD and the wider higher education sector.

Key Findings and Discussion Points

The rise of neurodiversity as both a conceptual and practical concern in higher education has led to a proliferation of interventions designed to support student engagement. Yet, as this scoping review compellingly illustrates, the empirical foundation underpinning these interventions remains patchy, inconsistent, and often atheoretical. Conducted using PRISMA guidelines and drawing from over 22,000 initial publications, the review identifies 60 relevant studies (25 quantitative, 26 qualitative, and 9 mixed methods) examining engagement-focused interventions for neurodivergent students. The diversity of methodologies and foci – from peer mentoring and therapeutic interventions to faculty training and accommodations – provides a rich, albeit fractured, terrain of evidence.

A consistent and well-supported finding is the positive impact of peer mentoring on academic and social adjustment for neurodivergent students, especially those who are Autistic. Studies by Siew et al. (2017), Rowe (2022) and Trevisan et al. (2021) echo earlier qualitative research (Van Hees et al., 2015; Cage et al., 2019) suggesting that peer-based approaches can reduce isolation, enhance self-efficacy, and support retention. Importantly, these findings resonate with Self-Determination Theory (Deci and Ryan, 2000), particularly the role of relatedness in fostering well-being and motivation.

Yet, the review also surfaces a more complex reality: social support is uneven, often dependent on chance encounters or institutional goodwill. Despite some promising initiatives, students frequently reported loneliness and social misunderstanding. This reveals a tension between the structural potential of peer support and the fragility of its delivery, particularly when programmes are not embedded in institutional culture.

Studies of adapted cognitive and behavioural therapies (e.g. dialectical behaviour therapy, cognitive behaviour therapy, mindfulness-based cognitive therapy) – though few in number – demonstrate preliminary efficacy in improving executive functioning, reducing anxiety, and enhancing self-regulation. However, there is a lack of clarity around the theoretical mechanisms of these interventions. This aligns with critiques in clinical literature that call for greater specificity in therapeutic theory and outcome mapping (e.g. Kazdin, 2007). Moreover, coaching models show promise in promoting goal completion and time management, key challenges for students with ADHD and executive function issues (Parker et al., 2011). However, scalability and cost-effectiveness remain largely unaddressed – leaving higher education leaders without clear implementation roadmaps.

Time management, stress regulation, and academic self-efficacy emerged as significant mediators of success. These findings dovetail with executive function literature (e.g. Barkley, 2012) and educational psychology research advocating for explicit strategy instruction. Notably, in a review paper, Skliarova et al. (2024) demonstrate the feasibility and positive effects of psychoeducational interventions for adults with ADHD and co-occurring mental illness. This points to the importance of transdisciplinary design in supporting neurodivergent learners. This reinforces the need to equip students with self-agency-enhancing tools. However, all too often such programmes are one-off or institution-specific, raising concerns about replicability and systemic equity.

Arguably, the most underdeveloped but urgent domain identified is staff knowledge and responsiveness. Many studies (e.g. Butcher and Lane, 2024; Ryder and Norwich, 2019) point to positive attitudes coupled with shallow or outdated understandings of neurodiversity – particularly dyslexia and autism. This gap contributes to stigma, reluctance to disclose, and ineffective accommodation practices. In response, Waisman et al. (2022) offer a promising model of co-produced training, combining universal design principles with neurodivergent-led content. The importance of coproduction and universal design cannot be overstated. These approaches shift responsibility from the individual to the institution, aligning with disability justice frameworks that advocate for structural rather than compensatory inclusion (Dolmage, 2017).

While accommodations such as extra time and alternative assessment formats are acknowledged as helpful, barriers to access – bureaucracy, stigma, and self-perception – remain significant. Echoing prior literature (Denhart, 2008; Cage and Howes, 2020), students often experience a conflict between needing accommodations and fearing the consequences of being perceived as 'different'. This has serious implications not only for equity but for mental health and retention. Merely offering accommodations is insufficient; institutions must consider how accessible and empowering these accommodations are perceived to be, and whether their use can be normalised across learning environments.

Importantly, only one study employed a participatory methodology (Waisman et al., 2022). Given the neurodiversity movement's emphasis on 'nothing about us without us', this signals a deep misalignment between the ethos of neurodiversity and its operationalisation in research. As such, one emergent implication is the need for methodological reform: embedding participatory, mixed-method, and longitudinal designs that capture the full texture of neurodivergent experience over time.

Too often in higher education institutions, it is not that there is no effort being made, it is that efforts are fragmented, under-theorised, and often institutionally siloed underscoring a need to move from piecemeal programmes to a coherent ecosystem of support, grounded in theory, co-created with neurodivergent communities, and measured with robust and replicable tools.
Arising from this, key actions are as follows:

1. Investment in longitudinal, multi-site trials of promising interventions like peer mentoring, coaching, and therapeutic supports.
2. Embedding coproduced training in universal design across all teaching and administrative levels.
3. Normalising accommodations through structural and cultural shifts that reduce stigma and bureaucratic hurdles.
4. Developing intersectional research that recognises how neurodivergence interacts with other identities and systems of disadvantage.
5. Building institutional metrics for inclusive practice, using frameworks like Fuller et al.'s (2004) model to map progress and identify gaps.

Building on the findings from the literature, the campus-wide survey provided a rich empirical dataset that moves the conversation from principles of neurodiversity to practice. The survey, which included responses from 747 students and staff, reveals a community largely aligned with neurodiversity-aware values: 85% of respondents were familiar with the term 'neurodiversity', and nearly half (46%) felt it described them. That nearly one in two members of a university community see themselves within the neurodivergent spectrum not only challenges long-held assumptions about the rarity of neurodivergent identities but also underscores the imperative to move from reactive supports to proactively inclusive design. However, a significant caveat applies in that the survey can be described as non-representative. Both students and staff self-selected for participation. Nonetheless, the findings remain meaningful, offering a valuable snapshot of campus experience.

These data support literature highlighting a growing trend of self-identification with neurodivergence, particularly among younger generations (Chapman, 2021). However, despite high levels of self-identification, disclosure rates remained relatively low – just 54% of students and 35% of staff who felt neurodiversity applied to them had disclosed their identity within UCD. This discrepancy echoes findings by Brown and Leigh (2018) and Kapp (2020), which indicate that stigma, institutional mistrust, and unclear pathways to disclosure deter neurodivergent individuals from seeking formal support.

Qualitative data from the survey affirms this interpretation. Respondents often cited burdensome processes, inconsistent follow-up, or fear of being misunderstood as barriers to disclosure. Others described disclosure as 'neutral', reflecting a broader shift identified in neurodiversity literature towards normalising identity over medicalisation (Botha et al., 2021). In this light, one of the most significant insights from the UCD survey is a preference for non-binary disclosure pathways. Participants described the need for informal, flexible routes that allow for phased self-identification – a finding that challenges institutional assumptions about binary categorisation and suggests a model for more inclusive and humane systems.

The survey also confirms the practical benefits and persistent gaps in support systems. While 32% of students and 21% of staff had accessed neurodiversity-related supports, with many finding them very helpful or excellent, other respondents described their experiences as bureaucratic or inconsistent or the supports as being difficult to access. This resonates with the 'accommodation paradox' described in higher education literature (Mallett and Runswick-Cole, 2014), where services designed to support difference can become exclusionary when overly reliant on formal diagnoses or inflexible procedures. The UCD data adds to this conversation by linking procedural complexity to executive dysfunction – a core trait for many neurodivergent individuals – thus showing how support systems can inadvertently amplify the barriers they are intended to dismantle.

Strong consensus emerged around the provision of reasonable accommodations, with over 90% of respondents supporting their use in teaching, assessment and employment contexts. Notably, the call for universal design principles over bespoke accommodations echoes key texts in inclusive pedagogy (Tobin and Behling, 2018; Hockings, 2010). Staff and students alike emphasised the importance of moving beyond compliance-based accommodations to proactively inclusive environments that benefit all learners and workers, not just those with disclosed differences. In the workplace, staff called for shorter meetings, quiet workspaces, and flexible formats – suggesting that universal design is not just pedagogical, but organisational.

When considering career progression, the findings are especially sobering. Ninety-four per cent of students and 92% of staff believed neurodiversity would impact students' future careers, and 78% believed it also affects staff progression. These perceptions reflect broader societal patterns in which neurodivergent individuals encounter hidden biases, particularly during recruitment and selection processes (Austin and Pisano, 2017; Doyle, 2020). The UCD survey underscores that interviews, informal norms, and unspoken expectations around communication and behaviour can act as structural barriers. Respondents described fear of stigma, assumptions of incompetence and the exhausting labour of code-switching as persistent features of academic and professional life.

Crucially, the data also shows a clear understanding among respondents that neurodiversity can be an asset – one that brings creativity, focus, and unique problem-solving approaches. This aligns with emerging literature on 'neurodivergent advantage' (Grant, 2010; Smith and Kirby, 2022), particularly in domains requiring lateral thinking or systems-based problem-solving. However, these advantages can only be realised in supportive contexts. As one respondent put it, 'The beauty of embracing a neurodiverse culture … is that it allows people to work to their strengths'. Without systemic scaffolding, such strengths may remain latent or unrecognised.

What emerges, then, is a picture of a university community that is intellectually and ethically ready to embrace neurodiversity – but that continues to operate within systems, structures, and assumptions shaped by neurotypical norms. The survey results point to critical leverage points for transformation. These include creating flexible disclosure mechanisms, embedding inclusive design into pedagogy and operations, resourcing targeted staff training, and ensuring that supports are streamlined, proactive, and person-centred. Moreover, the findings reaffirm the need for intersectional approaches that consider how gender, ethnicity, class, and neurodivergence interact to produce distinct experiences and barriers. As such the data suggests that the future of inclusion lies not in retrofitting existing systems to accommodate a minority, but in reimagining those systems altogether to reflect the diversity of minds that make up our universities and workplaces.

Methodological Innovation: Mapping Journeys as a Tool for Systems Change

A nuanced gap analysis employing four interconnected strands – policy review, journey mapping, stakeholder interviews and targeted focus groups was employed next. This approach reflects a systems thinking approach that foregrounds the complex interplay between people, processes, and institutional culture (Meadows, 2008; Senge, 2006).

Mapping both student and employee 'journeys' across lifecycle stages (recruitment, induction, support, and progression) demonstrates a novel form of inclusive systems auditing – a methodology that recognises not only where gaps exist, but how *experiences are shaped across time* and at intersecting points of engagement. In doing so, UCD moves beyond static access checklists and towards a dynamic model of developmental inclusivity, where needs evolve and systems must adapt accordingly.

Critically, this work applies the University for All pillars to a neurodiversity lens, embedding universal design not just in theory but in the structures of learning, support, environment, and digital access. It builds on work by Burgstahler (2015) and Rose and Meyer (2002), but adds a neuro-affirmative framing that recognises variation not as deficit but as design input – a principle foundation to the neurodiversity paradigm (Walker, 2021; Armstrong, 2010). The findings offer a candid and multi-layered portrait of a university in transition: one that aspires to be neurodiversity-friendly but still navigates an uneven terrain of awareness and purposeful, yet fragmented, delivery.

For employees, there is growing policy scaffolding – such as the inclusion of neurodiversity in disability employment policy and the availability of accommodations without diagnosis – but these are not always well communicated, integrated, or acted upon. Recruitment processes have evolved to acknowledge the role of social bias in interviews (Whelpley and May, 2023), and a neurodiversity-inclusive interview training module is an exemplar of institutional innovation. However, there remains a sense that support for staff lags behind that of students, a pattern echoed in broader higher education research (Brown and Leigh, 2018). While student-facing services have often been the vanguard of inclusive practice, staff needs – particularly around disclosure, accommodations, and progression – are under-explored. This underscores the imperative to apply whole-of-institution frameworks (UNESCO, 2020) and to cultivate inclusive leadership cultures that do not silo support into student services alone.

For students, strides via Access and Lifelong Learning and UDL strategies are apparent, as is a university and executive leadership commitment to neurodiversity. The integration of inclusive curriculum design, mainstream assistive technology (e.g. Ally for Brightspace) and social supports like the Access Leaders model, align with best practice globally (CAST, 2018; Griful-Freixenet et al., 2017). Importantly, the mapping reveals a commitment to mainstreaming supports to avoid the burdens of repeated disclosure, diagnosis-dependent access, and gatekeeping. This aligns with a growing push for post-diagnostic approaches in inclusive pedagogy, where support is provided based on need and preference, not solely on formal documentation (Denhart, 2008; Gillespie-Lynch et al., 2015). Still, capacity challenges loom large. The rise in neurodivergent student disclosure (e.g. over 2,600 students with disability supports, majority neurodivergent) means that systems designed for the few are now serving the many. This turns neurodiversity into a litmus test for the sustainability of inclusive systems. Can they adapt quickly enough? Are they resourced sufficiently? And most importantly – are they designed to be human in the face of scale?

One of the most powerful implications of this work is its alignment with contemporary critiques of institutional modernity: namely, that large systems risk becoming cold, bureaucratic, and dehumanising. In a world increasingly shaped by automation, standardisation, and remote interaction, neurodivergent experience reveals the cost of a one-size-fits-all approach (Han, 2015; Cacioppo and Patrick, 2008).

The mapping project calls for institutions to reclaim their human core. It shows that the essence of universal design is not homogeneity but built-in variability – a readiness to meet the individual as they are, not as the system expects them to be. This is the principle of 'personalisation at scale' – where structures enable individual tailoring without bureaucratic burden (Leadbeater, 2004). Such an approach is essential not just to neurodivergent inclusion, but to the future of equitable education and employment systems. If we can design systems that support those with the most complex or variable needs, we inherently create systems that are more humane for everyone.

Implications for Research, Policy, and Practice

This mapping study is both a diagnostic and a blueprint. Its implications are actionable, urgent, and scalable.

Research

- Invest in longitudinal tracking of neurodivergent student and staff experience across lifecycle stages.
- Examine the impact of mainstreaming supports on student outcomes and staff retention.
- Investigate co-produced, scalable models of tailored support (e.g. AI-assisted but human-guided accommodations).

Policy

- Integrate neurodiversity into all UCD strategies (e.g. recruitment, teaching, wellbeing).
- Move towards post-diagnostic eligibility for supports – needs-based, not paperwork-bound.
- Develop a whole-system neurodiversity framework, embedding design, dialogue and data at all levels.

Practice

- Expand training in neuro-affirming pedagogy and supervision, not only awareness.

- Co-create induction pathways, peer support networks, and accessible platforms with neurodivergent users.
- Institutionalise feedback loops with neurodivergent staff and student panels
shaping policy, tools, and space design.

Conclusion: The Evolution of Neurodiversity Inclusion

What this study ultimately reveals is that neurodiversity is not an accommodation issue – it is a systems issue. It asks universities to transform – not through
isolated reforms, but through adaptive, human, responsive evolution. In a
time when disconnection, burnout, and rigidity dominate institutional cultures, neurodiversity offers an alternative vision: one of *celebration, co-creation,*
and *compassionate complexity.*

The challenge now is not whether we will act, but how. Will we build systems that scale empathy as well as efficiency? Will we dare to see the difference
as design? And can we, in this process, create not only better institutions – but
a better, more human future?

*While all the ideas, content, and findings are the original work of the authors,
ChatGPT has been utilised to summarise and present aspects of this chapter.*

References

AHEAD. (2021) *Numbers of students with disabilities studying in higher education in
Ireland 2020/21.* Dublin: Association for Higher Education Access and Disability.

Armstrong, T. (2010) *The power of neurodiversity: Unleashing the advantages of your
differently wired brain.* Boston, MA: Da Capo Press.

Austin, R.D., and Pisano, G.P. (2017) 'Neurodiversity as a competitive advantage',
Harvard Business Review, 95(3), 96–103.

Barkley, R.A. (2012) 'Executive functions: What they are, how they work, and why
they evolved'. New York: Guilford Press.

Botha, M., Dibb, B., and Frost, D.M. (2021) '"Autism is me": An investigation of how
Autistic individuals make sense of autism and stigma', *Disability & Society,* 36(9),
1409–1431.

Botha, M., Hanlon, J., and Williams, G.L. (2022) 'Does language matter? Identity-first
versus person-first language use in autism research: A response to Vivanti', *Journal of
Autism and Developmental Disorders,* 52(2), 864–865.

Brown, N., and Leigh, J. (2018) 'Ableism in academia: Where are the disabled and ill
academics?', *Disability & Society,* 33(6), 985–989.

Burgstahler, S. (2015) *Universal design in higher education: From principles to practice*
(2nd edn.). Cambridge, MA: Harvard Education Press.

Butcher, L., and Lane, S. (2024) 'Neurodivergent (autism and ADHD) student experiences of access and inclusion in higher education: An ecological systems theory perspective'. *Higher Education.* https://doi.org/10.1007/s10734-024-01319-6

Cage, E., and Howes, J. (2020) 'Dropping out and moving on: A qualitative
study of Autistic people's experiences of university'. *Autism,* 24(7), 1664–1675.
DOI:10.1177/1362361320918750.

Cage, E., Di Monaco, J., and Newell, V. (2019) 'Experiences of autism acceptance and mental health in Autistic adults', *Journal of Autism and Developmental Disorders*, 48(2), 473–484.

Cacioppo, J.T., and Patrick, W. (2008) *Loneliness: Human nature and the need for social connection*. New York, NY: W.W. Norton & Company.

CAST. (2018) *Universal Design for Learning guidelines version 2.2*. Wakefield, MA: CAST.

Chapman, R. (2021) *Neurodiversity studies: A new critical paradigm*. London: Routledge.

Deci, E.L., and Ryan, R.M. (2000) 'The "what" and "why" of goal pursuits: Human needs and the self-determination of behavior', *Psychological Inquiry*, 11(4), 227–268.

Denhart, H. (2008) 'Deconstructing barriers: Perceptions of students labeled with learning disabilities in higher education', *Journal of Learning Disabilities*, 41(6), 483–497.

Dolmage, J.T. (2017) *Academic ableism: Disability and higher education*. Ann Arbor, MI: University of Michigan Press.

Doyle, N. (2020) 'Neurodiversity at work: A biopsychosocial model and the impact on working adults', *British Medical Bulletin*, 135(1), 108–125.

Fuller, M., Healey, M., Bradley, A., and Hall, T. (2004) 'Barriers to learning: A systematic study of the experience of disabled students in one university', *Studies in Higher Education*, 29(3), 303–318.

Gillespie-Lynch, K., Brooks, P.J., Someki, F., and Kapp, S.K. (2015) 'Whose expertise is it? Evidence for Autistic adults as critical autism experts', *Frontiers in Psychology*, 6, 1600.

Grant, D. (2010) *That's the way I think: Dyslexia, dyspraxia, ADHD and dyscalculia explained* (2nd ed.). London: Routledge.

Griful-Freixenet, J., Struyven, K., Verstichele, M., and Andries, C. (2017) 'Higher education students with disabilities speaking out: Perceived barriers and opportunities of the Universal Design for Learning framework', *Disability & Society*, 32(10), 1627–1649.

Han, B.C. (2015) *The burnout society*. Stanford, CA: Stanford University Press.

Hockings, C. (2010) 'Inclusive learning and teaching in higher education: A synthesis of research', *EvidenceNet*. York: Higher Education Academy.

Kazdin, A.E. (2007) 'Mediators and mechanisms of change in psychotherapy research', *Annual Review of Clinical Psychology*, 3, 1–27.

Kapp, S.K. (2020) *Autistic community and the neurodiversity movement: Stories from the frontline*. Singapore: Palgrave Macmillan.

Leadbeater, C. (2004) *Personalisation through participation: A new script for public services*. London: Demos.

Mallett, R., and Runswick-Cole, K. (2014) *Approaching disability: Critical issues and perspectives*. London: Routledge.

Meadows, D.H. (2008) *Thinking in systems: A primer*. White River Junction, VT: Chelsea Green Publishing.

Parker, D.R., Hoffman, S.F., Sawilowsky, S., and Rolands, L. (2011) 'Self-control in postsecondary settings: Students' perceptions of ADHD college coaching'. *Journal of Attention Disorders*, 17(3), 215–232.

Rose, D.H., and Meyer, A. (2002) *Teaching every student in the digital age: Universal design for learning*. Alexandria, VA: ASCD.

Rowe, M. (2022) 'Mentoring Autistic students in higher education: Practices and perspectives', *Disability & Society*, 37(7), 1174–1192.

Ryder, D., and Norwich, B. (2019) 'UK third level education lecturers' perspectives of dyslexia, student with dyslexia, and related disability provision'. *Journal of Research in Special Educational Needs*, 19, 161–172.

Senge, P.M. (2006) *The fifth discipline: The art and practice of the learning organization.* New York: Doubleday.

Siew, C.T., Mazzucchelli, T.G., Rooney, R., and Girdler, S. (2017) 'A specialist peer mentoring program for university students on the autism spectrum: A pilot study'. *PLoS One*, 12(7), e0180854.

Skliarova, T., Pedersen, H., Holsbrekken, Å., et al. (2024) 'Psychoeducational group interventions for adults diagnosed with attention-deficit/ hyperactivity disorder: a scoping review of feasibility, acceptability, and outcome measures'. *BMC Psychiatry*, 24, 463.

Smith, S., and Kirby, A. (2022) *Neurodiversity at work: Drive innovation, performance and productivity with a neurodiverse workforce.* London: Kogan Page.

Tobin, T.J., and Behling, K.T. (2018) *Reach everyone, teach everyone: Universal design for learning in higher education.* Morgantown, WV: West Virginia University Press.

Trevisan, D.A., Roberts, L.D., and Lin, A. (2021) 'Evaluation of a peer mentorship program for Autistic college students', *Autism in Adulthood*, 3(2), 187–194. https://doi.org/10.1089/aut.2019.0087

UCD EDI Neurodiversity Working Group. (2024) *Making UCD a neurodiversity friendly campus.* www.ucd.ie/equality/support/neurodiversity/report

UNESCO. (2020) *Global Education Monitoring Report 2020: Inclusion and education – All means all.* UNESCO Publishing. https://unesdoc.unesco.org/ark:/48223/pf0000373718

Van Hees, V., Moyson, T., and Roeyers, H. (2015) 'Higher education experiences of students with autism spectrum disorder: Challenges, benefits and support needs', *Journal of Autism and Developmental Disorders*, 45(6), 1673–1688. https://doi.org/10.1007/s10803-014-2324-2

Waisman, T.C., Williams, Z.J., Cage, E., Santhanam, S.P., Magiati, I., Dwyer, P., Stockwell, K.M., Kofner, B., Brown, H., Davidson, D., Herrell, J., Shore, S., Caudel, D., Gurbuz, E., and Gillespie-Lynch, K. (2022) 'Learning from the experts: Evaluating a participatory autism and universal design training for university educators', *Autism*, 27(2), 356–370. https://doi.org/10.1177/13623613221097207

Walker, N. (2021) *Neuroqueer heresies: Notes on the Neurodiversity Paradigm, Autistic empowerment, and postnormal possibilities.* Autonomous Press.

Whelpley, C.E., and May, C.P. (2023) 'Seeing is disliking: Evidence of bias against individuals with autism spectrum disorder in traditional job interviews', *Journal of Autism and Developmental Disorders*, 53(4), 1363–1374. https://doi.org/10.1007/s10803-022-05432-2

Part II

Programme Profiles

Section Foreword and Profiles of Nine Higher Education Programmes

Student Support Programmes

Common Ground, Unique Approaches and Lived Experience

Sandra Thom-Jones

Programme Profiles

The nine case studies in this section provide a broad range of perspectives and experiences on developing, implementing and evaluating programmes to support neurodivergent students in higher education. Some, such as the programme at USC Upstate, are in their early stages of development; others, such as the Royal College of Art, have been running for more than two decades. There are small programmes with enrolment in the single digits, such as UCAN at the University of Calgary; and there are large programmes, such as those at the University of Delaware and University of Tennessee.

Some of the case studies are programmes with a specific focus – typically peer mentoring for Autistic students, which is perhaps the most extensively implemented and researched form of support offered to this cohort (Duerksen et al., 2021).

Each of these programme profiles is informative on its own, with valuable information for those seeking to commence or expand their own initiatives. In bringing them together in one place, this book provides the opportunity for the reader to gain from the collective wisdom of these diverse programmes.

Programme Development

All of the programmes are based on sound theoretical models and educational frameworks. They have been developed, reviewed and evaluated by experts in curriculum design, programme development and educational psychology.

However, I would argue that there remains a need for more direct involvement of neurodivergent people in the development and implementation of programmes that are designed to improve our higher education experiences. Several of the case studies explicitly refer to actively seeking feedback from participating students and implementing their suggestions to improve programme offerings, but I think we can assume that all of these programmes follow this minimum level of participatory development (as it is embedded in standard educational practice). The UCAN Program at the University of Calgary has an

DOI: 10.4324/9781003495925-11

advisory group which includes Autistic people in the development, implementation and evaluation of the programme and I encourage other institutions to ensure that their programmes are guided by lived experience.

Programme Content

Of the nine profiles included in this section, six relate specifically or primarily to programmes for Autistic students. Two take a broader approach, targeting the neurodivergent student population as a whole (USC Upstate and Landmark College), and one focuses on SpLD (Royal College of Art). Institutions seeking to develop a programme should consider which approach will better meet the needs of their student body. The broad neurodiversity approach reaches more students, but focusing on a specific cohort enables you to offer more tailored support. In an ideal world, higher education institutions would offer a suite of neurodiversity programmes with specific offerings for Autistic students, those with ADHD, dyslexia and other wonderfully unique minds.

Two highly focused programmes included in this collection are the Career Connections programme at Landmark College, albeit a programme embedded within a unique institution established solely to serve neurodivergent students, and Curtin's Autism Academy for Software Quality Assurance, which focuses on Autistic adolescents with an interest in computers and programming.

Both the UCAN Program at the University of Calgary and the CSMP Program at Curtin University offer peer mentoring programmes for Autistic students (regular one-on-one meetings with a peer mentor, typically a psychology or health science student) and group social events. The Curtin CSMP has been running for over a decade and has been used as a model by many other Australian universities. There is evidence that peer mentoring provides a range of benefits for Autistic students, as well as for their mentors, but it does not address many of the larger systemic barriers experienced by Autistic students. (Note: This is *not* a criticism of these excellent programmes – keep reading to the 'Common Challenges' section.)

The University of Tennessee and the University of Delaware offer comprehensive programmes that address multiple aspects of the Autistic student's university experience. In addition to peer mentoring, students at both institutions are provided with a suite of supports across academic skill development, organisation and navigation, social engagement and career development. The University of Delaware also addresses structural barriers by embedding university-wide training in their programme to raise awareness of how to support Autistic students and colleagues.

There is an abundance of evidence that the barriers facing neurodivergent students in higher education are complex and multi-faceted (Borsotti et al., 2024). A programme that provided a truly inclusive experience would need to encompass multiple domains across the physical environment (Mostafa,

2021), learning and teaching (von Below et al., 2024), awareness and stigma (Wilson and Dallman, 2024), and many other aspects of university life.

Common Challenges

As I read through these profiles, I was struck by the consistency of the challenges experienced in establishing, growing and sustaining programmes to support neurodivergent students in higher education. Some of these challenges were explicitly identified by the authors, others were implicit in what they didn't say and some emerged from comparisons between the profiles. They also resonated with my own experiences in establishing and leading similar programmes, and in advising on programmes across multiple institutions.

Knowledge and awareness barriers pose significant challenges in multiple ways. The limited autism knowledge of institutional staff can create environments where it is difficult for programme developers to get buy-in from colleagues in other departments, and thus for programme components to lead to meaningful change outside of the immediate programme activities. This is exacerbated in communities where there is stigma associated with disability, or where stereotypical understandings of neurodivergence prevail. In these environments, which are the norm rather than the exception, many neurodivergent students do not feel safe to disclose. Programme staff commonly express frustration at the challenge in spreading awareness of the programmes and their offerings in a culture where disclosure is risky, discrimination is rife and community awareness of the diversity and strengths of neurodivergent individuals is limited.

Finding and retaining suitably qualified and dedicated staff is another common challenge. Programmes need to have a dedicated coordinator, with the expertise to manage complex programme elements, navigate the institutional context and negotiate with other stakeholders. Ideally, they should also have lived experience – although, sadly, that is uncommon in current higher education programmes. Mentoring programmes, a common element of almost all of the profiles, require the capacity to recruit and retain mentors who will consistently meet with mentees; a constant challenge when mentors are typically also students, with their own fluctuating personal and study demands.

I will not go through all of the challenges in detail, but ask readers to reflect on some of these as you read through the profiles. Issues such as institutional policies that make it difficult for neurodivergent students to access the resources they need, lack of support from senior leadership, the lack of benchmarks/clear guidelines on best practice, the disjointed nature of support available to students outside of these programmes and dealing with ethical issues around students' privacy while still being able to provide services.

Underpinning all of the challenges facing those who seek to establish and maintain high-quality programmes is the issue of having adequate and consistent funding. As an Autistic person who has supported many neurodivergent students through the higher education system and watched many others stumble and fall, it makes my heart break when I read of programmes like the Curtin CSMP that have had to cap places and implement a wait list due to staffing limitations and funding constraints. Readers will note that many of the profiles in this book – and so many more that aren't represented here – are doing amazing things on minimal funding. Imagine what they could do if they were adequately resourced.

Facilitators

It is not surprising that, in a number of instances, the facilitators are a mirror reflection of the challenges. When I look at the large-scale, multi-component programmes, they list as their facilitators factors that have reversed the challenges faced by other programmes.

The two largest programmes – Spectrum Scholars at the University of Delaware and Mosaic at the University of Tennessee at Chattanooga – have a large contingent of staff. The former has seven full-time staff supporting 30 students and the latter has five full-time and four part-time supporting 52 students. Several of the other programmes have less than half an FTE equivalent. Spectrum Scholars has a financial sponsor, and Mosaic has a fee for service model. The reality is that running programmes cost money.

Government policy is mentioned in some of the case studies, and implicit in others, as a facilitator. Many countries have introduced legislation which requires higher education providers to consider the needs of disabled students, and in some cases introduced enrolment quotas. In some instances, although not often enough, these policies are accompanied by funding, such as the Disabled Students Allowance in the UK.

Institutional support is touched upon in most of the case studies. This includes references to top-down, bottom-up and cross-unit support. Several discuss the importance of university partnerships – working with administrators, libraries, disability services, academic skills units, schools and faculties, student services and other parts of the organisation. Some note the synergy that occurs when those entities begin to recognise the two-way value of the partnership, seeing the programme as a valuable resource for information and training on working with and supporting neurodivergent students and staff. In my experience, what is absolutely critical is the top-level support. I have seen programmes thrive when senior leadership believes in and endorses the need to actively support our neurodivergent student population; and I have seen programmes wither when senior leadership sees these programmes as marginal or irrelevant.

Another critical facilitator is the meaningful involvement of neurodivergent people in all aspects of the programme, from the initial concept through programme development, implementation and evaluation. One of the benefits of the structure of this section of the book, in bringing together profiles of programmes at different stages of development, is that the reader can access exemplars of each stage. For example, the nascent USC Upstate case study provided as example of how the voices of neurodivergent students and staff can lead the development of a future programme. As noted above, the Calgary UCAN Program demonstrates the importance of including neurodivergent people in the advisory group. Similarly, the UTC Mosaic Program's Advisory Board includes current and graduate Mosaic students as well Autistic advocates and professionals.

What none of the case studies mention but is obvious to me – and I am sure will be obvious to readers – is the importance of programme champions. Each of these authors has written their case study for the same reason that they run their programme (and many of them were involved in the initial development): because they care deeply about the experiences of the neurodivergent students at their institutions. You can see this in the passion with which they write, in their commitment to ensuring a strengths-focus in their programmes, and in their advocacy for their students across their broader institutions.

Thoughts to Ponder

I would like to leave you with a few questions to ponder:

- How can we increase the evidence base for the value of these programmes? Whose responsibility is it to fund the research we need (and how do we encourage them to make the funding available)?
- How do we increase the involvement of neurodivergent people in the development, implementation and evaluation of these programmes? There are plenty of us out there in these institutions; how do we ensure a seat at the table?
- How do we address the huge cavern between secondary school and higher education? What policies, programmes and strategies can we put into place to ensure that neurodivergent students are supported to transition into higher education – and who needs to take responsibility for making it happen?

References

Borsotti, V., Begel, A., and Bjørn, P. (2024). 'Neurodiversity and the accessible university: Exploring organizational barriers, access labor and opportunities for change', *Proceedings of the ACM on Human-Computer Interaction*, 8(CSCW1): Article 172.

Duerksen, K., Besney, R., Ames, M., and McMorris, C.A. (2021). 'Supporting Autistic adults in postsecondary settings: A systematic review of peer mentorship programs', *Autism in Adulthood*, 3(1), 85–99.

Mostafa, M. (2021). *The autism friendly university design guide.* Dublin: Dublin City University.

von Below, R., Spaeth, E., and Horlin, C. (2024). 'Autism in higher education: Dissonance between educators' perceived knowledge and reported teaching behaviour', *International Journal of Inclusive Education*, 28(6), 940–957.

Wilson, K., and Dallman, A. (2024). 'Strategies for promoting neurodiversity and autism acceptance in higher education', *Journal of Diversity in Higher Education*. Advance online publication. https://doi.org/10.1037/dhe0000550

Royal College of Art, UK

An Example of SpLD Support at a UK Post-graduate Art and Design University

Qona Rankin

The role of Dyslexia Coordinator at the Royal College of Art (RCA) was established in August 2002, and I was appointed the following month on a 0.5 full-time equivalent (FTE) contract, later increased to 0.75 FTE, and in 2017 we appointed an additional specific learning differences (SpLD) tutor on a 0.375 FTE contract. Initially, we supported 850 students (80% in the UK and 20% from overseas). This has now grown to 2,500 students, with 20% in the UK, 50% from China, and 30% from other countries. The increase in Chinese students, in particular, is notable as SpLD awareness and support practices are limited in China.

Historically, our teaching had always been in person; however, COVID-19 necessitated online teaching, and while we prefer teaching face-to-face sessions, we still offer Zoom meetings for students who prefer them. Students often seek help with time management, organising research, planning writing sections, and presentations. We always ask students to bring a specific task with them to the session which we use as a vehicle to teach relevant strategies. We find that linking strategies to meaningful tasks is a more productive way of teaching.

I want to make clear that the perspectives I share in this chapter are rooted in the specific context of postgraduate art and design education. My understanding of broader academic practices at UK universities, particularly at the undergraduate level or across other disciplines, is quite limited.

In 2001, in recognition of the high incidence of dyslexia among students of art and design in the UK, the RCA, commissioned an investigation by Katherine Kindersley, a highly respected and experienced dyslexia consultant. The ensuing "Report on Dyslexia: Developing Provision and Support at the Royal College of Art", made a number of recommendations, including the appointment of a dyslexia co-ordinator and the formation of a dyslexia committee. In response to this the RCA formed a working party and produced an Action Plan (2002) and later that year a dyslexia co-ordinator was appointed. The purpose of the post was to develop, implement, co-ordinate, and monitor the delivery of support to RCA students and staff with dyslexia.

DOI: 10.4324/9781003495925-12

An audit of the previous two years revealed that the number of students enrolling with an assessment of dyslexia was about a quarter of the number who graduated with an assessment. In other words, only 25% of our dyslexic students were aware of their dyslexia when they enrolled. Clearly something needed to be done, firstly to raise awareness and secondly to arrange for screening and assessments.

At that time, the UK government provided the Disabled Students' Allowance (DSA) for UK and EU students diagnosed with dyslexia—this was, of course, before Brexit. The DSA was a generous provision, typically covering the cost of a laptop, specialised software (along with IT support to learn how to use it), and up to 30 sessions per year with a specialist dyslexia tutor, primarily focusing on reading and writing tasks. Given that 60% of our students were UK or EU students, once they were screened and assessed, their support would be financed and delivered externally to the RCA. However, matching this level of support internally was challenging, particularly with just one staff member working 2.5 days a week to support up to 114 students with varying needs. Nevertheless, we began by establishing inclusive teaching practices and offering regular staff training sessions, especially for those in the library and the Cultural and Historical Studies (CHS) team, which was responsible for the dissertation module. We also introduced small group workshops aligned with the CHS dissertation timetable, advised on "reasonable adjustments" for viva voce exams, and organised events to promote a positive outlook on SpLDs within creative practice which may be within architecture, fine art, communication, or design.

In addition to these initiatives, the coordinator's remaining time was spent working individually with MA students who struggled with specific aspects of their courses, helping them externalise their ideas in an acceptable format. PhD students also benefited from this support, particularly in planning, organising, and formatting their theses, as well as preparing for their viva voce presentations and subsequent Q&A sessions.

Our approach to support has always been tailored to the individual. We do not deliver a standardised program to the students we work with individually. Instead, we tailor our support to assist students with tasks that carry a mark, as these may not accurately reflect a student's ability due to their SpLD. We view each task as a vehicle for teaching, rather than teaching strategies in isolation. This approach is far more meaningful to the student. When planning these sessions, we consider the question, "What does the student need to know to fulfil their true potential with this particular task?"

It is always gratifying to receive positive feedback and many of our students are extremely generous in taking time to share their experiences with us. There is one message in particular that I refer to, especially if I am having doubts about our teaching methods.

All my life I had been told I was not academic. When I had the dyslexia test at the RCA it was a relief to discover there was an explanation for my struggles.

Before we handed in our dissertations, we were told that if we received an email from CHS (Cultural and Historical Studies) admin office telling us we had mail waiting in the office, that meant we had either failed or got a distinction. So, when I received such an email, I assumed I had failed but in fact I was awarded 1st class honours for my dissertation. Since then, I've become much more receptive and confident; it was like a roof being lifted of the sky. I was so relieved to discover I wasn't of low intelligence. Getting a distinction has enabled me to reframe my world and connect to a part of myself I didn't know existed.

Two decades later, our understanding of learning differences has deepened, and we now recognise the increasing instances of comorbidity. Reflecting this broader awareness, we have changed the title of the post to SpLD Coordinator. Today, many of our students have not only dyslexia but also dyspraxia, dysgraphia, and/or dyscalculia. ADHD and autism are also on the rise and although they require a diagnosis from a medical practitioner, they also significantly impact learning. Over the years, our student body has tripled, leading to an expansion of the SpLD coordinator role to nearly an FTE, with one post at three days a week and the other at 1.5 days per week.

It's not just the number of students that has increased; the demographic composition has shifted as well. Currently, only about 20% of our students are from the UK, with 80% being international students, half of whom are from China. This is highly significant because there is little awareness of SpLDs in China, and the term "disability" carries substantial stigma. Thus, part of our role now involves not only raising awareness of different learning difficulties but also reassuring students that at the RCA, there is absolutely no stigma attached to these conditions. Although only 20% of our students are now eligible for DSA support, this is not as problematic as it might sound, thanks to the remarkable advancements in new and emerging technologies, many of which are now available for free.

For instance, speech-to-text software has been transformative for individuals with dyslexia and/or dysgraphia. Programs such as Dragon Naturally Speaking and Google Voice Typing allow users to dictate text, which is then transcribed into written words, bypassing the challenges associated with writing and offering real-time spelling and grammar corrections. Conversely, text-to-speech software has also become more sophisticated, with programs like Kurzweil 3000 and Read&Write reading digital text aloud. These tools often include features such as text highlighting, which aids in comprehension and retention—a boon for adults in professional settings who need to process large volumes of information efficiently.

Another exciting development is in organisation and task management tools, particularly for individuals with ADHD or executive functioning difficulties. Apps like Todoist, Trello, and ClickUp offer customisable task lists and boards that can be color-coded, prioritised, and broken down into manageable steps. These platforms also often include reminders and deadline tracking, helping users stay on top of their commitments. Additionally, newer tools like MindMeister and Padlet support visual organisation of thoughts through mind mapping, which can be particularly helpful for people who struggle with linear thinking.

Another significant recent change at the RCA is that two years ago nearly all of our MAs became just one year and no longer required students to submit a 6,000–10,000 word dissertation, which was in many ways the hardest task for many of our SpLD students. Of course, students do still have to submit writing, to illustrate they understand critical theory and how to synthesise it, and the humanities MAs and research degrees still require a dissertation or thesis to be submitted. So that is another change. I spend more of my time working one-to-one with PhD students which can of course stretch over a number of years. It is extremely interesting to see how this group of students develops their research and find ways of expressing it through writing of course, but also websites, blogs, videos, podcasts, webinars, and so on none of which existed back in 2002.

Looking ahead, my hope is that if we succeed in creating all-inclusive teaching programs with integrated academic support, much of our current work will eventually become redundant. The advancements in artificial intelligence (AI) and machine learning hold great promise in this regard. AI-driven tools can analyse a user's typical mistakes and adapt their teaching methods accordingly, offering a personalised learning experience. This level of customisation is especially valuable for adults who have previously struggled with standardised educational approaches.

I am particularly excited about the potential of AI tools like ChatGPT, which I use regularly—not just to summarise lengthy papers but also to formulate relevant questions from texts. I also rely on it to help refine phrases or sentences when I'm stuck—not necessarily to copy its suggestions but to explore alternative structures. In teaching, I believe the focus should be on guiding students to use such tools responsibly, encouraging them to treat AI as a private tutor rather than merely a shortcut for copying and pasting.

I was fortunate to be able to use my teaching experiences to inform my academic research, creating a dynamic feedback loop that significantly enhanced both my research and teaching practices. Shortly after I began working at the RCA, several students whom I had been supporting with their dissertations approached me for additional help with their drawing skills. These students expressed that they found it challenging to draw accurately from observation and from their mind's eye, and they felt that this difficulty was disadvantaging them in their professional practice.

This feedback led me to reflect on the potential underlying factors that could be contributing to these challenges. I considered how cognitive and perceptual difficulties, such as a weak working memory, poor visual tracking, slower-than-average processing speed, lack of automaticity, visual perceptual difficulties, difficulties in concentration, and poor hand-eye coordination, could complicate the drawing process. For example, I observed a student with Specific Learning Difficulties (SpLD) struggling to draw the spine of a skeleton. The student expressed frustration that she had to continually look up from her paper because she kept forgetting the image, and each time she did so, she lost track of which rib she had been drawing. This experience highlighted how working memory deficits and poor tracking can significantly hinder the drawing process.

Driven by these observations, I managed to connect with a group of like-minded academics from other institutions who shared my interest in this area. Together, we formed a research group to explore these challenges further. We designed a series of drawing situations at both the RCA and Swansea College of Art, University of Wales Trinity Saint David, involving groups of students, some of whom had SpLDs. Our goal was to determine whether we could identify students with SpLDs based on their drawings. Remarkably, we were able to correctly identify these students 70% of the time, based on their drawings.

Our research findings were presented at various conferences, and we continued to engage in practice-based research. We discovered that, in addition to weak working memory, poor tracking, and slower processing speed, other factors also made drawing more challenging for students with SpLDs. Poor hand-eye coordination and visual stress often led to what I refer to as "hedge your bets" lines—fuzzy and imprecise marks on the paper. Visual perceptual difficulties manifested in unintended and distorted perspectives, while a lack of automaticity resulted in rigid, static drawings that lacked confidence and expressiveness.

The culmination of this research was a publication commissioned by Jessica Kingsley Publishers, co-authored by myself and Howard Riley, a member of our research group and then Professor of Drawing at Swansea College of Art. *Observational Drawing for Students with Dyslexia: Strategies, Tips and Inspiration* (published on February 18, 2021) represents a significant contribution to understanding the challenges faced by students with SpLDs in the context of drawing and offers insights into how educators can better support these students in developing their artistic skills.

Reflecting on the service we provided back in 2002, I feel confident that it was well-suited to the needs of the time. However, as the landscape of higher education has evolved, particularly in line with other higher education institutions (HEIs), academic roles have become increasingly burdened with administrative tasks. This shift raises questions about the long-term effectiveness of such an approach, and whether it best serves our core mission. That said, it's possible that these trends could reverse, or at least adapt, in the future.

One of the more immediate changes we've encountered is the UK government's recent reforms to student visa applications, which are reshaping the composition of our student body. This could lead to an increase in domestic students eligible for Disabled Students' Allowances (DSA) support. However, the regulations around DSA eligibility could also shift, introducing further complexity. The lasting impact of the COVID-19 pandemic has also fundamentally altered how we approach teaching and learning. Hybrid course delivery has become a mainstay, and this requires careful, ongoing consideration to ensure it meets the evolving needs of students.

What remains clear is that academic support must be agile and responsive. As educators and support staff, it is crucial that we stay vigilant and adaptable, ready to update both the content of our programs and the methods through which we deliver them. Continuous evaluation and a willingness to innovate will be essential in maintaining the relevance and quality of the support we offer.

In conclusion, my journey over the past 22 years at the Royal College of Art has been one of continuous learning, adaptation, and collaboration. The evolution of our approach to supporting students with SpLDs reflects the growing understanding of the diverse challenges these students face, particularly in the unique context of postgraduate art and design education. From the early days of addressing dyslexia to now encompassing a broader spectrum of learning differences, our efforts have been driven by a commitment to inclusivity and the belief that every student deserves the opportunity to reach their full potential. As we look to the future, the integration of new technologies and teaching methodologies offers exciting possibilities for further enhancing our support structures. I remain hopeful that our work will continue to evolve, ultimately leading to more inclusive educational practices that minimise barriers and empower all students (whatever their learning difference), to succeed.

USC Upstate, USA—Beyond Accommodations

Enabling Learners, Faculty, and Staff, Embracing Neurodiversity for All

Renu Pariyadath

Background

USC Upstate is a public regional university with nearly 5,000 students and about 800 faculty and staff members. Women make up about 68% of the student population. Approximately 50% of the student body is White, 30% African American, 8% Hispanic/Latino, and 3% Asian, with other racial and ethnic groups making up about 9% of the study body population. Over 50% of students receive some form of need-based grants or scholarships. As of the 2023–2024 school year, 210 students were registered by The Disability Services office (roughly 4% of the student population), including 54.3% White students, 35.7% African American students, 3.8% Asian/Pacific Islanders, and 3.3% Hispanic students. Of these, 88 represented neurodivergent learners, with the largest category served being ADHD (54), followed by learning disability[1] (19), and Autistic learners (25). Considering the national estimates on the prevalence of neurodivergence (CDC, 2024, 2019; Li et al., 2023), it may be inferred that a large part of our student body includes undisclosed neurodivergent learners and those without a formal diagnosis. This may be changing as awareness increases. Preliminary numbers of students registering with the Disability Services office in fall 2024 show that we have 151 registered neurodivergent students, a sizable increase over the previous year. There is currently no full-time equivalent staff dedicated to neurodiversity programming. Our Director of Neurodiversity is a faculty member with a reduced teaching load of six courses a year, down from the typical eight courses a year.

Our neurodiversity program started to take shape in 2022, when the provost's office created a neurodiversity task force consisting of faculty, staff, and administrators across campus, with the aim of providing a more neuroinclusive curriculum and programming. The group was tasked with examining the university's current climate surrounding neurodiversity and identifying best practices, and opportunities for training. While our Disability Services office has been providing accommodations for neurodivergent learners for years, faculty on campus are not often equipped to engage and support neurodivergent

DOI: 10.4324/9781003495925-13

learners in the classroom. In fact, aside from including a mandated statement on disability in syllabi, most faculty were unfamiliar with and not equipped to deal with the needs of learners served by our Disability Services office. An Access Committee that included faculty, staff, and administration ceased to operate around 2020 when key leaders on the committee transitioned to other universities. It was not clear to the task force if our institution was currently the university of choice in the region for prospective neurodivergent students and their families. Therefore, the primary recommendations by the task force were to (1) improve faculty buy-in on neurodiversity initiatives, (2) increase awareness about neurodiversity across campus, and (3) improve pre-arrival services for potential students and their families. To take forward the task force's recommendations, particularly the first two recommendations, the provost's office created a faculty fellow position focused on neurodiversity in the fall of 2023.

The Shift to a Neurodiversity Paradigm

From the outset it was evident that our neurodiversity program had to be neuroinclusive in the most expansive sense of the word, meaning that it had to not only be relevant to student success but also welcomed enthusiastically by faculty and staff. In researching other higher education institutions, we observe that most comprehensive neurodiversity programs on campus are typically learner-facing and focus on transitioning to college, providing support for academic goals, and gaining employment after graduation. While diversity, equity, and inclusion efforts in corporate settings offer insights into programming and support for neurodivergent employees, higher education tends to focus its neurodiversity programs exclusively on students. Being a teaching-focused university, full-time USC Upstate faculty often teach at least eight courses a year, and it is important that faculty not feel burdened by the prospect of adopting neurodiversity-focused approaches. And so, our neurodiversity program focuses on creating a neuroinclusive culture that strives to include faculty and staff and to embrace potential benefits for the campus community as a whole.

Dwyer et al. (2023) have recommended that leaders in Higher Education adopt a system-wide approach that considers not only disability-related functional barriers and accommodation needs, but also stigma, prejudice, identity, and culture. This cultural level shift is what we are aiming at achieving through training as well as considering the possibility that neurodivergent and neurotypical individuals within staff and faculty could also benefit from adopting the neurodiversity paradigm. Our approach has been to enable faculty and staff to adopt what Walker (2021) calls the "neurodiversity paradigm" rather than the stigmatising "pathology paradigm," through formal training and informal peer-to-peer collaboration. The neurodiversity paradigm, unlike the pathology paradigm, values neurodiversity as any other natural form of human diversity.

This assumes there is no "normal" human mind, and that the social dynamics we see at play regarding neurodiversity are similar to those that manifest with other forms of human diversity (Walker, 2021). The Stanford Neurodiversity Program provides a working model, focusing on neurodivergent individuals as a whole rather than only students and creating a workplace and a study environment where neurodiversity thrives. Our nascent programming efforts assume that all campus spaces inhabited by learners, faculty, staff, and administration hold the potential for neuroinclusion. While the Disability Services office provides individual supports and accommodations that are legally required, the neurodiversity program we are building aims at changing the culture surrounding neurodiversity and providing an inclusive educational and work environment for all campus stakeholders. We aim to establish a model for neuroinclusion where both employees and students are equal stakeholders, resulting in a campus that enables all. Below we discuss ways in which we have begun integrating the neurodiversity paradigm into our student success initiatives as well as formal and informal faculty and staff training.

Specific Features/Interventions of the Program and Their Potential Impact

As a first step to creating a neuroinclusive educational experience for learners, we partnered with Neurodiversity Hub who were experienced in helping neurodivergent graduates make a more seamless transition to an internship or job. A gap analysis rubric that Neurodiversity Hub provided to us forms the basis of our student-facing programming. We are in the process of building a dedicated team of campus neurodiversity leaders, including faculty, staff, and students, who will be tasked with the gap analysis.

In 2023, faculty and staff were first formally introduced to neurodiversity through our *Embracing Neurodiversity @ USC Upstate* fall faculty day. While designed primarily with faculty in mind, this day-long event was also open to staff. The event was organised by the Center for Academic Innovation & Faculty Support (CAIFS) and the Faculty Fellow for Neurodiversity, in consultation with the provost. The event was announced and invitations were sought for discussion panels. The idea was to gauge investment in neurodiversity among faculty and staff and identify individuals that might serve as ambassadors for neurodiversity in the spaces they worked on campus. Over 80 participants registered for the event and faculty and staff members who were advocates for their neurodivergent children, neurodivergent themselves, and/or researchers on neurodiversity expressed interest in serving as panelists. *Embracing Neurodiversity @ USC Upstate* started with the parent panel where faculty and staff who were advocates for their neurodivergent children shared their experiences about the stigma and challenges their children faced in K-12 settings. This was followed by a faculty panel where participants discussed their own experience of being neurodivergent at work or their research on neurodiversity. Topical lunch discussions followed the panels which allowed participants to choose a table on topics such as Dyslexia, ADHD, Autism, and so on, and ask questions of discussion leaders who were generally faculty-parent advocates. The afternoon session was the keynote by Kaelynn Partlow, who was featured in the Netflix show *Love on the Spectrum* and is a nationally recognised Autistic activist from South Carolina. This was followed by a Zoom session with The Director of Project LETS and a Peer Mental Health Advocate, Stefanie Kaufman-Mthimkhulu. The event concluded with a panel, which was an information session on services offered to neurodivergent students by Disability Services, Counseling Services, Career Management, Student Services, and Student Affairs. For most faculty and staff, this was the first exposure to topics such as masking, the increased stigma in the state of South Carolina, affordable testing offered on campus, and strategies for recognising, engaging, and including neurodivergent learners. The event was positively received and several participants requested that they be provided with more formal training and strategies for engaging neurodivergent learners.

Embracing Neurodiversity @ USC Upstate allowed those invested in neurodiversity on campus the opportunity to come together, discuss what they were each independently working on, and find community. The parent and faculty panelists from this event as well as the Director of Disability Services, the Director of Counseling Services and the Dean of Students were invited to join a campus-wide Neurodiversity Committee. This committee is currently working with the Director of Neurodiversity on curating resources on neurodiversity, for students, parents, faculty, staff, and administrators, which will be hosted as an open-access library guide. The committee is also immersed in a book club, collaboratively learning about and defining neurodiversity terminology and best practices. Once the committee begins to coalesce on the design for our campus neurodiversity program, we will undertake a gap analysis with parameters that integrate our university's focus on neurodivergent students as well as employees. We anticipate that this team of neurodivergent and neurotypical individuals, parent advocates, and student service professionals, will take the committee's work to their own departments and teams for critical feedback to build a more robust program.

Key Challenges and Enablers of Implementing the Program

As mentioned previously, a challenge has been the number of undisclosed neurodivergent members of the student body. The Disability Services office works to familiarise students with neurodiversity at the orientation stage and we are aware of the need to also provide pre-arrival services. A library extension is underway and several advocates on campus are working to provide a more visible quiet room and/or a sensory room. Currently, only students with legal documentation have access to the sensory/quiet room within the

Disability Services office. To better focus student needs inside the classroom, on campus and beyond graduation, the university has committed to neurodiversity in the newest iteration of its strategic priorities that are being drawn up as we write this. Within the strategic priority for student success, we are working to include the tactic: "Build a culture that supports neurodiversity."

While many universities work on faculty and staff training on neurodiversity through their DEI centres, we are working more closely with student services, CAIFS, and invested faculty and staff. This has allowed us to draw on the competencies of a range of neurodivergent and neurotypical individuals across campus. Our commitment to neurodiversity across the campus has been further cemented with the faculty fellow for diversity transitioning to the Director of Neurodiversity. Together with the Executive Director of CAIFS and the Director of Transformative and Inclusive Pedagogy, the new role will work on embedding neurodiversity as a value and practice across our campus.

Anticipated Outcomes of the Program

As our emergent neurodiversity program comes to fruition, we foresee a more welcoming study and work environment for students and employees alike. Looking forward, we hope to considerably reduce the stigma that leads neurodivergent students and employees to mask on campus. While there are existing neurodiversity-friendly options among private and state-level universities, we aim to become the college of choice for students within the metropolitan area we serve. Our vision is to create a campus environment that enables all.

Resultant Implications for Future Research and/or Application of Such a Program

We expect that our neurodiversity program will gradually lead to a campus where we will no longer need documented neurodivergence. Rather, all students will be offered a menu of options in course modalities, assignment formats, and a variety of options for transitioning into and out of college. Once a critical mass of faculty and staff on campus become fluent in recognising the barriers inherent in classroom and curricular expectations, the neurodiversity paradigm may be adopted at the department and college level.

Over the last year, *The Chronicle of Higher Education* has published a series of articles on making colleges attend to neurodiversity, including two essays, in particular, centred on faculty and staff neurodiversity. As with any workplace, embracing neurodiversity has obvious benefits for employees, such as consideration during hiring and promotion decisions as well as accommodations for courses or meeting formats. Autistic professor Irish (2023) recommends that universities become better aware of neurodivergence among faculty and staff and begin incorporating it into their DEI initiatives. In interviewing faculty and staff about their adult diagnoses, Pryal (2024) found that they reflected on being more empathetic teachers and advocates for neurodivergent learners, often opening up the space for students to seek and disclose their own diagnoses.

We hope that our effort to integrate student inclusion and employee wellness finds merit and is replicated on other campuses. Neurodivergent students need role models in higher education. Representation in the faculty body inculcates a sense of belonging among neurodivergent students. Less stigma and freedom to unmask among faculty leads to more inclusive spaces for learners as well.

Note

1   The author aligns with the social model of disability, which argues that disability is not an individual deficiency but a systemic oppression. Learners are disabled (by the education system) when their learning needs are not acknowledged or accommodated. Other terms the author considered here were "learning disabled," "learning differences," or listing dyslexia, dyspraxia, dysgraphia, etc., in full. Not having accurate data on the exact nature of disablement as leaner needs often overlap, the author chose to retain the category "learning disability" that the USC Upstate Disability Services office currently uses.

References

Centers for Disease Control and Prevention. (2019) *Disability and health related conditions* [online]. Centers for Disease Control and Prevention. https://www.cdc.gov/ncbddd/disabilityandhealth/relatedconditions.html

Centers for Disease Control and Prevention. (2024) *Data and statistics on autism spectrum disorder* [online]. Autism Spectrum Disorder (ASD). https://www.cdc.gov/autism/data-research/index.html

Dwyer, P., Mineo, E., Mifsud, K., Lindholm, C., Gurba, A., and Waisman, T. C. (2023) 'Building neurodiversity-inclusive postsecondary campuses: Recommendations for leaders in higher education', *Autism in Adulthood*, 5(1), 1–14. https://doi.org/10.1089/aut.2021.0042

Irish. (2023). 'How to make room for neurodivergent professors', *The Chronicle of Higher Education*. https://www.chronicle.com/article/how-to-make-room-for-neurodivergent-professors

Li, Y., Li, Q., Zheng, J., Zeng, X., Shen, T., Chen, Q., and Yang, W. (2023) 'Prevalence and trends in diagnosed learning disability among US children and adolescents from 1997 to 2021', *JAMA Pediatrics*, 177(9), 969. https://doi.org/10.1001/jamapediatrics.2023.2117

Pryal, K. R. G. (2024). 'Should you seek an adult diagnosis of neurodivergence?', *The Chronicle of Higher Education*. https://www.chronicle.com/article/should-you-seek-an-adult-diagnosis-of-neurodivergence

Walker, N. (2021). *Neuroqueer heresies: Notes on the neurodiversity paradigm, Autistic empowerment, and postnormal possibilities*. Fort Worth, TX: Autonomous Press.

University of Delaware, USA

Spectrum Scholars

Wes Garton, Adrienne Cornish Lucas and Jennifer Grelak

Context

As the number of Autistic students entering post-secondary education has grown, an increasing number of universities in the United States have begun offering services to empower these students in areas of self-advocacy and independence toward greater outcomes in college. The University of Delaware, located in the mid-Atlantic region of the Eastern US, serves approximately 25,000 students across ten colleges and schools. In 2018, an autism support initiative ("Spectrum Scholars") was launched to provide additional services to a select number of students. Over 30 students are currently supported by the initiative, with more added each year as part of a cohort model. Seven full-time staff members provide holistic services including executive function coaching, career counselling, and research related to Autistic identity and voice, delivered in-person and remotely to students during the university's academic semesters every year.

About Spectrum Scholars

The Spectrum Scholars college-to-career initiative supports Autistic undergraduate students enrolled at the University of Delaware. The support framework is based on a Multi-Tiered System of Support (MTSS) model, a comprehensive framework used by K-12 schools to provide academic and behavioural services and support for all students (Samuels, 2016). MTSS is an evidence-based approach that provides varying levels of support based on individual student needs (Samuels, 2016). The adaptation of this framework to a university setting recognises the challenges that Autistic students may face in higher education and aims to improve their academic, social, career, and personal outcomes.

Multi-Tiered System of Support

The MTSS framework originates from the integration of Response to Intervention and Positive Behavioral Interventions and Supports and aims to

DOI: 10.4324/9781003495925-14

identify struggling students early to provide timely assistance (Zhang et al., 2023). It is grounded in several core principles, including:

Schoolwide support: MTSS emphasises the importance of providing support to educators, administrators, and other key stakeholders within the educational environment (Zhang et al., 2023). This comprehensive support ensures that the system is equipped to meet the needs of all students.

Data-driven decision-making: A key component of MTSS is ongoing data collection and continuous assessment (Zhang et al., 2023). Data informs a personalised approach that continuously monitors progress and adjusts services and supports as needed.

Tiered levels of support: MTSS is structured around multiple tiers of support, with each tier providing increasingly intensive interventions (Zhang et al., 2023). These supports range from universal supports to more targeted and individualised interventions.

Universal screening: MTSS aims to identify student needs early through assessments at the beginning of the school year (Zhang et al., 2023). Regular screening and monitoring of student progress allows educators to identify students who need additional support and adjust interventions based on ongoing assessments.

Evidence-based practices: MTSS interventions and strategies are grounded in research and have demonstrated effectiveness (Zhang et al., 2023). The use of proven strategies ensures that student supports are reliable and replicable.

While the MTSS framework has been extensively studied and implemented within K-12 settings, its use within higher education is fairly new. The Spectrum Scholars initiative bridges this gap by drawing on the evidence-based practices used within K-12 to create a model that can be adapted to higher education. This approach provided Spectrum Scholars a foundation for developing the support systems for Autistic college students within the initiative.

Spectrum Scholars supports are organised into three tiers, following the MTSS guidelines, which provide increasingly intensive levels of support (refer Figure P3.1).

Tier 1: Universal Supports

Tier 1 supports are designed to create an inclusive campus culture that supports all students, staff, and faculty, including Autistic students. This level of support includes a broad range of activities aimed at raising awareness, knowledge, and skill among members of the campus community. Key components of this tier include training sessions, workshops, and presentations of best practices related to working with Autistic students. For example, Spectrum

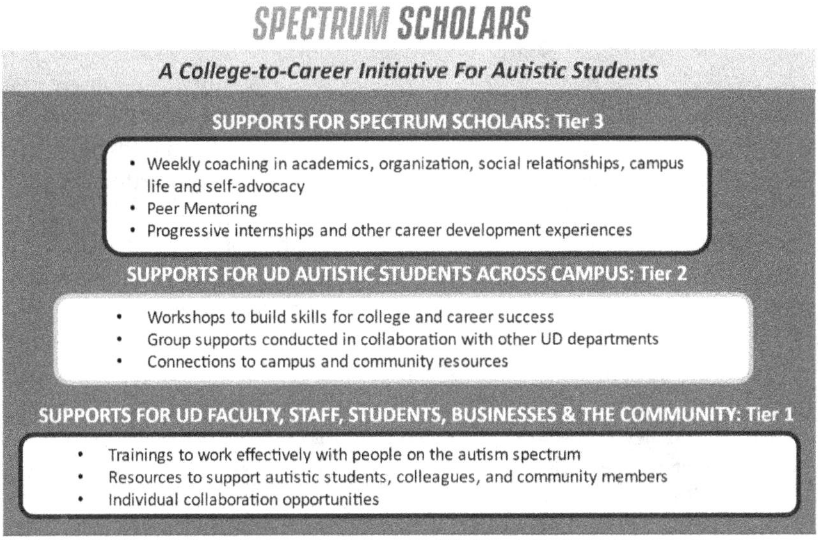

Figure P3.1 Spectrum Scholars initiative tiers of support.

Scholars provides training and "Tip Sheets" for faculty, including research and strategies for engaging with Autistic students. The initiative also provides training and resources to new resident assistants on supporting Autistic students living in campus housing.

This universal level of support is analogous to school-wide interventions in K-12 settings, where certain practices are implemented for the benefit of all students. The goal of Tier 1 support is to reduce barriers to participation and success, creating a more inclusive environment for all students.

Tier 2: Targeted Group Supports

Tier 2 supports neurodivergent matriculating students through workshops designed to develop essential skills for success in college and future careers. This tier also provides group support sessions in collaboration with various University of Delaware departments, facilitating connections to valuable campus and community resources.

For students who need more support than what is offered in Tier 1, Tier 2 provides targeted services and supports, which are offered through small group settings and drop-in services and are designed to address specific identified needs. One example of a Tier 2 intervention is the PEERS for Young Adults® curriculum, an evidence-based social skills initiative for Autistic young adults. Spectrum Scholars offered this initiative in collaboration with the university's Counseling Center and provided students with tools to help them navigate social situations. The PEERS for Young Adults® curriculum was implemented in 2019 and continued until a revised model was introduced in 2022. The new model, dubbed "Social Seminar," retained many evidence-based practices and interventions characteristic of PEERS®, while introducing novel features as well. Social Seminar is facilitated by Autistic individuals and provides space for students to practice neuro-affirming skills in a supportive group environment.

Tier 2 also includes partnerships with other campus organisations to provide additional resources and support across campus to neurodivergent students. These partnerships are informed by research in both secondary and postsecondary education. Examples include workshops offered on money management, creation of sensory-friendly spaces in collaboration with the university's career services centre, and voting literacy workshops offered in collaboration with the university library. These activities provide students with the additional support needed for academic and social success without requiring the extensive individualised interventions found in Tier 3.

Tier 3: Comprehensive Individualised Supports

Tier 3 is the most comprehensive level of support offered by the Spectrum Scholars initiative, offering comprehensive, person-centred support to a defined number of students admitted as part of an academic cohort. At this level, students receive one-on-one coaching that covers a wide range of areas, including academics, self-care, social engagement, and career development; these are elaborated below. The coaching process is guided by SMART (specific, measurable, attainable, relevant, and timely) goals that are determined each semester through collaboration between each student and their coach. This ensures the support is tailored to the student's needs and personal goals.

Tier 3 coaching domains are as follows:

Academics

A foundational element of the Spectrum Scholars initiative is its personalised academic support. Each participant receives tailored academic coaching and mentoring designed to meet their unique learning needs and academic objectives. The support aligns with the student's academic course of study and includes assistance from their assigned academic advisor, while incorporating essential competencies that all students should strive to develop during their educational journey.

Social Engagement

Acknowledging that social interaction can present challenges for Autistic individuals, the Spectrum Scholars initiative places significant emphasis on social skills development. The initiative offers structured training sessions that concentrate on communication, networking, and interpersonal relationships. These sessions often involve role-playing exercises, group discussions, and real-world scenarios to foster confidence and practical social skills. This intervention empowers students to handle social situations more effectively, which is crucial for both academic success and future career endeavours. Furthermore, students are encouraged to engage with campus and community resources and events.

Career Exploration

Transitioning from education to employment can pose significant challenges for Autistic individuals. The Spectrum Scholars initiative addresses these challenges by offering employment-related transition support that includes guidance on job searching, application processes, and workplace accommodations. These experiences enable students to acquire practical experience in various fields, establish professional networks, and clarify their career interests. Furthermore, the initiative provides career counselling services, resume workshops, and interview preparation to equip students with the necessary skills to confidently enter the workforce. Career Counselors work closely with students to identify potential obstacles and develop strategies to overcome them. This support ensures that students are well-prepared to transition from academic life to professional careers, thereby enhancing their prospects for long-term success.

Self-care

Self-care is essential for Autistic college students, who often encounter distinct challenges in both academic and social environments. Coaching in this domain is instrumental in helping students develop customised strategies for stress management, well-being maintenance, and effective balancing of various responsibilities. Coaches support students in establishing routines and identifying coping mechanisms that cater to their unique needs and preferences. By emphasising practices such as mindfulness, time management, and healthy lifestyle choices, coaching facilitates the integration of self-care into daily routines, ultimately promoting enhanced academic performance and personal growth.

Executive Functioning

Executive functioning challenges in Autistic college students frequently include difficulties with organisation, time management, and task initiation. These challenges can have a significant impact on both academic performance and daily life. Executive Functioning Coaching from Spectrum Scholars coaches serves as a valuable resource, offering personalised strategies to improve skills such as planning, prioritisation, and sustained focus. Coaches assist students in breaking tasks down into manageable steps, setting achievable goals, and utilising organisational tools like calendars and reminders. By promoting self-awareness and providing customised interventions, coaching in this area enables students to more effectively navigate the demands of higher education, build confidence, and pursue their academic and personal objectives. Tailored approaches ensure that the support provided is aligned with each student's specific needs.

Self-advocacy

Self-advocacy is essential for Autistic college students, as it enables them to articulate their needs and pursue the necessary support. Coaching within this domain enhances these skills by guiding students in recognising their strengths and challenges while navigating available resources. Spectrum Scholars coaches play a vital role in helping students build confidence to express their needs clearly, engage with professors and support staff, and effectively manage accommodations. Through methods such as role-playing, goal-setting, and the development of communication strategies, coaching empowers students to advocate for themselves with greater effectiveness. This support is integral to both academic success and personal growth throughout their college experience.

Interdependent Living

Interdependent living is essential for Autistic college students, as it allows them to balance independence with necessary support. Coaching can play a pivotal role in this process by assisting students in developing essential skills for managing daily tasks, including budgeting, meal planning, and time management. Spectrum Scholars coaches collaborate with students to identify specific areas where they may benefit from assistance and to formulate effective strategies for overcoming these challenges. By emphasising both self-sufficiency and the strategic use of available resources, coaching within this domain empowers students to adopt a balanced approach to independence. This tailored guidance enhances their confidence and resilience and facilitates a smoother transition to managing life responsibilities in a college environment.

Peer Mentoring

The initiative also incorporates peer mentoring as part of Tier 3 support. Research has shown that peer mentoring can be highly effective in improving outcomes for college students, both on and off the autism spectrum (Wu & Wang, 2022). By pairing students with mentors who have successfully navigated the college environment, the initiative provides an additional layer of practical and relatable support.

Rationale for the Multi-tiered Approach

The decision to adopt a multi-tiered approach within the Spectrum Scholars initiative was driven by the recognition that Autistic students often face unique challenges in higher education that are not fully addressed by traditional accommodations. These challenges can include difficulties with social interactions, executive functioning, and self-advocacy, all of which can impact a student's ability to succeed in a college environment.

By structuring the initiative as an MTSS framework, Spectrum Scholars ensures that support is accessible to all Autistic students at the university, regardless of their specific needs. The tiered approach allows for flexibility, with more intensive services available for students who need them.

Spectrum Scholars also prioritised the inclusion of Autistic students and staff in the initiative development. This collaborative approach respects and privileges the diverse experiences and perspectives of Autistic people, aligning with the initiative's commitment to inclusivity and its goal of creating a supportive campus environment for everyone.

Challenges and Enablers

Since its inception, Spectrum Scholars has undergone continuous quality improvement in response to expressed needs and preferences of students, staff, and the larger campus community as well as in concert with the growing evidence base regarding post-secondary programming for Autistic students, much of which has been generated by the full-time researcher embedded with the team. Originally, the initiative's primary financial sponsor envisioned that students would be drawn exclusively from computer science and engineering majors at the University of Delaware. Initial recruitment from these domains did not yield a sufficient number of Tier 3 participants, so the initiative pivoted to include students from other academic departments and majors. This evolution was enabled by key partners' understanding that the students' needs were different than originally anticipated, and inclusion across academic departments became normalised. The decision to branch out beyond the scope of the initiative's initial vision ultimately benefited the initiative and the student population by inviting Autistic students from all majors to consider applying. "Thinking outside the box" in this case was rather obvious and helped to challenge the stereotypical notion that Autistic college students are uniformly drawn to highly technical fields such as computer science and engineering. By including students from a wide range of backgrounds and academic interests, Spectrum Scholars reflected the diverse interests and aspirations of Autistic students accessing college. Another early challenge encountered by the initiative was the COVID-19 pandemic, which started only a few months after the inaugural cohort started their college experience. The need to move to a virtual learning environment overnight pressured the initiative's staff, students, and families. After the university's announcement that all university functions would remain remote, the initiative adopted Zoom and other virtual learning tools to ensure that services continued uninterrupted. These technologies proved to be essential to the initiative and have continued to enable the success of students in the initiative, as well as maximising accessibility with the advent of virtual and hybrid learning opportunities.

Other enablers of success include the initiative's stalwart campus partners. Since the beginning, Spectrum Scholars approached campus departments to offer collaborations and workshops that would benefit a larger number of students than those accessing Tier 3 services. Not only does collaboration benefit the overall campus community, but collaboration with campus partners has also fostered a greater sense of mutual trust, support, and common purpose in supporting students at the University of Delaware.

Outcomes

To date, Spectrum Scholars has had eight graduates, with 88% of graduates employed in full-time roles or continuing education. The initiative is proud of all students' accomplishments, which include students acquiring jobs at companies as diverse as JPMorgan Chase, Northrop Grumman, New York Life Trust Company, and DoorDash. Spectrum Scholars hopes to build off its successes by continuing to offer neurodivergent students at the University of Delaware with tiered services and support.

Implications for Initiative Development and Research

1. Inclusive educational practices: The success of initiatives supporting Autistic college students like Spectrum Scholars underscores the significance of fostering inclusive educational environments. This warrants the implementation of strategies such as Universal Design for Learning, flexible teaching methods, MTSS, accessible and inclusive resources, and customised academic advising. By widely adopting these practices, educational institutions can enhance support not only for Autistic students but also for individuals with diverse learning needs.
2. Workplace adaptations and accommodations: Insights gained from initiatives that support Autistic college students can inform workplace practices, making them more accommodating for neurodivergent employees. Strategies developed to support Autistic students in educational settings—such as clear communication, structured environments, and personalised support—can be effectively adapted for professional contexts. This approach promotes a more inclusive workforce and contributes to the success of Autistic individuals in their careers.

3. Policy development: The insights and experiences derived from initiatives supporting Autistic college students can inform policy development at both institutional and governmental levels. It is crucial to advocate for policies that guarantee accessibility (both programmatic and financial), reasonable accommodations, and antidiscrimination measures, thereby ensuring equal opportunities for neurodivergent individuals in education and employment.

4. Community and advocacy: Effective initiatives can serve as valuable models for advocacy efforts and community support initiatives. They highlight the importance of understanding and addressing the unique needs of Autistic individuals, which can drive broader societal change. Advocacy for similar initiatives across diverse educational contexts can help cultivate more supportive and inclusive environments for all students.

References

Samuels, C.A. (2016, December 13). 'What are multitiered systems of supports?', *Education Week*. www.edweek.org/policy-politics/what-are-multitiered-systems-of-supports/2016/12

Wu, T., & Wang, D. (2022). 'Peer mentoring support for students with autism in school settings: A concept analysis', *British Journal of Special Education*, 49(4), 561–581. https://doi.org/10.1111/1467-8578.12434

Zhang, J., Martella, R.C., Kang, S., & Yenioglu, B.Y. (2023). 'Response to Intervention (RtI)/Multi-Tiered Systems of Support (MTSS): A nationwide analysis', *Journal of Educational Leadership and Policy Studies*. https://eric.ed.gov/?id=EJ1396417

University of Calgary, Canada—Supporting Success in Post-secondary Settings for Neurodivergent Students

The UCAN Peer Mentorship Program

Carly McMorris, Mercedes Bagshawe, Nicole Eddy and Megan Ames

Background

The University of Calgary Autism and Neurodivergent (UCAN) Peer Mentorship Program was developed in 2021 and supported the first cohort of Autistic students in the winter of 2023. The University of Calgary (herein, UCalgary) is a large research-intensive university in Western Canada (Calgary, Alberta, Canada) and is in the top ten universities in Canada (according to the Center for World University Rankings; CWUR). With over 200 undergraduate, graduate, and professional degree programs, UCalgary comprises approximately 37,000 students and 1,850 academic staff. Of those, approximately 17% of the student population identifies as neurodivergent, including autism, attention-deficit/ hyperactivity disorder (ADHD), dyslexia, and so on (Stowe, O'Connell, Chew, Braun and Kaipainen, 2022).

UCAN is a peer mentorship program that provides individualised and flexible academic and non-academic supports to self-identifying Autistic and neurodivergent students registered at UCalgary. UCAN offers in-person one-to-one meetings with a graduate student either weekly or bi-weekly based on student preference, as well as in-person monthly group events or workshops. Since its conception, UCAN has served approximately 15 students in some capacity. The program is currently funded by a national research grant held by Dr. Carly McMorris, which supports the employment of a 0.2 full-time equivalent coordinator/staff and various aspects of implementing and evaluating the program. Given the clinical content (e.g. mental health concerns) that often arise during one-to-one meetings, a clinical supervisor is also needed for the program. The clinical supervisor meets bi-weekly with mentors to conduct group supervision around any clinical issues or problems that arise. Preliminary analyses demonstrate that students enrolled in UCAN are

DOI: 10.4324/9781003495925-15

moderately-to-highly satisfied with the program, and students report lower stress and stronger self-efficacy skills following their participation in UCAN.

Theory/Research Basis for the Program Approach and Features

There has been an increasing number of Autistic students attending post-secondary education; though graduation rates are lower (39% in 8 years) than that of non-Autistic students (~60% in 6 years; White et al., 2011; National Center for Education Statistics, 2018; Newman et al., 2011). Despite the many strengths possessed by Autistic students that can help facilitate post-secondary success (e.g. memory skills, detail oriented, originality and creativity, passionate interests, desire for knowledge, adherence to rules, ability to work long hours, and understand complex ideas; Anderson, Stephensen and Carter, 2017; Drake, 2017; Gobbo and Shmulsky, 2014; Gurbuz et al., 2019), there are unique challenges that can present within this environment (e.g. navigating campus, large classes, building social relationships, being flexible/dealing with unpredictability; Van Hees et al., 2015) that can impede student adjustment and adaptation (Barnhill, 2016). Indeed, co-occurring mental health challenges, such as anxiety and depression, that many Autistic individuals experience may further exacerbate difficulties (McMorris et al., 2018). Consequently, many Autistic students have been found to complete degrees at reduced rates (Barnhill, 2016), as well as having a reduced likelihood of obtaining secure employment (Roux et al., 2013), and are least likely to live independently (Anderson et al., 2014).

The diverse academic and non-academic needs of Autistic individuals, combined with the limited availability of appropriate services, can significantly hinder access to effective, autism-specific post-secondary supports and accommodations (Anderson et al., 2017; Drake, 2017; Newman et al., 2011). Indeed, our environmental scan of Canadian post-secondary institutions showed only 6% of institutions had at least one autism-specific support, the most common being information on the institution's website (Ames et al., 2022). Staff and administrators at institutions reported that while there is a strong desire to support Autistic students, many obstacles exist, including a lack of funding, knowledgeable staff, and institutional support (Coombs et al., 2023). Restrictive eligibility criteria, challenges in navigating a complex system, and the absence of neuro-affirming pedagogical practices, accommodations, and services all exacerbate the lack of adequate support, leaving Autistic students to struggle in the post-secondary setting (Ames et al., 2022; Cage et al., 2020; Coombs et al., 2023). Moreover, there are limited supports that address non-academic needs, such as understanding peer and instructor relationships, navigating the university environment, and developing university "know-how" (White et al., 2011; Newman et al., 2011; Ames et al., 2022); those that do exist may be restricted in their accessibility (e.g. overwhelming processes, unfamiliar environment, disclosure requirement; Newman et al., 2011).

Individualised supports, tailored to meet both academic and non-academic needs, are suggested as being the most effective for Autistic post-secondary students (Cage et al., 2020). Peer mentorship models have been identified as a cost-effective, individualised approach that promotes positive mental health in Autistic and neurodivergent post-secondary students (Duerksen et al., 2021). Such programs are associated with higher retention and graduation rates among mentees (Kiyama and Luca, 2014), more positive integration into post-secondary settings (Yomtov et al., 2015; Anderson et al., 2017), positive outcomes in social belonging, self-regulation skills, comfort in student role, and improvement in academic skills and performance (White et al., 2011).

One of the first multi-faceted peer mentorship programs specifically for Autistic post-secondary students (the **ASD M**entorship **P**rogram; **the AMP**; Ames et al., 2016) was developed and implemented by researchers at York University (Toronto, Ontario, Canada) in 2007. The AMP's mission was to help Autistic post-secondary students navigate the social and academic framework of campus life at a large university. Since then, several adaptations of the AMP and other peer mentorship approaches for Autistic post-secondary students have been developed globally.

In September 2021, in collaboration with existing services at UCalgary and alongside an advisory group comprised of Autistic students, academic faculty, university staff, and caregivers of Autistic post-secondary students, the **U**niversity of **C**algary's **A**utism and **N**eurodivergent (**UCAN**) Peer Support Program was developed. UCAN, informed by the AMP, is rooted in Tinto's (1993) model of student integration, which asserts that successful student outcomes depend on their integration into both academic and social systems. Thus, interventions aimed at improving student retention must focus on transforming the institution's academic and social environments to foster greater engagement and support. The inclusion of the advisory team ensures that UCAN is implemented according to UCalgary's context and existing support networks.

Reason Why This Approach, and Specific Elements of the Approach, Were Chosen

Overall, UCAN's mission is to offer a safe, supportive, and neuro-inclusive university-based peer network for Autistic and neurodivergent post-secondary students that promotes individual skill building through providing social support and a sense of belonging.

Research on peer mentorship programs identified one-on-one support as essential to addressing student-focused strengths and areas of growth (Duerksen et al., 2021). In a review of nine programs for Autistic post-secondary students (Anderson et al., 2017), students stressed the importance of having one-on-one support to assist with a range of difficulties (i.e. decision-making, study skills, daily living, and clarifying ambiguities). Students also highlighted peer mentorship groups as fostering support, belonging, and inclusion that extended beyond the post-secondary community (Anderson et al., 2017). The UCAN approach involves the following components:

- One-on-one individual support by a non-Autistic trained peer mentor
- Group-based social events and workshops
- Advisory board
- Program evaluation

Individual Meetings

Based on recommendations from previous research and collaborations with individuals with lived experiences, one-on-one meetings between a mentor (such as a psychology graduate student) and a mentee can offer a personalised, student-centred approach to skill development (Ames et al., 2016; Pillay and Bhat, 2012). Professionals in community colleges and post-secondary Autistic students suggest that accommodations for Autistic students need to be flexible and personalised, attending to the various needs of individuals. Manualized programs with "one-size-fits-all" outcome targets are not advisable for this population; thus, individualised supports that are flexible and can be continually adapted to meet one's needs are known to be most beneficial for Autistic students (Dwyer et al., 2023; Gelbar et al., 2014).

Peers, as opposed to service providers, staff, or faculty, are chosen in a peer mentorship model as they are better suited to act as role models, provide emotional support, and offer practical knowledge about post-secondary and classroom functioning. As with many peer mentorship frameworks, benefits can also be bi-directional, providing the mentor with additional training opportunities and capacity for working with the Autistic population. A significant barrier for Autistic and neurodivergent youth accessing mental health or healthcare services is clinicians not feeling capable or confident to provide adequate and appropriate service (Gallant et al., 2023). By acting as a mentor, clinicians-in-training are receiving specialised skills in implementing neuro-affirming approaches, which in turn will build capacity for future clinicians and ensure better access to supports and services for neurodivergent people.

Group Events and Workshops

Connection, acceptance, and social integration into the university community have been increasingly recognised as ways to foster success in post-secondary settings for Autistic and neurodivergent students. Consequently, through group-based activities, UCAN aims to create a welcoming, supportive, and inclusive environment where students can connect socially with other neurodivergent students. Group-based activities help to build peer networks, social supports, and foster connections between students. Psychosocial factors, including social activity and social connectedness, have been shown to predict academic performance and retention (Anderson et al., 2017). Some students whose self-identified goals are related to social interactions and building connections utilise group-based events to practice social skills (e.g. initiating conversations, engaging in small talk, making plans) that they have learned or practiced in their individual meetings. Given that group learning for Autistic students should focus on tasks and skill development rather than on disability or "deficits," UCAN also prioritises providing workshops or learning sessions on topics that are identified as areas of growth, such as managing finances and healthy relationships. Through group-based activities and workshops, UCAN fosters social connectedness within a safe, neuroinclusive community, while also providing valuable information that can support students' success.

Advisory Group

Consistent with various participatory action research approaches and the *Nothing about Us without Us* movement (Charlton, 1998), UCAN has embedded the voices of Autistic people, staff, and caregivers into the development and implementation of UCAN, along with identifying appropriate evaluation methods. This advisory group has been crucial in ensuring that the program's approach and components are strengths-based, accessible to all individuals on the autism spectrum, and align with the existing support network within the UCalgary context.

The Specific Features/Interventions of the Program and Their Impact

Prior to implementation, the UCAN Program underwent a six-month period of review and adaptation to ensure it would provide a needed service and would fit within the UCalgary landscape. A review of existing services and supports for UCalgary Autistic students was conducted. This review was performed in consultation with the advisory group and in partnership with existing service providers (e.g. the Accessibility Centre and the Wellness Centre). An assessment of Autistic students' academic and non-academic needs was also completed to ensure the UCAN Program filled an identified need. After highlighting gaps in supports and students' academic and non-academic needs, the UCAN team met with the advisory group to determine the aims and objectives of UCAN and develop an appropriate name, approach, and eligibility criteria for the program. Materials, approaches, and activities from the AMP manual (Ames et al., 2016) were also adapted and incorporated. These modifications and adaptations were then reviewed with the advisory group to ensure they aligned with needs of UCalgary neurodivergent students.

After ensuring UCAN fit the UCalgary campus, training materials for mentors were developed. Consistent with previous programs, graduate students in educational and clinical psychology programs were identified as appropriate mentors. Although the UCAN Program does not provide counselling services, graduate students in psychology were chosen as mentors as they have prior experience working with neurodivergent students and are equipped to manage significant mental health challenges or crises should they arise. To date, 17 mentors have been trained as part of the UCAN Program. As a team, mentors, program coordinator, and the clinical supervisor meet twice a month for supervision, where discussion is focused on topics and potential solutions raised by mentees during individual meetings. These sessions also provide an opportunity to brainstorm any administrative issues that have come up related to group events, meeting locations, recruitment of mentees, partnerships with existing programs, and documentation for crises.

Before being matched with a mentor, the program coordinator screens students who wish to be involved in UCAN and has an informal discussion about the student's experiences at the university, their goals (academic and non-academic), and what type of support they wish to get from UCAN. If students are a match for the program (i.e. identify as neurodivergent and are enrolled at UCalgary), students are sent a consent form, asked to provide basic demographic information, and answer questions related to their mental health and their experiences in post-secondary education. Mentees will complete the same measures at the end of the school year. All questionnaires are kept anonymous and used for research purposes to gain further understanding of the effectiveness of participating in UCAN.

Once matched, our mentors meet with UCAN mentees either weekly or bi-weekly based on student (mentee) preference. During the first meeting, mentors and mentees discuss boundaries, goals, and the types of support mentors can provide. It is important to note that all mentor/mentee interactions take place on UCalgary campus and that emergency contact cards are on file in the event of a crisis. Mentors in the UCAN Program are often seen as a coach, who helps their student navigate their post-secondary experience. The mentorship relationship and support provided is unique to each mentee depending upon the goals or support they are hoping to achieve through being involved in UCAN.

Group events, which are open to all neurodivergent students, are held on UCalgary campus each month and rotate between informative "lunch and learns" sessions (e.g. sex and healthy relationships, student advising and accommodations, and federal/provincial disability grants) and informal fun lunch activities (e.g. board games, painting, pizza lunches, canine therapy).

Key Challenges and Enablers of Implementing the Program

There were many crucial facilitators in implementing UCAN. In particular, the program has been supported by university partnerships; UCalgary administrators, advising staff, and leadership from the Student Accessibility Services, the Student Wellness Centre, and the Neurodiversity Support Office have provided instrumental support in recruiting neurodivergent students for the program. Working with other support offices within the university context that supports neurodivergent students has also helped in determining how to embed UCAN in existing supports while providing a distinct service. Further, UCAN's advisory group provides an unbiased review of the program implementation and to develop plans for the program to ensure it is sustainable on campus.

In addition to enablers, the program has also faced numerous challenges and learned important lessons. One of the biggest challenges has been effectively spreading awareness about UCAN and enrolling and serving a large number of students. With the increased focus on supporting neurodivergence at UCalgary, neurodivergent individuals are receiving several academic and non-academic supports (i.e. access to a sensory-friendly lounge or to neurodiversity support advisors). While this is a huge benefit and step in the right direction, it has limited the number of students who see a need for UCAN supports (which is a good thing!). Similarly, students have also been unsure about what additional support UCAN provides and how it is distinct from other services on campus. Students who were enrolled in UCAN were accessing several neuro-affirming supports at UCalgary and in the broader community. Thus, it became apparent that our recruitment strategies need to be more nuanced to distinguish UCAN from other programs and to reach individuals who needed support but were not currently receiving any.

A second challenge is related to staff and mentors; specifically, the need for dedicated staff with expertise in working with neurodivergent individuals to help coordinate the program. Ensuring the program coordinator has this expertise fosters a more inclusive and welcoming environment for neurodivergent folks, allowing for more specific clinical follow-up if needed, and supporting mentors in their interactions with mentees. Additionally, as mentors are graduate students, challenges have emerged in that students are themselves busy and there is a high turnover of graduate students available to take on mentorship positions. This has made consistent individual meetings between mentees and mentors difficult.

Outcomes of the Program

Over the period in which the UCAN Program has been piloted, there have been 15 Autistic or neurodivergent students enrolled and participated in the program in some capacity. Students who participated in UCAN expressed moderate to high satisfaction with the program, including social events and one-on-one meetings with their peers. Most students noted that they did not meet all the goals they had set for the year, but indicated that meeting with their mentor helped them work towards their goals. In addition to program satisfaction, students reported lower stress and stronger self-efficacy skills following their UCAN participation. Overall, these results highlight the potential benefit of peer mentorship for Autistic and neurodivergent youth in post-secondary education. The UCAN Program also provides unique opportunities for clinicians-in-training to learn how to work with a vulnerable, and often, misunderstood group, ensuring that our future psychologists will have the skills and expertise to better meet Autistic and neurodivergent mental health needs.

Based on the Experience of the Program, the Resultant Implications for Future Research, and/or Application of Such a Program

Preliminary data from UCAN demonstrates the demand, feasibility, and short-term effectiveness of a peer support model for Autistic and neurodivergent youth in higher education settings. Programs and supports, such as UCAN, and peer mentorship in general, may be a unique, feasible, and innovative way to promote academic success, mental health, and well-being and ensure that neurodivergent students graduate and thrive. Further research is needed to scale this work to support a larger group of neurodivergent students, as well as implementing a quasi-experimental study design to rigorously determine the efficacy of the UCAN Program over time for Autistic students relative to their neurotypical peers. More work is needed to understand whether there is an additional benefit of including neurodivergent students (versus neurotypical psychology graduate students) as mentors, as our advisory group and Autistic advocates have emphasised the value of having mentors and mentees that have a shared neurodivergent experience, while also balancing the unique mental health challenges these students often experience. Lastly, it is also essential for future research to determine the contextual barriers and facilitators for the long-term sustainability of peer mentor programs, such as UCAN, within the post-secondary landscape.

References

Ames, M.E., McMorris, C.A., Alli, L.N., and Bebko, J.M. (2016) 'Overview and evaluation of a mentorship program for university students with ASD', *Focus on Autism and Other Developmental Disabilities*, 31, 27–36.

Ames, M.E., Coombs, C.E.M., Duerksen, K., Vincent, J., and McMorris, C.A. (2022) 'Canadian mapping of autism-specific supports for postsecondary students', *Research in Autism Spectrum Disorder*, 90, 101899.

Anderson, K.A., Shattuck, P.T., Cooper, B.P., Roux, A.M., and Wagner, M. (2014) 'Prevalence and correlates of postsecondary residential status among young adults with an autism spectrum disorder', *Autism: The International Journal of Research and Practice*, 18(5), 562–570.

Anderson, A.H., Stephenson, J., and Carter, M. A. (2017) 'Systematic literature review of the experiences and supports of students with autism spectrum disorder in post-secondary education', *Research in Autism Spectrum Disorders*, 39, 33–53.

Barnhill, G.P. (2016) 'Supporting students with Asperger syndrome on college campuses: Current practices', *Focus on Autism and Other Developmental Disabilities*, 31(1), 3–15.

Cage, E., De Andres, M., and Mahoney, P. (2020) 'Understanding the factors that affect university completion for Autistic people', *Research in Autism Spectrum Disorders*, 72, 101519.

Charlton, J.I. (1998) *Nothing about Us without Us: Disability oppression and empowerment* (1st ed.). Berkeley, CA: University of California Press.

Coombs, E., Vincent, J., McMorris, C.A., and Ames, M.E. (2023) 'Barriers and facilitators to supporting Canadian Autistic postsecondary students: Experiences of accessible learning staff and administrators', *Research in Autism Spectrum Disorders*, 109. https://doi.org/10.2139/ssrn.4456013

Drake, S.M. (2017) *Academic success experiences of individuals with autism spectrum disorder* [Doctoral dissertation]. Minneapolis, MN: Walden University.

Duerksen, K., Besney, R., Ames, M., McMorris, C.A. (2021) 'Supporting Autistic adults in postsecondary settings: A systematic review of peer mentorship programs', *Autism in Adulthood*, 3(1) (online first).

Dwyer, P., Mineo, E., Mifsud, K., Lindholm, C., and Gurba, A. (2023) 'Building neurodiversity-inclusive postsecondary campuses: Recommendations for leaders in higher education', *Autism in Adulthood*, 5(1), 1–14.

Gallant, C., Roudbarani, F., Ibrahim, A., et al. (2023) 'Clinician knowledge, confidence, and treatment practices in their provision of psychotherapy to Autistic youth and youth with ADHD', *Journal of Autism and Developmental Disorders*, 53, 4214–4228.

Gelbar, N.W., Smith, I., and Reichow, B. (2014) 'Systematic review of articles describing experience and supports of individuals with autism enrolled in college and university programs', *Journal of Autism and Developmental Disorders*, 44, 2593–2601.

Gobbo, K., and Shmulsky, S. (2014) 'Faculty experience with college students with autism spectrum disorders: A qualitative study of challenges and solutions', *Focus on Autism and Other Developmental Disabilities*, 29(1), 3–22.

Gurbuz, E., Hanley, M., and Riby, D.M. (2019) 'University students with autism: The social and academic experiences of university in the UK', *Journal of Autism and Developmental Disorders*, 49(2), 617–631.

Kiyama, J., and Luca, S. (2014) 'Structured opportunities: Exploring the social and academic benefits for peer mentors in retention programs', *Journal of College Student Retention*, 15(4), 489–514.

McMorris, C.A., Baraskewich, J., Ames, M., Ncube, B., Shaikh, K., and Bebko, J.M. (2018) 'Mental health issues in post-secondary students with autism spectrum disorder: Experiences in accessing services', *International Journal of Mental Health and Addiction*, 17(3), 585–595.

National Center for Education Statistics. (2018) *Digest of education statistics.* https://nces.ed.gov/programs/digest/d18/tables/dt18_326.10.asp (accessed: 16 October 2020).

Newman, L., Wagner, M., Knokey, A.M., et al. (2011) *The post-high school outcomes of young adults with disabilities up to 8 years after high school: A report from the National Longitudinal Transition Study-2 (NLTS2).* https://eric.ed .gov/?id=ED524044 (accessed: 16 October 2020).

Pillay, Y., and Bhat, C.S. (2012) 'Facilitating support for students with Asperger's syndrome', *Journal of College Student Psychotherapy*, 26(2), 140–154.

Roux, A.M., Shattuck, P.T., Cooper, B.P., Anderson, K.A., Wagner, M., and Narendorf, S.C. (2013) 'Postsecondary employment experiences among young adults with an autism spectrum disorder', *Journal of the American Academy of Child & Adolescent Psychiatry*, 52(9), 931–937.

Stowe, L., O'Connell, J., Chew, S., Braun, R., and Kaipainen, E. (2022) *Equitable pathways to experiential learning*. University of Calgary, Taylor Institute for Teaching and Learning, Office of Experiential Learning.

Tinto, V. (1993) *Leaving college: Rethinking the causes and cures of student attrition* (2nd ed.). Chicago, IL: University of Chicago Press.

Van Hees, V., Moyson, T., and Roeyers, H. (2015) 'Higher education experiences of students with autism spectrum disorder: Challenges, benefits, and support needs', *Journal of Autism and Developmental Disorders*, 45(6), 1673–1688.

White, S.W., Ollendick, T.H., and Bray, B.C. (2011) 'College students on the autism spectrum: Prevalence and associated problems', *Autism*, 15(6), 683–701.

Yomtov, D., Plunkett, S., Efrat, R., and Marin, A. (2015) Can peer mentors improve first-year experiences of university students? *Journal of College Student Retention: Research, Theory & Practice*, 19(1), 25–44.

Universiti Kebangsaan Malaysia

Elevating Career Support for
Students Displaying a Number of
Autistic Traits

Mohd Syazwan Zainal

Background

This chapter explores the challenges faced by students displaying several Autistic traits (referred to in this profile as "high Autistic traits") in Malaysian universities, emphasising the critical need for tailored support and data-driven strategies. High Autistic traits refer to characteristics associated with autism that are more pronounced, including difficulties with social communication, rigid or repetitive behaviors, heightened sensory sensitivities, and intense focus on specific interests, even if the individual does not have a formal Autism diagnosis. (The editors note that this language may not align with the Neurodiversity Paradigm, but that this was the approach and terminology used in this study.) The lack of data on Autistic students, especially in public universities, is a significant concern, with many students remaining under-diagnosed or having hidden statuses due to societal stigma, limited awareness, and subtle presentations of Autistic traits. Factors such as unrecognised symptoms during childhood and a lack of accessible diagnostic services in educational contexts contribute to this underrepresentation. Aligned with the theme of this book, this profile highlights key findings from a study conducted on nearly 1,400 undergraduate students at a public university in Malaysia, representing a population of approximately 20,000 students. The study also explored their learning experiences and how these contributed to shaping their career self-efficacy, as the ultimate goal after graduation is to transition into the job market. Comparisons were made between groups with low and high Autistic traits. Using a preliminary and unvalidated instrument—the new version of the AQ-28 Malays—this study found that over 30% of the sampled students exhibited high Autistic traits. Although the translated tool has not yet undergone full validation and was used exclusively for this study, the findings indicate a potentially higher prevalence of students with high Autistic traits compared to figures reported in other countries using validated instruments. Besides that, the majority of students in this high Autistic traits category are enrolled in science-related fields, aligning with both the composition of the study sample and patterns observed in international research.

DOI: 10.4324/9781003495925-16

Additionally, students with high Autistic traits face notable barriers in developing career self-efficacy, often due to challenges in social communication and limited involvement in career-related activities. Despite external encouragement boosting their confidence, these students often struggle to translate personal achievements into career readiness. This highlights the critical need for personalised feedback, structured reflection opportunities, and explicit career guidance tailored to their unique strengths and challenges. Besides that, integrating practical experiences such as internships and mentorship programs can help bridge the gap between academic success and professional preparedness. Addressing these gaps is essential not only for fostering inclusive academic environments but also for empowering neurodivergent students to confidently transition into fulfilling careers.

Discussion

In the dynamic environment of Malaysian university campuses, students from diverse backgrounds converge, each contributing unique perspectives and experiences. Among these are students displaying high levels of Autistic traits—a group whose specific needs and characteristics often go unnoticed. This lack of recognition is partly attributed to the scarcity of data and statistics capturing the presence of Autistic students, particularly in Malaysian public universities (Low et al., 2024; Zainal et al., 2024a). Factors such as undisclosed diagnoses, underdiagnosis, and misdiagnosis contribute to this gap. Societal stigma, limited awareness, and the subtle presentation of Autistic traits, especially in high-functioning individuals, exacerbate the issue (Zener, 2019). Additionally, the lack of accessible diagnostic services within educational settings complicates identification (Hine et al., 2020). These challenges underscore the urgent need for greater awareness and systemic efforts to address the hidden realities faced by students with high Autistic traits in Malaysian universities.

Through the research conducted, the study sought to understand neurodivergent conditions by categorising students into two distinct groups: those with high Autistic traits and those with lower levels. Although the instrument used was not clinical (Zainal et al., 2024a), the assessment found that approximately 33% of the students fell into the high Autistic traits category, regardless of whether they had a formal diagnosis. Notably, only one student in this group had a confirmed autism diagnosis, while ten others suspected they might be on the spectrum but had not received formal confirmation. This gap between high Autistic traits and formal diagnosis highlights potential issues in identification and awareness among students. Several factors may contribute to this discrepancy, including reluctance to seek formal assessments, unrecognised symptoms during childhood, or limited access to resources and support systems that encourage diagnostic evaluations (Hus & Segal, 2021). Additionally, many individuals with high Autistic traits develop coping strategies that mask their challenges, making it less likely for them to be referred for assessments (Oswald et al., 2018). These findings underscore the need for universities to improve awareness and provide accessible pathways for students to seek appropriate evaluations and support.

Universities play a crucial role in supporting students with diverse needs, and providing accessible diagnostic resources and tailored support services is essential in helping students better understand and manage their traits. In this study, some students with high Autistic traits reported having documented medical histories, highlighting the potential overlap between Autistic traits and other health conditions. This intersection points to the importance of comprehensive support systems that address both academic and health-related challenges (Sefotho and Onyishi, 2020). Co-occurring conditions such as anxiety, depression, and sensory processing difficulties can further complicate the recognition and support of students with Autistic traits, reinforcing the need for holistic approaches to ensure both academic success and personal well-being (Shattuck et al., 2011).

This study also highlighted substantial differences between the two groups (high and low Autistic traits) across various domains of Autistic traits, extending beyond mere academic scores to affect multiple aspects of behaviour and cognition. This finding emphasises the diverse ways Autistic traits can manifest, influencing how students interact with their environment and pursue their studies (McLeod et al., 2021). The variability in how Autistic traits manifest can occur due to individual differences in sensory processing, communication styles, and cognitive preferences (American Psychiatric Association, 2013). These differences impact how students engage with their academic environment, highlighting the need for personalised support strategies that accommodate diverse needs (Shattuck et al., 2011). Understanding these profiles is not just an academic exercise—it has real implications for how universities support their students. By acknowledging the varied manifestations of Autistic traits and providing tailored support, educational institutions can foster an environment where all students, regardless of their traits, have the opportunity to succeed and thrive (McLeod et al., 2021). This approach not only benefits the students directly but also enriches the academic community as a whole by embracing and supporting diversity in all its forms.

By addressing these challenges and implementing targeted strategies, universities in Malaysia can create environments where students with high Autistic traits are empowered to thrive academically, socially, and professionally. Tailored interventions and collaborations are essential in unlocking the full potential of neurodivergent students, fostering a culture of inclusion that benefits the entire academic community. At present, two related articles have been published in Malaysian-indexed journals, providing general insights into the findings of the study (Zainal et al., 2024a, 2024b). The study has been presented at the university level to address issues of student diversity, potential underdiagnosis, and strategies to enhance support services for neurodivergent or Autistic students. This effort aligns with Malaysia's national agenda to enhance disability services in higher education. The findings have raised awareness among university stakeholders, emphasising the limited research on Autistic traits in Malaysia, particularly within universities. Building on this, the author has been awarded a national grant to explore the levels of Autistic traits among adolescents in boarding schools, focusing on their academic experiences and adaptation processes in determining their post-school pathways. This is especially relevant, as many Autistic students tend to pursue science-related fields at the university level.

Conclusion

This study underscores the critical need for Malaysian universities to address the unique challenges faced by students with high Autistic traits. Significant gaps in institutional support, including the absence of comprehensive data on the prevalence of these students, highlight systemic issues. Barriers such as societal stigma, underdiagnosis, and the under-recognition of Autistic traits—particularly in females—further emphasise the need for targeted interventions. Addressing these challenges is essential to improving academic success, personal development, and career preparedness for neurodivergent students. Malaysian universities have a pivotal role in bridging these gaps by enhancing data collection, improving diagnostic accessibility, and establishing comprehensive support systems. Gender-sensitive approaches, inclusive curricula, and tailored career counselling are essential to meeting the diverse needs of neurodivergent students. Additionally, fostering collaborative partnerships with the broader community can strengthen these efforts, ensuring that initiatives are impactful and sustainable. By prioritising inclusivity and understanding, universities can create environments that empower neurodivergent students to thrive. These efforts not only enhance the well-being and success of the students themselves but also enrich the academic community, fostering a more equitable, diverse, and dynamic educational landscape. Such commitments to inclusivity are vital in ensuring that all students, regardless of their neurodivergent traits, have the opportunity to excel and contribute meaningfully to society.

References

American Psychiatric Association. (2013) *Diagnostic and* statistical manual of mental disorders *(DSM-5)* (5th ed.). Washington DC: American Psychiatric Publishing. https://doi.org/10.4324/9780203772287-23

Hine, J.F., Allin, J., Allman, A., Black, M., Browning, B., Ramsey, B., Swanson, A., Warren, Z.E., Zawoyski, A., and Allen, W. (2020) 'Increasing access to autism spectrum disorder diagnostic consultation in rural and underserved communities: Streamlined evaluation within primary care', *Journal of Developmental & Behavioral Pediatrics*, 41, 16–22.

Hus, Y., and Segal, O. (2021) 'Challenges surrounding the diagnosis of autism in children', *Neuropsychiatric Disease and Treatment*, 17, 3509–3529. https://doi.org/10.2147/NDT.S282569

Low, H.M., Zainal, M.S., Pang, J.C., Ang, Y., and de Vries, M. (2024) 'Self-reported Autistic traits and psychosocial outcomes among university students in Malaysia', *Autism*, 28, 174–186. https://doi.org/10.1177/13623613231167501

McLeod, J.D., Hawbaker, A., and Meanwell, E. (2021) 'The health of college students on the autism spectrum as compared to their neurotypical peers', *Autism*, 25, 719–730. https://doi.org/10.1177/1362361320926070

Oswald, T.M., Winder-Patel, B., Ruder, S., Xing, G., Stahmer, A., and Solomon, M. (2018) 'A pilot randomized controlled trial of the ACCESS program: A group intervention to improve social, adaptive functioning, stress coping, and self-determination outcomes in young adults with autism spectrum disorder', *Journal of Autism and Developmental Disorders*, 48, 1742–1760. https://doi.org/10.1007/s10803-017-3421-9

Sefotho, M.M., and Onyishi, C.N. (2020) 'Transition to higher education for students with autism: Challenges and support needs', *International Journal of Higher Education*, 10, 201. https://doi.org/10.5430/ijhe.v10n1p201

Shattuck, P.T., Wagner, M., Narendorf, S., Sterzing, P., and Hensley, M. (2011) 'Post-high school service use among young adults with an autism spectrum disorder', *Archives of Pediatrics & Adolescent Medicine*, 165, 141–146. https://doi.org/10.1001/archpediatrics.2010.279

Zainal, M.S., Low, H.M., and Ismail, H.N. (2024a) 'Autistic profiles among undergraduate students in Malaysia: A descriptive analysis', *Jurnal Pendidikan Bitara*, 17, 2821–3173. https://doi.org/https://doi.org/10.37134/bitara.vol17.sp.10.2024

Zainal, M.S., Low, H.M., and Ismail, H.N. (2024b) 'The relationship of learning experience and career self-efficacy among undergraduate students from a public university in Malaysia', *Jurnal Pendidikan*, 49, 84–91. https://doi.org/10.17576/JPEN

Zener, D. (2019) 'Journey to diagnosis for women with autism', *Advances in Autism*. https://doi.org/10.1108/AIA-10-2018-0041

Curtin University, Western Australia

Specialist Mentoring Program

Jasmine McDonald and Sylvanna Mirichlis

Program Background

The Curtin University Specialist Mentoring Program (CSMP) was founded in 2014 at Western Australia's largest university situated in Perth, Western Australia. As of 2023, Curtin University had more than 60,000 enrolled students across its Australian and international campuses. This presently includes 3,628 students who had reported a disability (Curtin University, 2023). The program was devised to address educational inequity particularly experienced by Autistic tertiary students, one of the most potentially talented, yet disadvantaged, disability groups studying at university.

Research has shown that the number of Autistic students accessing tertiary education in Australia has continuously increased, with these students facing unique challenges in their academic and personal lives (Autism Spectrum Australia, 2012; Hastwell et al., 2013; Hedley et al., 2018; Howlin, 2013, 2021; Howlin and Magiati, 2017; Owen et al., 2016; White, Ollendick, and Bray, 2011). Generalised disability supports, such as reasonable adjustments in their nominated courses, had been found to be insufficient for Autistic students, reflecting a need for systemic change (Gelbar, Smith, and Reichow, 2014; van Hees, Moyson, and Roeyers, 2014). Australian Bureau of Statistics' (ABS) data continuously indicated that Autistic individuals were less likely than any other disability group to complete an educational qualification beyond high school. Recent ABS data have indicated that only 8.1% of Autistic Australians had completed a bachelor degree or higher, compared with 16.1% of those with a disability and 31.2% of those without a disability (AMCoP, 2020, p. 1).

Furthermore, Autistic students were found to experience higher rates of attrition and burnout, as well as generally poorer mental health than their allistic peers (Autism Spectrum Australia, 2012; Cage and McManemy, 2022). These results reflected the enduring disadvantage experienced by Autistic adults who were more likely than their allistic counterparts to experience difficulties in employment, social relationships, physical and mental health, and quality of life (Howlin, 2013, 2021). These inequities have remained persistent despite the substantial cognitive abilities and talents commonly found

DOI: 10.4324/9781003495925-17

amongst the Autistic population indicating a significant loss of intellectual potential within the Australian tertiary and employment sector (Meilleur, Jelenic, and Mottron, 2015).

In response to the potentially high number of Autistic students studying at Curtin University, Dr. Jasmine McDonald and Dr. Theresa Kidd were tasked in 2013, to devise a program to more effectively support Autistic students studying at the university. McDonald and Kidd's comprehensive experience with neurodivergence within their own families, in their employment and own research situated them well to lead such a project (McDonald, 2010, 2014; McDonald and Lopes, 2014; Kidd and Kaczmarek, 2010). This coincided with the university's responsibility to provide educational equity for all disabled students in response to Australian legislative requirements set out in the Disability Discrimination Act (1992) and the Disability Standards for Education (2005) and their own successive Disability Access and Inclusion Plans and Student Support Policies.

Program Aims and Components

In response to these inequities and the university's legal responsibilities, CSMP was created by adapting components of a small number of successful international tertiary peer mentoring programs specifically designed to support Autistic students (Bebko, Schroeder, and Ames, 2011; Hastwell et al., 2013; Mowat, Cooper, and Gilson, 2011; Wolf, Brown, and Bork, 2009). The core components of the mentoring program are illustrated in Figure P6.1.

The program's overall aim was to increase educational equity and decrease disadvantage by fostering Autistic students' academic potential, well-being, and independence. The peer mentoring approach adopted was akin to that

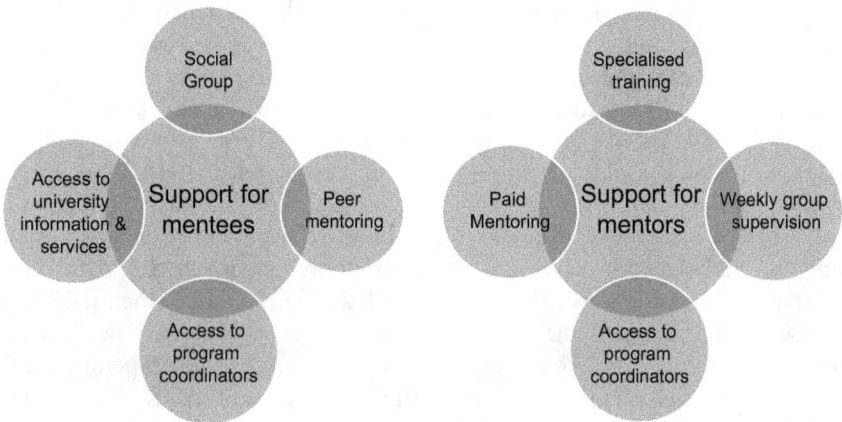

Figure P6.1 Core components of CSMP.

of a coaching relationship with mentors and mentees being carefully matched based upon such criteria as the mentee's needs, goals, interests, and areas of study. Mentors work collaboratively with their mentees to identify and address their academic, career, and personal goals. Mentors and mentees organise weekly online/face-to-face meetings focusing on their mentee's unique requirements. As a duty of care measure, mentors provide fortnightly reports detailing their mentee's progress and attend weekly online group supervision overseen by experienced coordinators.

Peer mentors are recruited by the coordinators throughout the year from a pool of competitive postgraduate and honours Curtin University students with the majority studying Health Science courses. All mentors are provided with comprehensive evidenced-informed training and with resources such as the Mentor Toolkit (McDonald et al., 2016c). The Toolkit is revised yearly to ensure mentors are prepared to support their Autistic mentees appropriately with best practice materials and methods. Mentors use person-centred/strengths-based practice including an understanding of collaborative decision making, role boundaries, goal setting, employment, and critical mental health support. Training includes contributions by CSMP coordinators/mentees/mentors, registered psychologists, and career advisors to afford new mentors with a well-informed start to their mentoring career.

With the support of the program coordinators, a social group is collaboratively organised by a committee of mentees and mentors who build a sense of community and provide a safe socialising space for members of the program. The group meets weekly to enjoy games, discussions, excursions, and guest speakers and is a fundamental part of CSMP.

Impacts and Outcomes of the Program

In 2014, CSMP began with five mentees and by the end of the year was providing mentoring to 17 students. This mentee pool nearly doubled the following year to 32 students (McDonald et al., 2016b). From 2017 to 2023 the program experienced an average new intake growth rate of 34.7% per year (Mirichlis, 2024). Across the decade only one full-time equivalent coordinator position was allocated despite the ever-increasing number of mentees supported by the program growing from five to upwards of 75. The size of the program was eventually capped in 2022 at 75 mentees, accompanied by the implementation of a waitlist due to a lack of appropriate resourcing to manage the increasing demand for the program (Mirichlis, 2024).

As depicted in Figure P6.2, there has been a steady retention of mentees within the program, ranging from approximately 66–78% retained, including a retention of 73.3% of mentees retained from the end of 2022 to November 2023. Of those who did not continue with the program into 2023, 12% pursued further studies and 14.7% had graduated from their studies (Mirichlis, 2024).

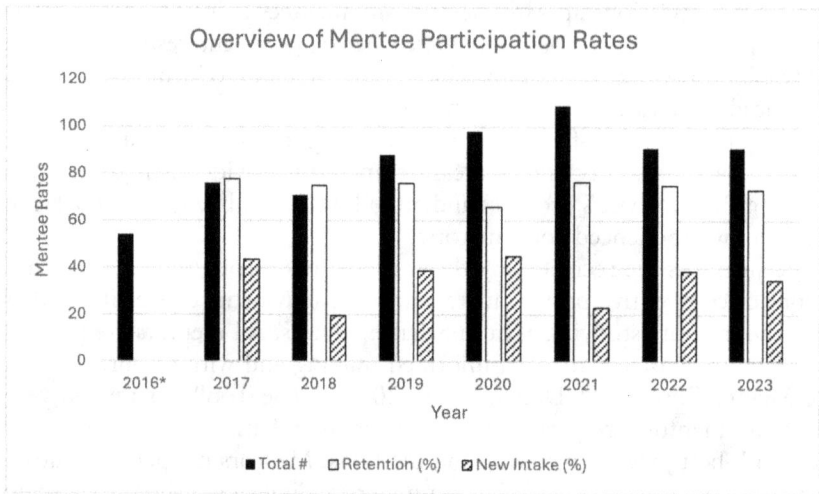

Figure P6.2 Mentee participation rates.

At the request of the Autism Cooperative Research Centre for Living with Autism (Autism CRC) and based on the initial success of CSMP, a manualised version of CSMP was developed covering the training, mentee, mentor, and coordinator experience. In 2016, these resources became freely available on the Autism CRC website (Autism CRC, 2016; McDonald et al., 2016a, 2016b, 2016c).

Internal and external mixed method evaluations of CSMP have consistently demonstrated the positive impact that the program makes to the educational experiences and outcomes of Autistic students and their mentors (Hamilton, 2015; Hamilton et al., 2016; Siew, 2014; Siew et al., 2017). External evaluations of the program indicated its efficacy with reports of mentees experiencing increased support, decreased social communication apprehension, and high satisfaction with the program (Siew, 2014; Siew et al., 2017). Mentors indicated that they gained valuable training, supervision support, leadership experience, and career-related skills, including specialist communications, increased confidence working with Autistic students, advocacy skills, increased awareness of the benefits of diversity, and the skills to appropriately support that diversity (Hamilton, 2015; Hamilton et al., 2016).

Following the success of CSMP and based on the Autism CRC manualised program, a similar service was established at the University of Western Australia in 2015/16 (McDonald et al., 2016a, 2016b, 2016c). Evaluations of both programs indicated that specialised training for mentors and support for mentee social interaction and their specific communication needs were beneficial (Thompson et al., 2018). The modeling and roleplaying integrated into the mentee-mentor partnership was also found to be crucial to the positive changes achieved (Thompson et al., 2020). Parents reported that the program worked to bridge the gap between university participation and the broader environment for young Autistic adults. Parents also attributed maturation and improvement in their relationship with their offspring at university to their involvement in these mentoring programs (Thompson et al., 2021). This evaluative work has highlighted that despite discriminatory assumptions sometimes made about Autistic students, they are indeed capable of participating and thriving in tertiary education when supported appropriately (Thompson et al., 2018).

Most recently, in a 2023 annual internal mentee and mentor feedback survey, Mirichlis (2024) reported that mentees rated CSMP to be at least "very good" M = 3.17, SD = 0.92 (out of a possible score of 4). In terms of usefulness in achieving their goals, on average mentees rated CSMP as between moderately and very useful (M = 3.7, SD = 1.20), with 62.5% reporting CSMP to be at least very useful in helping them to work toward their goals. On average mentees reported their mentors to be somewhat helpful in increasing their employability (M = 2.58, SD = 1.31).

Nine mentees reported gaining some form of employment experience during 2023 including three internships. On average mentees reported that their mentor helped them to engage with university life moderately well (M = 2.95, SD = 1.27). Mentees reported receiving support from their mentors in the following areas:

- University belonging: connecting with services available at university, and joining Student Guild clubs
- Social communication: interacting with strangers, communicating with academic staff, social skills, relationship advice, building relationships with peers, and dealing with conflict
- Academic skills: group work/projects, presentations, planning, prioritising, organising, study skills, time management, and referencing
- Mental health: knowledge about emotions and emotion management, stress relief, and accessing Curtin Counseling
- Employability: networking, work opportunities, and workplace/meeting etiquette

On average mentors rated CSMP 8.63 (SD = 1.30) out of a possible ten (being "excellent"), with 84.21% rating the program as at least "very good." Mentors indicated that their experience in the program helped them to develop skills that they could transfer into their profession (M = 4.11, out of a possible 5, SD = 1.02). Mentors reported gaining skills and knowledge in communication, active listening, and rapport building; organisation; and psychological literacy, neurodiversity, empathy, and self-awareness.

Challenges

In a 2022 report, the Australian Federal Government listed tertiary institutions that have trailed peer mentoring programs inclusive of Curtin University, the Australian National University, the University of Newcastle, the University of

Tasmania, and the Australian Catholic University's Autism Inclusion Program (SSCoA, 2022). The report indicated that some of these programs have utilised the range of Autism CRC free resources developed by Curtin University. Tertiary peer mentoring programs were identified as a mechanism for support during the transition into and ongoing participation in higher education, with such programs found to be significantly beneficial for Autistic students (SSCoA, 2022).

Despite the significance of peer mentoring programs discussed in the report, several significant challenges were also identified. Namely, uncertainty of funding was flagged as a major barrier to future-proofing these supports with a call being made for the Australian Federal Government to establish a funding pathway dedicated to such programs (SSCoA, 2022). Additionally, it was recommended that a review of the specialist mentoring programs across the tertiary education sector be conducted to generate benchmarks for quality practice and to support informed decision-making for Autistic people when considering university options (SSCoA, 2022).

The report also identified barriers to identifying students who may benefit from these supports due to the proportion of non-disclosure of diagnoses by Autistic students for fear of discrimination. The committee recommended that autism awareness should be integrated into the professional development of all university staff including those in teaching, administrative, and support roles (SSCoA, 2022).

With its ever-growing evidence base over the past ten years, the CSMP experience has increasingly proven its value for this cohort of tertiary Autistic students. Unfortunately, resourcing educational equity has proven inadequate and insecure, depriving many young people of their educational and life potential. This subsequently robs Australia of what could be their best intellectual potential. As reiterated in the Australian Federal Government report (SSCoA, 2022), the provision of ongoing staff professional development in inclusive educational practice must also accompany any evidence-based programs for this cohort of Autistic students. Without this contextual change, Autistic students will continue to struggle to find a sense of belonging and flourish in tertiary education.

References

Autism Mentoring Community of Practice (AMCoP). (2020) *Submission to the 2020 review of the disability standards for education 2005.* www.education.gov.au/disability-standards-education-2005/consultations/consultations-2020-review-disability-standards-education-2005/submission/10758 (accessed: 10 October 2024).

Autism Cooperative Research Centre. (2016) *Peer mentoring program for Autistic university students.* www.autismcrc.com.au/knowledge-centre/reports/peer-mentoring-program-autistic-university-students (accessed: 10 October 2024).

Autism Spectrum Australia. (2012) *We belong: Investigating the experiences, aspirations and needs of adults with Asperger's disorder and high functioning autism.* www.aspect. org.au/uploads/documents/Research/Autism_Spectrum_WE_BELONG_Rese arch_Report-FINAL_LR_R.pdf (accessed: 22 October 2024).

Bebko, J., Schroeder, J., and Ames, M. (2011) *A mentoring program for students with Asperger & ASDs.* https://campusmentalhealth.ca/wp-content/uploads/2018/ 03/A-Mentoring-Program-for-Students-with-Asperger-and-ASDs.pdf

Cage, E., and McManemy, E. (2022) 'Burn out and dropping out: A comparison of the experiences of Autistic and non-Autistic students during the COVID-19 pandemic', *Frontiers in Psychology*, 12(792945), 1–16. DOI:10.3389/fpsyg.2021.79294.

Curtin University. (2023), *Annual report 2023.* www.curtin.edu.au/file/pdf/curtin-university-annual-report-2023.pdf (accessed: 1 November 2024).

Gelbar, N.W., Smith, I., and Reichow, B. (2014) 'Systematic review of articles describing experience and supports of individuals with autism enrolled in college and university programs', *Journal of Autism and Developmental Disorders*, 44(10), 2593–2601. DOI:10.1007/s10803-014-2135-5.

Hamilton, J. (2015) Training and experience of mentors working with tertiary students with an autism spectrum disorder. Master of Psychology (Clinical) dissertation. Perth, WA: Curtin University.

Hamilton, J., Stevens, G., and Girdler, S. (2016) 'Becoming a mentor: The impact of training and the experience of mentoring university students on the autism spectrum', *PLoS One*, 11(4). DOI:10.1371/journal.pone.0153204.

Hastwell, J., Harding, J., Martin, N., and Baron-Cohen, S. (2013) *Asperger syndrome student project, 2009–12: Final project report.* www.admin.cam.ac.uk/univ/disabil ity/asperger/project.html

Hedley, D., Uljarevic, M., Foley, K., Richdale, A., and Trollor, J. (2018) 'Risk and protective factors underlying depression and suicidal ideation in autism spectrum disorder', *Depression and Anxiety*, 35, 648–657. DOI:10.1002/da.22759.

van Hees, V., Moyson, T., and Roeyers, H. (2014) 'Higher education experiences of students with autism spectrum disorder: Challenges, benefits and support needs', *Journal of Autism and Developmental Disorders*, 45, 1673–1688. DOI:10.1007/ s10803-014-2324-2.

Howlin, P. (2013) 'Social disadvantage & exclusion: Adults with autism lag far behind employment prospects', *Child & Adolescent Psychiatry*, 52(9), 897–899. DOI:10.1016/j.jaac.2013.06.010.

Howlin, P. (2021) 'Adults with autism: Changes in understanding since DSM-111', *Journal of Autism and Developmental Disorders*, 51(12), 4291–4308. DOI:10.1007/ s10803-020-04847-z.

Howlin, P., and Magiati, I. (2017) 'Autism spectrum disorder: Outcomes in adulthood', *Current Opinion in Psychiatry*, 30(2), 69–76. DOI:10.1097/ YCO.0000000000000308.

Kidd, T., and Kaczmarek, E. (2010) 'The experiences of mothers home educating their children with autism spectrum disorder', *Issues in Educational Research*, 20(3), 257–275.

McDonald, J. (2010) Seeking progressive fit: A constructivist grounded theory and autoethnographic study investigating how parents deal with the education of their child with an autism spectrum disorder (ASD) over time. Unpublished Doctor of Philosophy Thesis, The University of Western Australia.

McDonald, J. (2014) *How parents deal with the education of their child on the autism spectrum: The stories and research they don't and won't tell you.* Rotterdam: Sense Publishers.

McDonald, J., and Lopes, E. (2014) 'How parents home educate their children with an autism spectrum disorder with the support of the Schools of Isolated and Distance Education', *International Journal of Inclusive Education*, 18(1), 1–17. DOI:10.1080/13603116.2012.751634.

McDonald, J., Kidd, T., Ting Siew, C., Hamilton, J., Unwin, L., Thompson, C., Evans, K., Black, M., D'Abrera, J., and Girdler, S. (2016a) *Specialist peer mentoring module: Mentee information booklet.* www.autismcrc.com.au/sites/default/files/inline-files/Peer_mentoring_-_Module_Mentee_Information_Booklet.pdf (accessed: 22 October 2024).

McDonald, J., Kidd, T., Ting Siew, C., Hamilton, J., Unwin, L., Thompson, C., Evans, K., Black, M., D'Abrera, J., and Girdler, S. (2016b) *Specialist peer mentoring module: Program coordinator manual.* www.autismcrc.com.au/sites/default/files/inline-files/Peer_mentoring_-_Module_Coordinator_Manual.pdf (accessed: 22 October 2024).

McDonald, J., Kidd, T., Ting Siew, C., Hamilton, J., Unwin, L., Thompson, C., Evans, K., Black, M., D'Abrera, J., and Girdler, S. (2016c) *Specialist peer mentoring module: Specialist mentor toolkit.* www.autismcrc.com.au/sites/default/files/inline-files/Peer_mentoring_-_Module_Specialist_Mentor_Toolkit.pdf (accessed: 22 October 2024).

Meilleur, A.-A., Jelenic, P., and Mottron, L. (2015) 'Prevalence of clinically and empirically defined talents and strengths in autism', *Journal of Autism Development Disorders*, 45(5). DOI:10.1007/s10803-014-2296-2.

Mirichlis, S. (2024) 'Autism mentoring program coordinator manual', *PsychArchives*. https://doi.org/10.23668/psycharchives.15522

Mowat, C., Cooper, A., and Gilson, L. (2011) *Supporting students on the autism spectrum: Student mentor guidelines.* www.autism.org.uk/~/media/NAS/Documents/Workingwith/Education/NAS-Student-Mentor-Guide_LowRes.ashx (accessed: 22 October 2024).

Owen, C., McCann, D., Rayner, C., Devereaux, C., Sheehan, F., and Quarmby, L. (2016) *Supporting students with autism spectrum disorder in higher education.* www.ncsehe.edu.au/wpcontent/uploads/2016/03/Supporting-Students-with-Autism-Spectrum-Disorder-in-Higher-Education.pdf (accessed: 22 October 2024).

Senate Select Committee on Autism (SSCoA). (2022) *Support and life outcomes for Autistic Australians.* www.aph.gov.au/Parliamentary_Business/Committees/Senate/Autism/autism/Report (accessed: 10 October 2024).

Siew, C. (2014) An evaluation of the Curtin Specialist Mentoring Program for university students on the autism spectrum. Unpublished Master of Psychology (Clinical) Dissertation, Perth, WA: Curtin University.

Siew, C., Mazzucchelli, T., Rooney, R., and Girdler, S. (2017) 'A specialist peer mentoring program for university students on the autism spectrum: A pilot study', *PLoS One*, 12(7). DOI:10.1371/journal.pone.0180854.

Thompson, C., Falkmer, T., Evans, K., Bölte, S., and Girdler, S. (2018) 'A realist evaluation of peer mentoring support for university students with autism', *British Journal of Special Education*, 45(4). DOI:10.1111/1467-8578.12241.

Thompson, C., McDonald, J., Kidd, T., Falkmer, T., Bölte, S., and Girdler, S. (2020) ' "I don't want to be a patient": Peer mentoring partnership fosters communication for Autistic university students', *Scandinavian Journal of Occupational Therapy*, 1(16). DOI:10.1080/11038128.2020.1738545.

Thompson, C., Milbourn, B., Taylor, J., Falkmer, T., Bölte, S., Evans, K., and Girdler, S. (2021) 'Experiences of parents of specialist peer mentored Autistic university students', *Developmental Neurorehabilitation*, 24(6), 368–378. DOI:10.1080/17518423.2021.1886190.

White, S., Ollendick, T., and Bray, B. (2011) 'College students on the autism spectrum: Prevalence and associated problems', *Autism*, 15, 683–701. DOI:10.1177/1362361310393363.

Wolf, L., Thierfeld Brown, J., and Kukiela Bork, G. (2009) *Students with Asperger syndrome: A guide for college personnel.* Shawnee, KS: Autism Asperger Publishing Co.

Curtin University, Western Australia

AASQA Program

Ben Milbourn, Tele Tan, Elinda Ai Lim Lee, Susan Hall, Lucy Simons and Sonya Girdler

Overview

Launched in 2016, the Autism Academy for Software Quality Assurance (AASQA) is an innovative Australian program designed to support Autistic adolescents in gaining information and communication technology (ICT) related and work readiness skills to support successful employment outcomes (Lee et al., 2019). The program offered by Curtin University in Western Australia has supported approximately 680 Autistic adolescents to date. The program is supported by community volunteers, university students, as well as paid staff (1.6 full-time equivalent). The team provides face-to-face mentorship and support to Autistic youth through a range of technology activities, including CoderDojo (coding clubs), hackathons, career tasting, international software testing qualifications examination, work placement, and work-integrated learning internship scholarships. The program adopts a philosophy of "nothing about us without us", striving to co-produce programs and research where possible.

Australian Context

In 2022 in Australia, 290,900 individuals were diagnosed as Autistic (Australian Bureau of Statistics [ABS], 2024), a neurodevelopmental condition characterised by focused interests and repetitive behaviours in the presence of social communication challenges (American Psychiatric Association [APA], 2013). The prevalence of autism diagnoses in Australia is increasing, evidenced by a 41.8% increase in individuals with autism diagnoses between 2018 and 2022 (ABS, 2024), suggesting a growing need for services to support Autistic individuals to flourish and experience improved quality of life (Merrington et al., 2024).

DOI: 10.4324/9781003495925-18

Strengths, Skills, and Employment

Keen attention to detail, strong memory, technical and mathematic skills, trustworthiness, and loyalty have been consistently identified as strengths of many Autistic individuals (de Schipper et al., 2016; Cope and Remington, 2022). While not all Autistic individuals may share technology interests, Autistic individuals, and employers have highlighted these skills as assets in the workplace (Scott et al., 2019; Cope and Remington, 2022). This is not to stereotype based on particular skill sets or assumptions regarding technical skills but to identify a niche for those who do have these skills. It is also important to acknowledge that in an employment situation, it should not be necessary for an Autistic individual to deliver additional value or skills over and above their peers to secure a job. Autistic individuals continue to face challenges in obtaining and maintaining employment (Chen et al., 2015; Wilczynski et al., 2013). In Australia, less than half (38%) of Autistic adults of working age (15–64) are employed. This employment rate is lower than people with and without a disability, with employment rates of 53.4% and 84.1%, respectively (ABS, 2019), highlighting the need for employment support for Autistic individuals. Inequitable employment opportunities can negatively impact Autistic adults' self-esteem, sense of purpose, and personal independence, contributing to economic hardship (Hedley et al., 2017).

The AASQA Program

The AASQA Program—created by the Curtin Autism Research Group at Curtin University—differs from other approaches focused on the remediation of viewed impairments. Instead, Autistic individuals' strengths are championed, providing the opportunity for skill development in inclusive environments (Lee et al., 2020; Jones et al., 2018). Acknowledging it "takes a village to raise a child", the AASQA Program focuses on developing and fostering an interest in science, technology, engineering, and math (STEM) education. The AASQA Program aims to assist young Autistic individuals in accessing further training and valued employment in ICT and related fields through supported pathways (Girdler et al., 2023; Lee et al., 2019).

In partnership with a dedicated "village" including educators, volunteers, community groups, government agencies, funding bodies, and business partners, AASQA delivers a free service for Autistic individuals aged 12–18 years old, collectively benefitting Autistic individuals, their families, industry, and the community (Girdler at al., 2023).

Program Features

The AASQA Program focuses on three key aspects (Crooks, 2023):

- High school student outreach
- ICT training and education support
- Work experience opportunities and internships for young Autistic individuals

CoderDojo

The AASQA CoderDojo Program is part of the CoderDojo Western Australian network of coding which delivers a strengths-based extra-curricular program for young Autistic individuals (called ninjas) interested in coding and computers (Lee et al., 2019). CoderDojo sessions run for two hours on Saturdays during the Curtin University semester, for approximately 10 weeks (Lee et al., 2023). Within this program, ninjas are guided by trained volunteer facilitators in a safe and inclusive environment that enables them to harness their skills and interests (Lee et al., 2019, 2020). Technical support is provided by trained facilitators or mentors who have experience in or are enrolled in computer science, software engineering, or cybersecurity university courses (Lee et al., 2023). Allied health students work alongside the ninjas, promoting the development of their emotional regulation and social communication skills (Jones et al., 2023a). Ninjas can choose between groups of various topics based on the facilitator's technical skills. These groups have previously focused on coding, Arduino, Lego Robotics, or Nao Robotics (Lee et al., 2019).

The AASQA CoderDojo has also seen previous ninjas return to the program as mentors, supporting younger students, and continuing to develop their skills in ICT fields.

Work Experience

Older students (aged 15–18) within the AASQA Program are offered the opportunity to participate in AASQA's work experience program (Girdler et al., 2023; Jones et al., 2021). AASQA collaborates with the Australian Computer Society Foundation (ACS) and the Autism Association of Western Australia to deliver this program in which participants can access scholarships and be supported to overcome employment barriers through personalised plans and job coaching (Crooks, 2023).

During work experience, participants attend a short-term placement of five to ten, seven-hour days in ICT-related organisations. The placements expose participants to workplaces that match their interests, strengths, skills, and abilities (Lee et al., 2019). The program aims to prepare young Autistic individuals to manage the transition from high school to post-school areas, and enter the workforce (Lee et al., 2019, Jones et al., 2023a). Education on workplace expectations is provided by Autism service providers who give an overview of the job tasks before the commencement of the placement (Lee et al., 2019). They then provide ongoing phone or in-person support to participants.

AASQA facilitates autism awareness workshops for interested host organisations (Lee et al., 2019). Job tasks undertaken by young Autistic individuals vary across worksites and provide them with opportunities to build upon the skills developed through the CoderDojo Program.

Internships

Participants who pursue undergraduate-level studies are provided support obtaining and participating in internships that offer paid employment for up to 12 months. In the internship program, AASQA collaborates with the ACS to support participants and workplaces through the interview and onboarding process. Support includes clearly defining participants' roles, identifying well-suited job tasks, and the provision of education and resources to create autism-friendly working environments (Crooks, 2023; Girdler et al., 2023). AASQA and ACS assist employers in supporting and caring for young Autistic individuals in the workplace, providing Autistic individuals with the opportunity to develop innovative working approaches as they build their careers in ICT fields.

Outcomes

The AASQA Program has demonstrated many collective, positive outcomes, benefitting Autistic individuals, industry, and the community. On their journey, AASQA has supported Autistic individuals to secure and thrive in meaningful employment, while developing technical, social, and work-readiness skills. The AASQA Program was commenced in 2016. By the end of 2022, 581 young Autistic individuals had been trained through AASQA, supported over time by dedicated volunteer mentors (Girdler et al., 2023). Within the growing program, 45 participants have pursued tertiary education, and 106 participants completed valuable internships. More than two-thirds (70%) of interns have remained in their positions (Girdler et al., 2023). (Note that there is currently no official system to collect these numbers, and we are reliant on either parents informing us of their students' acceptance or our own efforts to assist students through Curtin's portfolio pathway system into the first-year multidisciplinary course. Hence the numbers may be understated.) AASQA's "village" continues to grow as new participants and mentors commenced with the program in 2024.

Researched outcomes of the program thus far have predominantly focused on the perspectives of participants' parents. Parents have identified positive impacts on their children's social interactions and relationships, well-being, sense of belonging, and self-esteem (Lee et al., 2020, 2023). The AASQA Program is consistently valued for providing a safe, supportive environment where participants can be themselves while engaging in special interest groups with other Autistic individuals with shared passions (Lee et al., 2020, 2023).

AASQA's work experience placements supported participants and their parents to better identify their strengths and potential in the workplace, leading to increased confidence in participants' abilities, and a strengthened career direction (Lee et al., 2019). Employers and supervisors consistently identified multiple benefits of hosting work experience students including enhanced workplace productivity, new working approaches, and an increased understanding and awareness of autism (Lee et al., 2019).

AASQA remains committed to empowering Autistic individuals, recognising their strengths and unique skills. Through creating strong partnerships with industry and community members, AASQA strives to best support Autistic individuals' future transitions to valued employment, working toward an inclusive society for all (Girdler et al., 2023).

Enablers and Challenges of the Program

AASQA's Programs have supported the achievement of positive outcomes for participants and the wider community. Key features of AASQA's Programs acknowledge and respect the unique ways that Autistic individuals' sense, think, socialise, and communicate, forming its strengths-based approach (Donaldson et al., 2017). Aligning activity and employment opportunities with the interests and skills of Autistic individuals has been identified to improve their wellbeing and quality of life (Courchesne et al., 2020).

CoderDojo Environment

Jones et al. (2021) highlight the importance of considering the environment in relation to ninjas' sensory needs. Previously, noise and overcrowding in CoderDojo sessions have caused frustration among some ninjas. Changes to the physical environment through the addition of quiet break-out rooms, along with support from OT student mentors encouraged ninjas to self-manage their sensory needs and provided opportunities for the development of emotional regulation skills (Jones et al., 2021; Lee et al., 2019).

While developing valuable STEM skills, ninjas also learn social skills within a "real" setting, surrounded by other Autistic individuals with many shared interests and experiences (Girdler et al., 2023; Jones et al., 2018). Parents and ninjas have noted this less structured approach promotes communication on shared interests between the ninjas. Shared experiences and interests aid the formation of authentic friendships, motivating the ninjas to continue participating in the program (Jones et al., 2021).

Ninjas shared that program mentors inspired them to consider future study and employment opportunities in ICT fields through sharing their experiences of studying and working in industry (Ashburner et al., 2018; Jones et al., 2021). The knowledge and expertise of the many dedicated volunteer mentors, some of whom were Autistic individuals themselves, guided the creation of the varied groups within the CoderDojo Program and provided a personalised, evolving experience for the ninjas (Girlder et al., 2023). However, given many mentors were university students, with varying availability across the university semester, the consistency of group activity choices, as well as the schedule of sessions varied (Jones et al., 2018).

Workplace Environments

As explained by Chang et al. (2023), the employment interview is one of the most commonly used selection tools and may be particularly challenging for young Autistic individuals due to unpredictable, open-ended questions, and expectations, often in an unfamiliar environment. Collaborative support throughout the interview and onboarding process sets up the participants for success in the AASQA work experience and internship programs while building job readiness skills (Crooks, 2023; Girdler et al., 2023). Collaboration in the onboarding process can also help identify suitable job tasks for participants. Previously, without a strong understanding of the student's ICT-related skills and knowledge, host organisations were not able to accurately assess and allocate suitable job tasks that were adequately challenging for participants (Lee et al., 2019).

AASQA has facilitated autism awareness training for host organisations to support the creation of inclusive workplaces that celebrate and respect Autistic individuals' strengths (Efeoğlu and Kılınçarslan, 2024; Lee et al., 2019; Vitelli, 2024). Organisations are supported to identify and implement reasonable accommodations for program participants, including the creation of quiet workplaces, comprehensive job instructions, and flexibility in job tasks (Wilkinson, 2023). These accommodations are key to establishing an inclusive and supportive workplace culture for the participants and employees and boosting business productivity (Lee et al., 2019).

The autism awareness training also enabled worksite employees and management to better understand and respect Autistic individuals, support their diverse needs, dispelling misunderstandings, and prejudices regarding autism (Petty et al., 2022). Research highlighted that understanding of autism is linked to reduced stigma, in turn supporting Autistic individuals' well-being, and positively impacting not only participants and workplaces but also the wider community (Lee et al., 2019).

Considerations for Program Implementation

- When creating programs to meet Autistic individuals' needs, identify, and utilise their interests and strengths to support engagement and enhance confidence and well-being (Jones et al., 2021).
- Consider and match the interests of participants and mentors and provide the participants with activity choices to support the development of rapport, motivation, and attendance (Jones et al., 2018, 2023b).

Liam's lived experience of the AASQA Program

Liam credits his decision to join the AASQA Program as one that resulted in a series of opportunities that have led him to where he is today.

During high school, Liam said he developed a keen interest in coding and software development. "Year 10 was the year I worked out that what I really wanted to do in life was software development … something to do with typing code". Coding was Liam's way of creating, and coding projects gave this creation purpose. "As long as I have a computer, I can always code, I can always create … that was something missing from my life before that point". These interests led Liam to become a founding member of the AASQA Program in 2016. "I was doing CoderDojo before that and then Tele Tan made one specifically for Autistic individuals, I was like that's great, that's perfect, that's where I fit in". For Liam, the CoderDojo sessions were a dedicated time each week where he could develop his skills and work on coding projects in a supportive, inclusive environment with guidance from experienced coders and software developers. "It's great having a place where … I would go and I would have support from very much more experienced people to help me".

After two years in the program, Liam became the first ninja to transition to a mentor role and spent the next five years teaching and guiding other ninjas. This was not Liam's only first, as soon after in his final year of high school he was offered an opportunity to sit the internationally recognised, complex software testing exam, the International Software Testing Qualifications Board (ISTQB) Foundation Level Qualification. "I was a little hesitant at first … but I was like, look, this qualification is internationally recognised, if you get this, it's technically a post-university level". Liam became the first person under the age of 18 to pass the exam and receive a qualification typically achieved by individuals with undergraduate degrees and industry experience, "…and I hadn't even graduated high school yet". For Liam, this qualification was a key part of his journey, he shared, "Without AASQA I wouldn't have got the ISTQB qualification … that led onto a whole bunch of chain reaction events like getting a job". One of those other chain reaction events included entering university, for which Liam applied via the portfolio pathway.

The role of CoderDojo mentor allowed Liam to learn more about himself, his interests, and his strengths in what he describes as a "mostly risk-free environment". In staying connected through the AASQA Program, Liam was able to obtain an internship, and through his dedication and hard work transitioned into a permanent position with the same company. The opportunities did not end there, and through the AASQA Program Liam has also been invited to attend talks and ministerial events and today remains a strong advocate of this innovative program that champions the strengths of Autistic individuals and supports varied pathways into ICT employment.

- Train facilitators and mentors in varied teaching strategies to enable the adoption of individualised and collaborative approaches (Jones et al., 2018, 2023b).
- Through consultation with participants, identify their sensory needs, and provide environments that meet these needs. This may include access to a "quiet room" to encourage participants to self-manage their sensory needs as required (Jones et al., 2021).
- Provide opportunities for participants to showcase their projects and the skills they have developed to reinforce their individual value (Jones et al., 2023b).
- Provide autism awareness training to host organisations to develop appropriate job tasks and work environments for participants and reduce workplace stigma (Efeoğlu and Kılınçarslan, 2024; Vitelli, 2024).
- Partner with organisations to provide individualised job coaching and develop participants' work readiness skills to create pathways toward valued employment (Crooks, 2023; Girdler et al., 2023).
- Strength-based approaches and mentoring (aspects of the AASQA Program) have also been used in other areas of practice including Autistic youth digital arts programs (Lee et al., 2024).

Summary

Identifying the need for employment supports for Autistic individuals, AASQA created a program for Autistic adolescents, who championed their strengths and interests, to support the development of ICT-related and work-readiness skills. The CoderDojo coding sessions, work experience and internships that are a part of AASQA's Program, have improved participant well-being, self-esteem, confidence, and career direction while supporting workplaces' understanding of autism and their development of new and inclusive working approaches. An inclusive, supportive environment with a network of trained mentors and professionals who provide individualised mentorship to ninjas is highly valuable. These people and their approaches support the program's positive outcomes as AASQA strives to achieve their mission of enhancing the lives and employment outcomes of Autistic individuals.

References

Australian Bureau of Statistics. (2019) *Disability, ageing and carers, Australia: Summary of findings*. www.abs.gov.au/statistics/health/disability/disability-ageing-and-carers-australia-summary-findings/2018#autism-in-australia (accessed: 27 August 2024).

Australian Bureau of Statistics. (2024) *Disability, ageing and carers, Australia: Summary of findings*. www.abs.gov.au/statistics/health/disability/disability-ageing-and-carers-australia-summary-findings/latest-release (accessed: 27 August 2024).

American Psychiatric Association. (2013) *Diagnostic and statistical manual of mental disorders: DSM-5* (5th ed.). American Psychiatric Association. DOI:10.1176/appi.books.9780890425596.

Ashburner, J., Bobir, N., and van Dooren, K. (2018) 'Evaluation of an innovative interest-based post-school transition programme for young people with autism spectrum disorder', *International Journal of Disability, Development and Education*, 65(3), 262–285. DOI:10.1080/1034912X.2017.1403012.

Chang, H., Saleh, M., Bruyère, S., Vogus, T., and Inge, K. (2023) 'Making the employment interview work for a neurodiverse workforce: Perspectives of individuals on the autism spectrum, employers and service providers', *Journal of Vocational Rehabilitation*, 59(1), 107–122. DOI:10.3233/JVR-230031.

Chen, J., Leader, G., Sung, C., and Leahy, M. (2015) 'Trends in employment for individuals with autism spectrum disorder: A review of the research literature', *Review Journal of Autism and Developmental Disorders*, 2(2), 115–127. DOI:10.1007/s40489-014-0041-6.

Cope, R., and Remington, A. (2022) 'The strengths and abilities of Autistic people in the workplace', *Autism in Adulthood*, 4(1), 22–31. DOI:10.1089/aut.2021.0037.

Courchesne, V., Langlois, V., Gregoire, P., St-Denis, A., Bouvet, L., Ostrolenk, A., and Mottron, L. (2020) 'Interests and strengths in autism, useful but misunderstood: A pragmatic case-study.' *Frontiers in Psychology*, 11, 569339. DOI:10.3389/fpsyg.2020.569339.

Crooks, J. (2023) Supporting the autism academy. Australian Computer Society Foundation. www.acsfoundation.com.au/post/supporting-the-autism-academy (accessed: 27 August 2024).

de Schipper, E., Mahdi, S., de Vries, P., Granlund, M., Holtmann, M., Karande, S., Almodayfer, O., Shulman, C., Tonge, B., Wong, V., Zwaigenbaum, L., and Bölte, S. (2016) 'Functioning and disability in autism spectrum disorder: A worldwide survey of experts', *Autism Research*, 9(9), 959–969. DOI:10.1002/aur.1592.

Donaldson, A.L., Krejcha, K., and McMillin, A. (2017) 'A strengths-based approach to autism: Neurodiversity and partnering with the autism community', *Perspectives of the ASHA Special Interest Groups*, 2(1), 56–68. DOI:10.1044/persp2.SIG1.56.

Efeoğlu, İ.E., and Kılınçarslan, Ö. (2024) 'How do individuals with autism participate in work life? A study on inclusive employability', *Equality, Diversity, and Inclusion: An International Journal*, 43(2), 173–187. DOI:10.1108/edi-09-2022-0254.

Girdler, S., Milbourn, B., and Tan, T. (2023) Unleashing the power of neurodiversity. Accreditation Council for Entrepreneurial and Engaged Universities (ACEEU). www.aceeu.org/news/spotlightarticle/id/60 (accessed 27 August 2024).

Hedley, D., Cai, R., Uljarevic, M., Wilmot, M., Spoor, J., Richdale, A., and Dissanayake, C. (2017) 'Transition to work: Perspectives from the autism spectrum', *Autism: The International Journal of Research and Practice*, 22(5), 528–541. DOI:10.1177/1362361316687697.

Jones, M., Falmer, M., Milbourn, B., Tan, T., Sheehy, L., Bölte, S., and Girdler, S. (2018) *A strength-based program for adolescents with autism*, BCEC Research Report No.17/18. https://bcec.edu.au/assets/A-strength-based-program-for-adolescents-with-autism.pdf (accessed 1 August 2024).

Jones, M., Falkmer, M., Milbourn, B., Tan, T., Bölte, S., and Girdler, S. (2021) 'Identifying the essential components of strength-based technology clubs for adolescents with autism spectrum disorder', *Developmental Neurorehabilitation*, 24(5), 323–336. DOI:10.1080/17518423.2021.1886192.

Jones, M., Falkmer, M., Milbourn, B., Tan, T., Bölte, S., and Girdler, S. (2023a) 'The core elements of strengths-based technology programs for youth on the autism spectrum: A systematic review of qualitative evidence', *Review Journal of Autism and Developmental Disorders*, 10(3), 441–457. DOI:10.1007/s40489-022-00302-0.

Jones, M., Milbourn, B., Falkmer, M., Vinci, B., Tan, T., Bölte, S., and Girdler, S. (2023b) 'A practical framework for delivering strengths based technology clubs for Autistic adolescents', *Autism in Adulthood*, 5(4), 356–365. DOI:10.1089/aut.2022.0038.

Lee, E., Black, M., Tan, T., Falkmer, T., and Girdler, S. (2019) ' "I'm destined to ace this": Work experience placement during high school for individuals with autism spectrum disorder', *Journal of Autism and Developmental Disorders*, 49(8), 3089–3101. DOI:10.1007/s10803-019-04024-x.

Lee, E., Black, M., Falkmer, M., Tan, T., Sheehy, L., Bölte, S., and Girdler, S. (2020) ' "We can see a bright future": Parents' perceptions of the outcomes of participating in a strengths-based program for adolescents with autism spectrum disorder', *Journal of Autism and Developmental Disorders*, 50(9), 3179–3194. DOI:10.1007/s10803-020-04411-9.

Lee, E., Scott, M., Black, M., D'Arcy, E., Tan, T., Sheehy, L., Bölte, S., and Girdler, S. (2023) ' "He sees his autism as a strength, not a deficit now": A repeated cross-sectional study investigating the impact of strengths-based programs on Autistic adolescents', *Journal of Autism and Developmental Disorders*, 54(5), 1656–1671. DOI:10.1007/s10803-022-05881-9.

Lee, E.A.L., Milbourn, B., Afsharnejad, B., Chitty, E., Jannings, A.-M., Kealy, R., McWhirter, T., and Girdler, S. (2024). ' "We are all bringing, like a unique sort of perspective": The core elements of a strengths-based digital arts mentoring program for Autistic adolescents from the perspective of their mentors', *Australian Occupational Therapy Journal*, 1–17. https://doi.org/10.1111/1440-1630.12980

Merrington, H., Gibbs, V., Haas, K., Clark, T., Robinson, A., AlAnsari, M., and Pellicano, E. (2024) 'What matters most? An exploration of quality of life through the everyday experiences of Autistic young people and adults', *Autism in Adulthood* [Preprint]. DOI:10.1089/aut.2023.0127.

Petty, S., Richardson, H., Eccles, N., and Tunstall, L. (2022) 'Supporting Autistic employees: Understanding and confidence in UK workplaces', *Industry and Higher Education*, 37(3), 448–454. DOI:10.1177/09504222221124505.

Scott, M., Milbourn, B., Falkmer, M., Black, M., Bölte, S., Halladay, A., Matthew, L., Taylor, J., and Girdler, S. (2019) 'Factors impacting employment for people with autism spectrum disorder: A scoping review', *Autism: The International Journal of Research and Practice*, 23(4), 869–901. DOI:10.1177/1362361318787789.

Vitelli, R. (2024) *Autism: Your questions answered*. New York, NY: Bloomsbury.

Wilczynski, S., Trammell, B., and Clarke, L. (2013) 'Improving employment outcomes among adolescents and adults on the autism spectrum', *Psychology in the Schools*, 50(9), 876–887. DOI:10.1002/pits.21718.

Wilkinson, G. (2023) 'Designing Autistic friendly workplaces', *The Architects' Journal*, 6. www.architectsjournal.co.uk/news/opinion/the-regs-designing-autistic-friendly-workplaces

University of Tennessee at Chattanooga, USA

Mosaic Program

Amy Rutherford, Mary-Elizabeth Goodman and Anne Hill

Introduction

Mosaic is a multifaceted and comprehensive program developed to support the holistic needs of Autistic students at the University of Tennessee at Chattanooga (UTC). UTC is a mid-sized public university with nearly 12,000 students currently enrolled. For the Fall 2024 semester, there were 52 students in the Mosaic Program. All students in the program are actively working to earn a college degree.

There are four pillars on which the Mosaic Program is built; these are a credit-bearing curriculum, coaching, peer/professional mentoring, and supervised study hours. Students agree to engage in all four components when joining the program. In addition, programming is offered to educate and enhance the student experience, and Mosaic partners with student-led groups to provide more opportunities for socialisation and engagement.

The Mosaic staff is composed of five full-time and five part-time employees. Most of our offerings are in-person with the occasional virtual meeting. This program was founded in 2008 and was developed out of the request and expressed needs of Autistic students. All aspects of the program are informed and led by student feedback. If student input guides our work, then how do we gather the student voices? One way is by asking students directly for feedback. We receive feedback daily through student interactions and intentionally through surveys. We also capture student feedback weekly while documenting coaching meetings. Coaching surveys collect data on student well-being, academic progress, career competencies, and referrals to campus resources. We also document students' social commitments with peer mentors. Finally, we engage with students and mentors in the classroom through seminars and written assignments.

Initial Offerings and Program Development

The Mosaic Program was born out of a specific need. Autistic students wanted more supports than they received through the Americans with Disabilities Act

DOI: 10.4324/9781003495925-19

(ADA). The ADA made the college platform accessible but did not include social supports and there were gaps with academic fluency. Initially, Mosaic started with four students.

There were several iterations of the program as we pivoted to meet student requests. In 2008, the program started with counselling groups, social skills groups, and living learning communities. Early in the program development, the team created a business model. Then academic-based coaching was incorporated. In 2010, the program consulted with Dr Jane Thierfeld Brown, who has been foundational in the development of college support programs for four decades. Dr Thierfeld Brown is an Assistant Clinical Professor at Yale Child Study, Yale Medical School, and is the Director of College Autism Spectrum (College Autism Spectrum, 2024). At that time, there were only a handful of college autism-support programs throughout the USA. Dr Thierfeld Brown evaluated the current structure, as well as the campus environment, and gave insight into what the future could hold for the program. It has shaped our current practices.

Mosaic graduates and other professional Autistic self-advocates in the community also contribute significantly as members of the Mosaic Advisory Board, shaping program evolution with the perspective and hindsight from their lived experiences. The Mosaic Advisory Board comprises solely of current students, graduated students, program family members (past and present), Autistic professionals and autism service providers in the region. From the beginning, those with lived experiences have guided the development of the program and continue to do so.

Mosaic is a fee-for-service program—where the fees are charged for participation in the program and paid by families, philanthropic sources, and contributions from the Vocational Rehabilitation (VR) program—and is entirely self-sustaining. Revenue is based on student fees; and we are able to make the program accessible through a robust partnership with VR, with whom we have shared goals. VR is a US-federally funded, state-run program that strives to connect Americans with disabilities with gainful employment commensurate with their skills while maximising independence.

There were few resources or research studies examining post-secondary autism support in 2010. The articles of the time were just discovering that college-bound Autistic students (unlike many students at the time requesting resources) have a range of needs across many areas (VanBergeijk, Klin & Volkmar, 2008). These observations are not surprising to people in the field today. Journals noted Autistic students frequently needed support navigating adjustments to major life changes, living independently, dealing with downtime, prioritising assignments and studying, living with roommates, managing group work, self-advocating, regulating emotion, meeting deadlines, and communicating across different contexts (Hewitt, 2011; Glennon and Marks, 2010). In addition, papers were starting to note that the autism spectrum is, indeed, a wide spectrum and relative strengths vary widely from student to student (Weiss & Rohland, 2015). Further complicating the college landscape was the fact that many faculty members were not familiar with autism (Barnhill, 2014).

Mission Statement and Program Description

Mosaic strives to give students an authentic college experience while providing a supportive and challenging environment that cultivates interpersonal, intrapersonal, educational, and professional growth. It is our mission to foster independence and the development of community with the ultimate goal of gainful employment in the students' chosen career.

The Mosaic Program comprises four primary components. Each of these works in concert with the others to provide a comprehensive program. These components include: a fully established curriculum linked to a credit-bearing course, weekly coaching, peer/professional mentoring, and supervised study hours. In this manner, we provide academic, organisational, and social support, while also touching base with each student multiple times per week.

Our first component is a credit-bearing curriculum. Mosaic students enrol in a four-year, credit-bearing course of study (with an optional fifth year) dedicated to developing the skills needed to navigate through college and career after graduation. The optional fifth year was developed to support students requiring more time to earn their degree. Each subsequent year builds on the skills developed during the previous year. The first-year curriculum focuses on understanding the social rules of a college campus and community (Rigler, Rutherford and Quinn, 2015a). Students learn how to navigate situations that arise with roommates, professors, and more. The second-year curriculum encompasses a strengths-based approach to understanding self-perception, exploring the autism diagnosis, societal stigmas, and building identity (Rigler, Rutherford and Quinn, 2015b). The third- and fourth-year curriculums work to strengthen career interests and hone the soft skills needed to find and maintain employment (Rigler, Rutherford and Quinn, 2015c, 2016). Our staff promotes the strengths of Autistic talent regionally while expediting student internships, employment, and professional mentoring. In the fifth-year curriculum, students focus on maintaining a healthy work-life balance, while continuing to seek work experience through volunteering, part-time employment, campus research, and other opportunities.

Coaching is the second component of the program. Mosaic students meet at least once a week with a coach to prioritise and develop a game plan for the week. Every session with a coach focuses on each student's individual needs at the meeting, while emphasising academic and social engagement. Coaching might include developing time management strategies, processing roommate or communication difficulties, planning the workload for the coming week, and/or connecting the student with on-campus resources like tutoring or the writing centre. Grades are frequently checked with each student to help monitor academic progress and provide accountability. Our services are customised, and we are flexible with timing (providing more meetings or check-ins as dictated by students' changing needs). Our coaching practices are centred on a person-focused and solution-oriented approach, and we often use motivational interviewing techniques to elicit positive changes in students. It's important to note that coaching is not the same as counselling, though our coaches can help connect students with a counsellor if needed.

The third component of the program is peer mentoring. Initially, students are partnered with a trained peer mentor. Mentors are students who display leadership and social understanding on the college campus and have an interest in autism. Mentors are vetted through an application and interview process. The mentoring relationship fosters on-campus engagement and provides peer support as our students navigate social situations. In the latter years of a student's college career, we try to pair students with a professional mentor in their field, to help provide career guidance as our students begin to navigate the transition into the workforce.

The fourth and final component of the program is supervised study hours. Mosaic students must complete four hours of supervised study per week in designated spaces. This allows coaches to determine if students are making use of good study habits, or if distractions are interfering with productivity. It also allows coaches to ascertain if more academic support is needed while helping students who are struggling. Supervised study time also allows students to naturally develop support systems amongst themselves and with others in the community. Meeting the study hour goals every week is part of each student's classroom grade. Internal tracking metrics have determined that Mosaic students who regularly attend supervised study hours consistently earn higher grades than their less consistent peers.

Extended study hours give Mosaic students exclusive access to our sensory-inclusive space in the evening, providing a supportive environment for their academic success. Additionally, we have partnered with various departments to offer specialised writing and math support. To make these sessions even more engaging, we host themed study nights based on student feedback, such as ice cream socials, taco Tuesdays, therapy dog nights, and more throughout the semester.

A Few Programming Highlights

The Mosaic Events Committee (MEC) was formed in 2016 to fulfil student requests to bring activities and volunteer opportunities to the Mosaic Program. While not a core component, this organisation is an extension of the Mosaic Program and gives students the opportunity to enhance their leadership, communication, and teamwork skills. MEC responsibilities include creating, delegating, and implementing events for Mosaic students and their peer mentors. The MEC includes students from each cohort in the Mosaic Program. The goal here is to provide students with an opportunity to develop leadership, and for students to have active voices in programming. These efforts foster a sense of community, which is not something that can be taught but develops naturally.

The Annual Reverse Career Fair is a culminating event at UTC Mosaic. It is an opportunity for our students to engage in a more comfortable career fair format. All our Juniors, Seniors, and any graduates still seeking employment have a booth to share their strengths, talents, and skills while employers have a chance to walk around and meet each student. This provides our Mosaic students with the opportunity to showcase their strengths to local businesses and organisations for potential internship or employment opportunities. It also provides companies and organisations with the opportunity to recruit high-quality candidates in multiple disciplines.

Impacts

The Mosaic staff have supported hundreds of college students as they earn college degrees. This depth of experience has honed the program components while striving to meet a series of goals. The program's initial concern is to minimise the distress of transition to a post-secondary institution. We recognise that this is a fragile time in the life of a neurodivergent individual, who is often moving away from the family home for the first time while simultaneously trying to chart a path with augmented freedom and more demanding academic rigour. Most of our students are deeply anxious when confronted with such changes. The program provides scaffolding for new students and seeks to lessen executive functioning impacts while encouraging community among cohorts.

One of the program's biggest impacts is helping students build confidence in themselves and helping them find a community. We contradict the negative narrative that students have received throughout their lives. We encourage advocacy, independence, autonomy, and resilience. We strengthen students' independent living skills and help them bounce back from setbacks. We help our students navigate the complexities of different relationships. For students that are easily trusting, we help them be not as naïve. We work to actively reduce cognitive distortions and help students break out of negative reactions to events. Success imparts on students that they can and do pivot and recover from unexpected challenges.

A benefit of support programs that have been established for a long time is the development of an extensive pool of graduates. Alumni are usually not only willing but want to give back. Alumni can strengthen a program's outreach in the workforce. Alumni are a unique resource for our current students and provide hope along with guidance.

Another way to measure impacts is to consider if the program fosters peer support. There is strength in students leading other students and the facilitation of conversation around shared experiences. Often, for Mosaic students, this is the first space where that has ever happened. Sometimes, a great deal is communicated through the mentoring component where both parties lean into each other and grow. We have found that staff rapport with students can also enhance success in a program. The student/coaching relationship must be collaborative and not dictatorial.

It is also critical to have institutional support to optimise day-to-day operations. Mosaic students must navigate the systems set up within the university. Everyone on campus needs to be open and willing to understand and accommodate different learners. Consider the different offices on campus; they support Mosaic students as well. They often intervene when resolving social miscues or miscommunications. They support mental health impacts. They provide testing accommodations. And in return, our staff have become a campus-wide resource for autism education. Faculty and staff reach out for guidance and information.

Higher education measures outcomes in student retention, graduation rates, and employment rates. The Mosaic Program measures outcomes somewhat differently. The mission of Mosaic is to hone the skills that are transferable to the workforce. Another goal of the program is to bolster the resilience and communication skills of our students so that they can thrive in a postgraduate setting. Earning a college degree is a sizeable accomplishment; but that, in itself, is not making a difference in post-degree employment statistics for Autistic adults. If we are not honing the skills needed to navigate the workforce while boosting the ability to self-advocate for needed accommodations, then we are not providing a complete service. We aim to improve outcomes across the lifespan.

Sustainability, Growth, and Other Considerations

What we do will not translate to every campus without adaptation. When implementing a new program, one must assess the campus culture, dynamic, and the specific goals to be addressed. Much preliminary groundwork is necessary to bring a neurodiversity support program to fruition.

There are several things that went well in the implementation of the Mosaic Program, which has often been shaped through a series of trials and errors. Sustainability and scalability were something we have really done well. As the program streamlined student supports, it gradually grew within natural tolerances. We have been fortunate to find good student candidates organically.

Other critical issues to consider when building your program are funding, institutional support, staffing, and staffing turnover. It is essential to establish a good business plan that includes at least a five-year sustainability plan and varied funding sources. Additionally, it can be difficult to find and retain staff with lean budgets, and training/continuing education is essential in providing the best services. There is always more to learn and understand. When making staffing decisions, one should consider the impacts of a collegiate environment on staff and coaching capacity.

Finally, there are ethical considerations to keep in mind when protecting students' privacy and protection from disclosure on campus. We must take steps to maintain peer-to-peer confidentiality and campus-wide confidentiality. We do notice that when students fully engage in our program components, a sense of belonging develops, and often students proudly present themselves as Autistic self-advocates.

Future Considerations and Goals

When looking to provide seamless student services, one must strive to bridge the gaps. One gap is the silos that exist. The elementary and secondary schooling community is an entity within itself, and so are the post-secondary educational institutions. We need to work harder on communication and shared goals from high school to college and from college to the workforce. We could radically improve these transitions by bridging the gaps. This is our main priority moving forward. Institutional knowledge about where neurodivergent college students fall through the cracks in college should inform the services and training they receive in elementary, middle, and high school. In addition, program alumni come back for support and there is little capacity to serve them. We have developed trusting relationships to help these former students, but we currently do not have pathways to provide the career guidance and workplace navigation solutions they want. Programs need to incorporate methods to continue supporting alumni. If alumni struggle and need resources, how do they access those? We need to start the planning and conversations now to establish a better way to connect graduates with resources in the future.

Another consideration is supporting students who find that a four-year degree is not the right path for them. Programs and colleges define success based on graduation and retention rates. We pride ourselves on retention rates averaging 85% with a five-year graduation rate of 80%. But we also define success much more broadly. What happens with students who find they are not a good match for the collegiate path? How do we help them exit on good terms? How do we ensure they access the support needed for their next steps?

We need to help students exit well. One way to initiate improvements is by hosting alumni events so that departed students maintain their sense of community. We could also strengthen career supports for these students who might find a trade to be a better fit. Additional resources are needed for those who choose a vocational path that is not offered at our institution. Many of those who choose to step away from the program have done so with a solid plan or job replacement.

After several years of development, the current comprehensive Mosaic Program has worked hard to maintain high standards in serving Autistic students who choose UTC. We have maintained student voices as a foundation to program expansion and program development. We have a neurodivergent staff with a strong connection to student needs. We have the resources to continue providing support to Autistic students for the long term due to our sustainability efforts, determination, and supportive university partnerships.

References

Barnhill, G.P. (2014) 'Supporting students with Asperger syndrome on college campuses', *Focus on Autism and Other Developmental Disabilities*, 31(1), 3–15. https://doi.org/10.1177/1088357614523121

College Autism Spectrum. (2024) *Our team—College Autism Spectrum* [online]. https://collegeautismspectrum.com/team/ (accessed: 3 January 2025).

Glennon, T., and Marks, A. (2010). 'Transitioning to college issues for students with an autism spectrum disorder in the clinic' [online]. https://centerforpediatrictherapy.com/wp-content/uploads/2013/11/Transitioning-to-College.pdf (accessed: 6 November 2024).

Hewitt, L.E. (2011) 'Perspectives on support needs of individuals with autism spectrum disorders', *Topics in Language Disorders*, 31(3), 273–285. https://doi.org/10.1097/tld.0b013e318227fd19

Rigler, M., Rutherford, A., and Quinn, E. (2015a) *Developing identity, strengths, and self-perception for young adults with autism spectrum disorder*. London: Jessica Kingsley Publishers.

Rigler, M., Rutherford, A., and Quinn, E. (2015b) *Independence, social, and study strategies for young adults with autism spectrum disorder: The BASICS college curriculum*. London: Jessica Kingsley Publishers.

Rigler, M., Rutherford, A., and Quinn, E. (2015c) *Turning skills and strengths into careers for young adults with autism spectrum disorder*. London: Jessica Kingsley Publishers.

Rigler, M., Rutherford, A., and Quinn, E. (2016) *Developing workplace skills for young adults with autism spectrum disorder: The BASICS college curriculum*. London: Jessica Kingsley Publishers.

VanBergeijk, E., Klin, A., and Volkmar, F. (2008) 'Supporting more able students on the autism spectrum: College and beyond', *Journal of Autism and Developmental Disorders*, 38(7), 1359–1370 [online]. https://doi.org/10.1007/s10803-007-0524-8

Weiss, A.L., and Rohland, P. (2015) 'Implementing a communication coaching program for students with autism spectrum disorders in postsecondary education', *Topics in Language Disorders*, 35(4), 345–361. https://doi.org/10.1097/tld.0000000000000071

Landmark College, USA

Programming for Fostering Career Connections among Neurodivergent College Students

Jan Coplan, Adam R. Lalor, Marlee Bickford-Bushey and Rebecca W. Matte

Background

Among the many goals of higher education in the United States is the preparation of students to be contributing members of society through gainful employment (Financial Value Transparency, 2023). This preparation is important to neurodivergent students as neurodivergent people are unemployed and underemployed at higher rates than neurotypical people (Roux et al., 2015). This is despite evidence noting the many strengths and skills that neurodivergent people bring to the workforce (Stenn et al., 2023). So, what may be done in higher education to better support neurodivergent students in obtaining higher education at greater rates?

Historically, minimal if any career-related knowledge and skill development has focused on the needs of neurodivergent students in higher education (Oswald et al., 2015). While attention is given to the career preparation of neurodivergent secondary students covered under the Individuals with Disabilities Education Act who are preparing to transition directly to the workforce, less career preparation is typically afforded to college-bound neurodivergent students (Morningstar et al., 2023). As such neurodivergent college graduates must usually navigate the transition to career with little identity-specific guidance. This chapter describes a comprehensive program called Career Connections that is specifically designed to support the career development needs of neurodivergent college students, namely, learning disabled, attention-deficit/hyperactivity disorder (ADHD), and Autistic students. Student outcomes and the portability of the program to other institutions of higher education will be discussed.

Landmark College Career Connections Programs

Prior to discussing the Career Connections Programs, it is important to understand the unique educational environment in which it is situated: Landmark College (LC). LC is the first institution of higher education founded solely to serve neurodivergent students diagnosed with learning disabilities, ADHD,

DOI: 10.4324/9781003495925-20

and autism. Founded in 1985, LC is an educational community where students enrol to develop and hone their academic and social-emotional skills as they pursue associate's and baccalaureate degrees. The LC education focuses on enhancing student skills while providing opportunities for students to improve upon areas that they find more challenging. Situated in Putney, Vermont, LC is more than an academic community. LC is a cultural community that supports students as they explore neurodiversity culture and identity.

Internationally recognised as a leader in neurodivergent education, LC students enrol from around the world for its unparalleled education. Additionally, many enrol as online students through the LC Online Program. As enrolled students, a variety of services are provided to students to support their educational and social-emotional development including academic coaching, social pragmatics, tutoring, identity-based programming, life skills support, and career preparation and development services.

Career Connections Department Overview

Career Connections is the department at LC charged with serving students as they chart their path toward career and post-college life. Comprised of four, full-time professional staff members, Career Connections originated in 2014 shortly after the College added an accredited bachelor's degree program. The mission of the office is to facilitate career exploration, support the graduate school application process, and enhance workforce preparation. Landmark is a small college with a total student population of roughly 480 students. In any semester roughly 50% of the student body is engaged with our office and its programming. Our office employs four full-time career counsellors including the director. In addition to 1:1 meetings the program offers robust programming which meets the needs of all college students but is designed intentionally with the neurodivergent student in mind. These programs are available to students both in-person and virtually.

Career Connections is guided by the Comprehensive Career Readiness (CCR) Program formulated by LC in 2019. CCR is designed to support students in developing both career and life readiness skills including self-advocacy, civic engagement, financial literacy, personal accountability, problem-solving, and effective interpersonal communication.

The CCR Program was built with the unique needs of the neurodivergent student in mind. The foundation of this program is the eight career readiness competencies supported by the National Association of Colleges and Employers: career and self-development, leadership, communication, professionalism, critical thinking, teamwork, equity and inclusion, and technology (NACE, 2024). Additionally, Career Connections grounds its programmatic offerings in two primary theories which will be discussed in the next sections.

Theoretical Underpinnings of Career Connections

The world of work is not a uniform experience. Each person enters the workplace with their own unique story shaped by a variety of different factors that have presented themselves throughout an individual's life and educational journey. Culturally, the neurodivergent experience is also far from monolithic and encompasses a wide range of experiences influenced by intersecting factors such as diagnosis, socioeconomic status, race, ethnicity, religion/spirituality, and sexual orientation. Despite each person experiencing neurodivergence in their own way, many individuals in the neurodivergent community (and within professions) share common experiences and motivations that bind them together and create a sense of community and cultural belonging. Theories often serve as a powerful tool for contextualising common experiences in life, education, and the workplace. Two primary theories undergird the programs and services offered by Career Connections: Chickering's (1969) Seven Vectors of College Student Development and Maslow's (1943) motivational hierarchy.

Arthur Chickering's theory is one of the most prominent college student development theories in higher education. Over the decades, it has been examined through different lenses including neurodivergence (Gouws, 2022; Stamp, 2020). The theory's focus on the undergraduate student experience makes it an important tool for constructing internship and career readiness programs. Chickering posits that for a student to be successful within higher education they must achieve competence within seven vectors (i.e. domains or areas). The use of the term *vectors* refers to the ongoing work that must be undertaken in these domains of growth, again, making it a powerful tool for career readiness. The Seven Vectors are as follows: developing competence, managing emotions, moving through autonomy toward interdependence, developing mature interpersonal relationships, establishing identity, developing purpose, and developing integrity (Chickering and Reisser, 1993). While all vectors are important for success in higher education, there are a few that should be highlighted given their importance for career readiness as related to neurodivergent individuals.

Chickering's first vector, developing competence, is explained as a period where a student develops not only intellectual, physical, and manual skills but also interpersonal competencies by wrestling with and moving through growth tasks which affirm their sense of competence in a domain. The ability to develop competence is often fostered through tasks such as peer review processes for assignments and interactions with different departments within a college or university. This is in contrast to the secondary education setting where many interactions are often centralised through a special education teacher or service provider. These types of growth tasks can be more challenging for some neurodivergent students to navigate as they transition to postsecondary education. These skills are also important career competencies. For example, skills are developed and refined during the process of interviewing and accepting feedback presented in a performance evaluation. It is important to support the development of these skills in a career readiness program.

Managing emotions is the second vector in Chickering's model. This competency can be challenging for many neurodivergent college students who may encounter issues with sensory regulation in multiple areas such as dining or residence halls (Eveleth, 2012). This translates as a career readiness skill as students will need to negotiate similar sensory challenges in a new workspace. Emotional management skills can be enhanced by developing a distress tolerance plan to help identify potential triggers and self-regulation strategies and coaching students to update the plan as old challenges fade and new ones arise. Career coaching can further assist neurodivergent individuals in this domain through the development of transitional phrases that help to promote self-advocacy during a student's career journey. For example, coaching students to use phrases such as "that is a great question and I would like to take a moment to think about that" helps the student develop advocacy skills when they need additional processing time or time for recall. Similarly, such a skill would translate to the workplace setting if a neurodivergent employee encountered environments with high sensory demands.

Growth tasks in the remaining vectors should be addressed with similar intentionality. Many of the areas of growth examined in college student development overlap with those measuring the career readiness of neurodivergent college students for success in internships. Clear and explicit coaching in these domains will better prepare neurodivergent students for the transition to the workplace.

As conversations about career readiness subside, the topic of workplace and living environments often becomes a focus. It is at this time that theories such as Maslow's motivational hierarchy (i.e. hierarchy of needs) can assist students setting better-informed hopes and expectations for workplace fit and reasonable accommodations. Maslow's motivational hierarchy is typically depicted as a pyramid with basic needs forming the foundation (refer Figure P9.1). This lower level includes the subcategories of *physiological needs* and *safety needs* which include the basics such as food, clothing, shelter, health, and employment security (Sharf, 2013). Maslow's physiological need is even more important to consider when looking at certain demographics. Far from the movie stereotype of a college student, these basic needs are not guaranteed. In fact, it is estimated that between 33% and 51% of college students in the United States are food insecure and an estimated 1.5 million college students in the United States experience homelessness (McKibben et al., 2023). Disabled individuals including those who are neurodivergent experience pay inequity through wage gaps and legal sub-minimum wage work programs (Ruppel, 2024). It is therefore critical to work with students to consider employment

What is your highest potential?
What would you need to accomplish in your lifetime to consider it a "life well lived"?

Potential   How do you see yourself fitting into the world/global citizenry?

What will feel like success for you?

Self-Esteem
What will feel like success for you?

What will feel like success for you?
What value would you like to bring to the environment?
What is the best thing that can happen?
What else?

Social
What are your social needs?

What might you need to do to maintain your existing relationships or set boundaries as necessary? How might you build relationships in and and outside of the workplace? What timeline would you expect for new relationships? How do you feel connected to others?

Safety
What are your safety/security needs?

What are environmental factors that support feelings of calm & safety? What do you have in your home that would be most important to replicate in a new space?

Physiological
What are your basic physiological needs?

Consider your basic needs. What are your needs with regard to: Food? Shelter? Clothing? Sleep? How might you address these in the new environment?

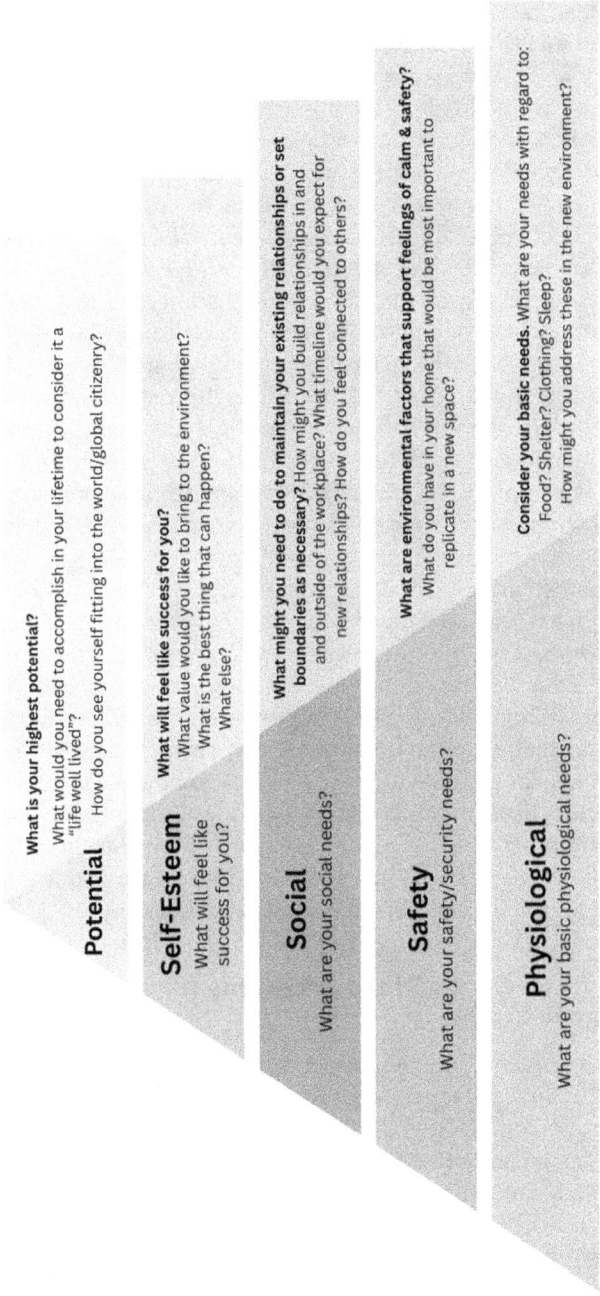

Figure P9.1 Coaching questions targeting Maslow's hierarchy of needs.

and internship options that would provide them with opportunities for the desired level of autonomy, professional success, and socioeconomic growth. Career coaching can support neurodivergent students in thinking through these basic needs.

The third and fourth tiers of Maslow's hierarchy, categorised as *psychological needs*, consist of *love and belonging needs* and *esteem needs*. These growth areas are important in considering how to support the development of internal coping strategies when encountering workplace dynamics and workplace stress. Many neurodivergent employees report feeling isolated in workplace settings (Weber et al., 2024). These occurrences often result from things like miscommunication between neurotypical and neurodivergent employees, also known as the double empathy problem. A lack of supervisor knowledge about neurodiversity and/or placement in a job that is not well matched with the abilities and interests of the neurodivergent employee can lead to workplace challenges including avoidant behaviour among neurodivergent employees and interns (Iqbal et al., 2024). Many studies have affirmed that neurodivergent individuals strive for the same emotional and social connections as "neurotypical individuals" including social connections inside and outside of the workplace (Crompton et al., 2020). Social connections are a crucial factor that can lead to employees choosing to stay or leave a place of employment or internship opportunity (Rothausen et al., 2015). This is why it is important for many students to not only examine and plan for what might happen within the workplace but what also happens during the weekends. This might mean deliberately exploring what location gives students ample access to quality of life and areas in the workplace; and even third spaces (i.e. locations where a person can relate or bond with a particular community such as churches, gyms, coffee shops) in which they can build confidence, respect, and self-esteem.

As a neurodivergent individual considers life beyond college, it is important that career advisors broaden the scope of their questioning to include multiple dimensions and domains of a student's life that will be impacted by the transition. Neurodivergent students benefit from more directive questioning that targets growth tasks identified through Maslow's Hierarchy.

Signature Career Connections Programs for Neurodivergent Students

Neurodivergent students face numerous barriers to employment and often have little or no paid work experience (Kwon et al., 2023). This lack of experience makes it more difficult for them to secure internships and envision, let alone develop, a career path. To address these concerns, LC developed a robust, scaffolded, and neuroinclusive approach to career readiness. Students have several ways of accessing and engaging with the Career Connections office including a dedicated career counsellor, programming, and workshops. These options help students with identifying and addressing their unique needs, strengths, and challenges as they engage in their career development. Career Connections incorporates a supportive, strengths-based approach to each step of the career development process: from career exploration and identifying a major to salary negotiation and discussing disability disclosure.

The Career Connections staff work collaboratively with departments across campus and online to engage students at various entry points during their LC journey including career coaching, an array of workshops, class visits, administering skill and strengths assessments (e.g. the Birkman, Clifton Strengths Finder), and programming for alumni. The signature programs offered by the LC Career Connections office are the Employment Readiness Experience (ERE) and the Comprehensive Internship Program.

Employment Readiness Experience

Knowing the barriers neurodivergent students face, Career Connections created the ERE. The ERE is a short-term, credit-bearing, on-campus paid work program. This experience allows neurodivergent students to develop professional skills and refine career interests within a low-risk developmental environment under the supervision of LC staff who understand neurodivergence. Additionally, students have the opportunity to work with a job coach who visits them while they are engaged in the ERE work experience. The program specifically serves those students who do not currently demonstrate the professional skills and/or confidence to successfully perform an internship or work in the greater community. The primary goal of the program is to address the career development needs of neurodivergent students, help neurodivergent students uncover their strengths as employees, and develop career literacy. Examples of short-term projects and tasks engaged in by ERE students include developing and using graphic design skills to create flyers, data entry and analytics, and learning and surveying new online platforms to improve department use and application.

ERE Program Outcomes

Through the careful collection of data and post-program debriefing, the ERE has undergone continuous evaluation since 2017. Post-program surveys of ERE students have shown that 75–90% of students self-reported improvements in working independently, managing projects, problem-solving, planning and organisation, communicating, and professionalism. Eighty percent of participants strongly agreed that their input and skills were valued in the workplace. All students also agreed that their job coach offered helpful insights about improving professionalism. Additionally, students cited experiencing growth in their technical skills. Of note is that several ERE participants reported receiving employment offers from their ERE supervisor for the next semester based on strong performance and growth in their positions. The program also demonstrated success in adapting to a virtual environment during the height of the COVID-19 pandemic. Thus far, 50% of participants have either successfully completed a credit-bearing internship or earned employment. Perhaps most telling is that 86% of participants agreed that the ERE made them feel better prepared to enter the job market. Although anecdotal, there also appears to be an increased interest in employment and confidence related to future employment.

Comprehensive Internship Program

An internship at LC is a career-related, credit-bearing experience that can provide mentorship, training, and exposure to employment in a given field. Career Connections is committed to providing the resources required for students to access experiential learning opportunities and put into practice what they are learning in the classroom. The internship serves as an essential opportunity for a student to experience the demands of the world of work and compare them to the demands of the classroom. The environment, whether remote or in person, exposes students to challenges that inform their career goals, the need to self-advocate, and the importance of researching opportunities to evaluate whether they are "good fits" that will support their various needs. Students have shared that the internship is where they realised their level of commitment to their professional growth, the need to be accountable, and the consequences when they are not professional. Often motivated by earning a salary and the level of independence, LC student interns flourish.

LC requires that students complete an alternative learning experience to meet graduation requirements. Often, the preferred method of doing so is an internship. Several degrees, for example, the business degree, require that students complete an internship. In recent years, there has been a significant increase in the number of students interested in internships. While positive, this increase has revealed barriers and prompted creative solutions and opportunities. As a rural college in Vermont with limited public transportation students have less ability to secure external internships in the surrounding community. Given this challenge, many neurodivergent students have been offered opportunities on campus. The internship placements vary but often include research assistants, coordinator roles in our diversity and inclusion centres, and other internship positions in campus departments including admissions, health services, marketing and communications, and Career Connections. This provides the necessary supervision some of our students need.

Career Connections is also dedicated to procuring internship opportunities with companies, organisations, corporations, and small businesses that align with student interests and career goals. Many of these internships are with companies who wish to hire a neurodivergent workforce. The Director of Career Connections is tasked with developing partnerships that seek to recruit neurodivergent students and graduates from LC and other institutions. These partners have led to impactful campus visits and hiring, while also helping to educate the campus community about the strengths of neurodiversity in the workplace.

Internships are often a pivotal experience exposing the student to the expectations of a professional environment and the importance of self-advocacy. Students report that their internship activates their executive functioning skills in a different manner than their academic work. They also see themselves as having the ability to succeed and be valued within an employment setting, thereby gaining a new sense of belonging.

Whether or not the internship experience goes as expected, pairing it with post-experience reflection fosters a deeper sense of career maturity. While most students view their experience as a success, students are given the right to struggle and the right to "fail." LC Career Connections staff offer a safe environment to process the internship experience and what can be done differently in the future. During internships, students become aware of the myriad ways they can engage in an industry of interest and the many career options available to them. Because students are encouraged to engage with Career Connections early in their academic program, they have time to (a) refine their career goals, (b) develop new skills through coursework and other career development opportunities, and (c) potentially engage in another internship.

Comprehensive Internship Program Outcomes

Internship placement and outcomes are strong. Since 2016 over 450 students have successfully completed an internship. During that time only two students withdrew from their placements. Internship withdrawal is a typical part of the data set in any program and Career Connections is pleased that the attrition numbers remain low. The low rate of attrition is attributed to two key factors: robust career coaching before, during, and after the experience and intentional procurement of neuroinclusive internship placements. Internship supervisors and company partners have commented that Career Connections staff know LC students well, strongly support their growth and provide the tools for partnering organisations to host successful experiences for neurodivergent students.

Portability and Implications for Research

Much can be gleaned from the Career Connections Program by career professionals and researchers. Without question, LC is a unique institution of higher education which begs the question of portability of the philosophy and programs of the Career Connections department. As described, the theoretical foundations of the programs and services offered are those used by a wide variety of colleges and universities. The work of NACE, Chickering, and Maslow are broad and, frankly, have been used by higher education staff at traditional colleges and universities (i.e. not solely neurodivergent serving). Still, programs geared specifically toward neurodivergent students are uncommon in higher education. Resources in the form of time, staffing, funding, and professional development would be critical to other colleges and universities developing ERE and Comprehensive Internship Programs on their campuses. As countries are becoming more aware of post-college career outcomes and being held more accountable for demonstrating the value of a higher education, the return on the investment of establishing an ERE or a Comprehensive Internship Program for neurodivergent students will only increase.

Despite early assessment of the ERE and Comprehensive Internship Program, further research is needed. Although data on the perceived benefit of Career Connections Programs is important, at present it is not possible to make claims regarding efficacy of the programs. As such, research is needed to determine the effects of the ERE and Comprehensive Internship Program on student career outcomes. Additionally, research exploring whether differences exist across different demographic groups of neurodivergent students would be meaningful and allow for program revisions related to cultural relevance. Systematic research that explores the perceptions of supervisors of ERE and Comprehensive Internship Program supervisors would also be beneficial. What training do they need? What additional training do they believe would benefit ERE and Comprehensive Internship Program students? Do these training needs vary by industry? Answering these and other questions will be important to the continuous improvement of these programs.

Conclusion

The LC Career Connections Program is unlike that of any other higher education career preparation program. With its focus on meeting the career development needs of a broad array of cognitive profiles using a scaffolded, strengths-based approach, the Career Connections Programs have benefitted many neurodivergent LC students. Initial findings from assessments of the ERE and Comprehensive Internship Program support this and provide early evidence that targeted career development programs for neurodivergent students are beneficial in the higher education environment.

References

Chickering, A.W. (1969) *Education and identity.* San Francisco, CA: Jossey-Bass.

Chickering, A.W., and Reisser, L. (1993) Education and identity (2nd ed.). San Francisco, CA: Jossey-Bass.

Crompton, C.J., Ropar, D., Evans-Williams, C.V., Flynn, E.G., and Fletcher-Watson, S. (2020) 'Autistic peer-to-peer information transfer is highly effective', *Autism*, 24(7), 1704–1712. https://doi.org/10.1177/1362361320919286

Eveleth, A. (2012) 'Sensory regulation', In E. Ashkenazy and M. Latimer (eds.), *Navigating college: A handbook on self-advocacy written for Autistic students from Autistic adults* (pp. 45–47). Autistic Self Advocacy Network.

Financial Value Transparency. (2023) *Financial value transparency and gainful employment, 88 F.R. 70004* (proposed October 10, 2023) (to be codified at 34 CFR Parts 600 and 668). www.federalregister.gov/documents/2023/10/10/2023-20385/financial-value-transparency-and-gainful-employment

Gouws, E. (2022) 'Experiencing university life as an Autistic student: A critical autoethnography' (Publication No. 30700128) [Doctoral Dissertation], University of Pretoria (South Africa), ProQuest Dissertations and Theses.

Iqbal, Q., Volpone, S.D., and Piwowar-Sulej, K. (2024) 'Workforce neurodiversity and workplace avoidance behavior: The role of inclusive leadership, relational energy, and self-control demands', *Human Resource Management*, 1–21. https://doi.org/10.1002/hrm.22249

Kwon, C.K., Guadalupe, S.S., Archer, M., and Groomes, D.A. (2023) 'Understanding career development pathways of college students with disabilities using CRIP theory and the theory of whole self', *Journal of Diversity in Higher Education*, 16(4), 520–525. https://doi.org/10.1037/dhe0000464

Maslow, A.H. (1943) 'A theory of human motivation', *Psychological Review*, 50, 370–396. https://doi.org/10.1037/h0054346

McKibben, B., Wu, J., and Abelson, S. (2023) *New federal data confirm that college students face significant—and unacceptable—basic needs insecurity*. Philadelphia, PA: Temple University. https://hope.temple.edu/npsas

Morningstar, M.E., Lombardi, A., Mazzotti, V.L., Buddeke, K., Langdon, S., Taconet, A., ... and Kwiatek, S.M. (2022) 'Perspectives of college and career readiness among educational stakeholders', *Journal of Disability Policy Studies*, 1–11. https://doi.org/10.1177/10442073231177405

National Association of Colleges and Employers (NACE). (2024) *Competencies for a career-ready workforce*. www.naceweb.org/docs/default-source/default-document-library/2024/resources/nace-career-readiness-competencies-revised-apr-2024.pdf?sfvrsn=1e695024_6

Oswald, G.R., Huber, M.J., and Bonza, A. (2015) 'Effective job-seeking preparation and employment services for college students with disabilities', *Journal of Postsecondary Education and Disability*, 28(3), 375–382.

Rothausen, T.J., Henderson, K.E., Arnold, J.K., and Malshe, A. (2015) 'Should I stay or should I go? Identity and well-being in sensemaking about retention and turnover', *Journal of Management*, 43(7), 2357–2385. https://doi.org/10.1177/0149206315569312

Roux, A.M., Shattuck, P.T., Rast, J.E., Rava, J.A., and Anderson, K.A. (2015) *National autism indicators report: Transition into young adulthood*. Philadelphia, PA: AJ Drexel Autism Institute, Drexel University. https://drexel.edu/~/media/Files/autismoutcomes/publications/National%20Autism%20Indicators%20Report%20-%20July%202015.ashx

Ruppel, E.H. (2024) How work becomes invisible: The erosion of the wage floor for workers with disabilities. *American Sociological Review*, 1–30. https://doi.org/10.1177/00031224241268201

Sharf, R.S. (2013) Advances in theories of career development. In W.B. Walsh, M.L. Savickas, and P.J. Hartung (eds.), *Handbook of vocational psychology: Theory, research, and practice* (4th ed., pp. 3–32). London: Routledge.

Stamp, L.M. (2020) 'Neurodivergent learners' career identity development: A narrative study investigating the lived experiences of a cohort of neurodivergent learners (Publication No. 27831796)' [Doctoral dissertation], Northeastern University, ProQuest Dissertations and Theses.

Stenn, T., Lalor, A.R., Coplan, J., and Osterholt, D.A. (2023) 'Managing neurodiversity inclusion in today's entrepreneurial-styled workplace', In *Managing for social justice: Harnessing management theory and practice for collective good* (pp. 455–486). Cham, Switzerland: Springer International Publishing.

Weber, C., Krieger, B., Häne, E., Yarker, J., and McDowall, A. (2024) 'Physical workplace adjustments to support neurodivergent workers: A systematic review', *Applied Psychology*, 73(3), 910–962. https://doi.org/10.1111/apps.12431

Epilogue

Discourse

The discourse on neurodiversity within higher education and employment is increasingly nuanced, yet a fundamental gap persists between policy and practice. This disconnect stems from an implicit privileging of neurotypical frameworks, reinforcing a hegemony that continues to marginalise neurodivergent individuals despite efforts towards inclusivity. The strategies currently employed largely focus on adapting neurodivergent students and staff to existing structures rather than transforming these structures to be truly accessible. This knowledge-based and practical gap calls for a critical reassessment of how higher education institutions and workplaces conceptualise and implement support mechanisms.

Bronfenbrenner's bioecological model, as explored in the discussion on designing for neurodiversity in higher education, provides a valuable lens for understanding the interactions between neurodivergent students and their environments. However, while this model underscores the importance of institutional adaptation, much of the current discourse still places undue responsibility on the neurodivergent individual to navigate a system that was never designed with them in mind. The emphasis on Universal Design, while beneficial, often falls short of challenging the ingrained assumptions about what constitutes an effective learning environment. Flexible learning options and robust support services are presented as solutions, yet without addressing neurotypical hegemony, these initiatives might not lead to real, lasting change.

Dyslexia and attention-deficit/hyperactivity disorder (ADHD), two of the most prevalent neuro-variations in higher education, illustrate the consequences of this systemic oversight. The Australian context for dyslexic students reveals a stark reality: despite the widespread prevalence, institutional recognition remains inadequate, forcing students to navigate convoluted bureaucratic processes for minimal support. The reliance on family and peers further underscores the institutional lack of support. Similarly, the UK-based discussion on ADHD highlights how classification as a specific learning difference (SpLD) diminishes the visibility of ADHD as a distinct neuro-variation. The lack of streamlined diagnosis and intervention mechanisms places neurodivergent students in an unhelpful position, where access to support is contingent on navigating systems built for neurotypical users.

The co-design model employed in the refurbishment of the TL Robertson Library at Curtin University represents a step forward. However, it should not be construed that existing spaces need only be repurposed, as this potentially perpetuates a limited approach to accessibility. Ideally, inclusivity and availability should be embedded as foundational principles from the outset.

Assistive technology (AT) is often heralded as a great equalizer, yet its implementation remains fraught with institutional and financial barriers. The discussion of AT in higher education highlights the dual-edged nature of such tools: while they offer crucial support, they also risk increasing the visibility of impairments, reinforcing stigma rather than alleviating it. Moreover, mainstream AT integration remains slow, reflecting a broader reluctance to normalise neurodivergent needs as part of the standard educational infrastructure. Until AT is embedded into learning environments as a baseline requirement rather than an individualised accommodation, its full potential for reducing inequity will remain unrealised.

The Neurodiversity Placements Program (NPP) at La Trobe University exemplifies a strength-based approach that seeks to challenge the medical model of disability. However, even within this model, institutional inertia and fluctuating priorities limit sustained cultural change. A truly neurodiversity-affirming framework must acknowledge that the barriers faced by neurodivergent individuals are not simply logistical but deeply embedded in normative expectations of communication, productivity, and professionalism – expectations that support neurotypical dominance.

The UCD Neurodiversity-Friendly Campus project highlights key challenges and opportunities in fostering an inclusive academic environment. While 81% of students and 77% of staff reported personal experiences related to neurodiversity, only 46% believed the term applied to themselves. Institutional obstacles, including rigid diagnosis requirements and limited staff awareness, hinder accessibility. Participants emphasised the need for flexible accommodations, inclusive assessment, and awareness initiatives. A cultural shift towards genuine inclusivity – through education, environmental design, and institutional change – is essential. Addressing stigma, fostering open dialogue, and embedding neurodiversity in policies and procedures will help create a truly supportive academic community.

Across the profiles of student support programs in higher education institutions in various countries, a recurring theme emerges: the success of these initiatives is contingent upon dedicated individuals and localised efforts rather than systemic institutional commitment. Programs such as the Spectrum Scholars Initiative at the University of Delaware or the Mosaic Program at the University of Tennessee at Chattanooga offer promising models, yet their effectiveness is potentially constrained by the broader structural limitations of individual institutions. The fact that neurodiversity-focused initiatives remain the exception rather than the rule speaks to the enduring dominance of neurotypical hegemony within educational institutions.

The same challenges extend into employment pathways, where neurodivergent students frequently encounter exclusionary hiring practices and workplace cultures. Programs such as the AASQA initiative in Australia or the Career Connections Program at Landmark College in the USA highlight the necessity of tailored career support, yet these remain patchwork solutions to a systemic issue. Without a fundamental shift in how professional competence and workplace success are defined, neurodivergent individuals will continue to be evaluated against neurotypical benchmarks that fail to account for their strengths.

Ultimately, the analysis of neurodiversity inclusion in higher education and employment underscores a critical truth: true inclusion cannot be achieved through adaptation alone. The current approach, which focuses on helping neurodivergent individuals 'fit in' rather than reimagining environments that work for all, is fundamentally flawed. To bridge the gap between policy and lived experience, institutions must dismantle the structures that uphold neurotypical privilege and hegemonic norms. This requires a radical rethinking of pedagogical practices, assessment methods, workplace expectations, and support systems.

Neurodivergent individuals do not need to be 'accommodated' within a neurotypical world; rather, the world itself must evolve to reflect the full spectrum of human cognition. Until institutions move beyond superficial inclusivity measures and engage in genuine structural transformation, the promise of neurodiversity in higher education and employment will remain unfulfilled.

The Path Forward

As we conclude this exploration of neurodiversity and higher education, we turn our attention to the path forward. The material in this book has illuminated both the challenges faced by neurodivergent students and the transformative potential of inclusive practices. This epilogue serves as a call to action, outlining the essential elements required to build a sustainable and thriving ecosystem for neurodiversity within higher education settings. With this, we can move beyond mere inclusion, advocating for a fundamental shift in perspective and practice, one that embraces neurodiversity as a valuable and integral part of the academic landscape.

So how do we move forward and what are the essential elements required to create a sustainable ecosystem for neurodiversity in higher education?

Institutional culture, driven by leadership, is paramount. It is crucial to ascertain whether a commitment to neurodiversity is evident at the highest levels of administration, such as with the President or Vice-Chancellor of the university or other institution. This necessitates examining whether the institution strategically prioritises and values diversity across its community – encompassing students, researchers, lecturers, and all other staff. While the rhetoric and strategic statements may present a promising agenda for equity and inclusion, research suggests a potential gap between these intentions and the implementation of concrete programs and actions (Quigley et al., 2024; Frawley et al., 2018). Therefore, continued vigilance and a focus on demonstrable outcomes are crucial.

Another key element that flows from this is to create awareness and acceptance and reframe the narrative around neurodiversity among those working and studying in higher education institutions. We need to remember that everyone's brain is uniquely wired, and we each perceive the world differently. That is what neurodiversity is all about. It is therefore suggested to adopt neurodiversity as the default operating framework.

Creating awareness and acceptance and reframing the narrative can be progressed through a range of initiatives, including:

- reviewing disability and other student-facing and staff employment policies and procedures to ensure they appropriately embrace the neurodiversity paradigm (Walker, 2014).
- running awareness and accessibility training for academics and professional staff, including emphasising the importance of supporting a range of different learning and communication styles and implementing inclusive teaching strategies.
- running neurodivergent-specific student orientation sessions.
- creating and supporting neurodivergent-friendly social groups or clubs, and running events and programs to foster community and reduce isolation.
- offering peer mentoring programs where neurodivergent students support each other.
- providing principles and guidance for academic staff on running accessible lectures and tutorials.
- upskilling 'peer learning advisors' and student services personnel so that there is dedicated, educated, and experienced support for neurodivergent students.
- partnering with companies that support neurodivergent hiring and can offer career coaching, interview preparation, and internship opportunities.
- implementing sensory-friendly employer networking events and careers fairs that support the effective engagement of all participants.
- being part of a community of practice with other higher education institutions – such as www.NeurodiversityHub.org, which has developed a 'Model Program of Activities' that higher education institutions can use to benchmark themselves on their journey to neuro-inclusion.

- providing comprehensive 'neurodivergent-aware' Employee Assistance Programs and Student Assistance Programs, particularly given the mental health issues of many students.

It is also relevant to consider the concept of 'availability' (Mostafa et al., 2023) of different workspaces and learning spaces and approaches, as opposed to their 'inclusivity'. The problem with 'inclusion' as a concept is that it assumes that someone is currently 'excluded', and, unfortunately, there can then be a stigma attached to 'including' them. However, if there is 'availability' of a range of alternatives to choose from, a more engaged, energising environment can be created. These alternatives could be achieved via:

- providing a diversity of spaces and virtual tools.
- ensuring clear signage, visual schedules, and accessible navigation aids.
- establishing a coordinated, multi-site research study, with a large and diverse student population of participants, to generate clear, measurable outcomes and compelling evidence to inform the development and implementation of workable, evidence-based programs and initiatives for higher education.
- utilising research to guide the design of work and learning environments for all, incorporating sensory-friendly, low-stimulation areas with adjustable lighting and dedicated 'escape spaces' for relaxation and decompression.
- considering universal design for learning principles in course design and delivery.
- increasing the involvement of neurodivergent students and staff in the development, implementation, and evaluation of program offerings.
- providing different options for how students can interact with and learn from the course material, including providing multiple learning formats (e.g. recorded lectures, transcripts, visual aids, providing copies of lecture slide decks ahead of time to facilitate note taking etc.) and alternative communication options (e.g. text-based, AAC-friendly etc.).
- offering alternative assessment options for all, such as oral exams, alternative mediums for responding (e.g. visual or presentation-based), extended deadlines, or project-based evaluations.
- providing easy-to-access learning and assessment accommodation request processes with minimal bureaucratic barriers.

In closing, the journey towards a neurodiversity-affirming higher education institution is not a destination, but a continuous process of evolution and adaptation. By embracing the principles of 'availability' over mere 'inclusion', institutions can cultivate environments where diverse minds not only feel welcomed but are empowered to thrive. The recommendations outlined – from leadership commitment and policy revisions to practical adjustments in teaching and support – represent tangible steps towards this vision.

The success of these initiatives hinges on a fundamental shift in perspective: recognising, embracing, and celebrating neurodiversity as the norm, not the exception. By fostering awareness, understanding and acceptance, providing accessible resources, and celebrating the unique contributions of neurodivergent individuals, higher education institutions can unlock the full potential of their student and staff populations. This, in turn, will create a more equitable, innovative, and enriching academic experience for all. Ultimately, the creation of a sustainable ecosystem for neurodiversity requires a collective commitment to ongoing learning, collaboration, and a genuine respect for the diverse ways in which individuals experience and interact with the world.

Conflict of Interest Statement

One of the editors of this volume is associated with the Neurodiversity Hub community of practice, which is mentioned in the Epilogue and some of the contributions. However, the respective editor has not received personal financial or material benefit from this endeavour and declares no conflict of interest regarding this book.

References

Frawley, T., Meehan, A., and De Brún, A. (2018) 'Impact of organisational change for leaders in mental health', *Journal of Health Organization and Management*, 32(8), 980–1001. https://doi.org/10.1108/JHOM-08-2018-0220

Mostafa, M., Baumeister, R., Ramsgaard Thomsen, M., and Tamke, M., eds. (2023) *Design for inclusivity: Proceedings of the UIA World Congress of Architects Copenhagen 2023.* Springer. Sustainable Development Goals Series. https://doi.org/10.1007/978-3-031-36302-3

Quigley, E., O'Hanlon, M., Brandes, M., Kennedy, R., & Gavin, B. (2024). Neurodiversity and third-level education: A lacuna between the strength-based paradigm shift and the lived experience. Neurodiversity, 2. https://doi.org/10.1177/27546330241277427 (Original work published 2024)

Walker, N. (2014) *Neurodiversity: Some basic terms and definitions.* https://neuroqueer.com/neurodiversity-terms-and-definitions/

Index

For Product Safety Concerns and Information please contact our EU
representative GPSR@taylorandfrancis.com
Taylor & Francis Verlag GmbH, Kaufingerstraße 24, 80331 München, Germany

www.ingramcontent.com/pod-product-compliance
Lightning Source LLC
Chambersburg PA
CBHW050640280326
41932CB00015B/2725